REFUGEE

UNSETTLED AS I ROAM: MY ENDLESS SEARCH FOR A HOME

AZMAT ASHRAF

FriesenPress

Suite 300 - 990 Fort St
Victoria, BC, V8V 3K2
Canada

www.friesenpress.com

First Edition — 2020

Cover Photo by David Marcu on Unsplash

ISBN
978-1-5255-6382-9 (Hardcover)
978-1-5255-6383-6 (Paperback)
978-1-5255-6384-3 (eBook)

1. BIOGRAPHY & AUTOBIOGRAPHY, PERSONAL MEMOIRS

Distributed to the trade by The Ingram Book Company

A true story of a family's search for a home over three generations, told by one family member, in his own words. Dedicated to the courage and resilience of millions of refugees around the world.

TABLE OF CONTENTS

Foreword

The lottery of birth decides where we are born. No one has a say, and no one can fix it, yet it can be utterly cruel on some for no fault of their own. For centuries parts of humanity have been persecuted, evicted, and forced to flee. Beyond the headlines, the pain and suffering of these people go largely unnoticed except by men and women of exceptional courage who stand up to protect them, often risking their own lives. Both the victims and those who stand by them need to be understood, and their resilience in the face of insurmountable odds should be celebrated.

SIXTH MIGRATION

Have you lived a life. . . and where is it, where is it?
—AARON ZEITLIN from *A Visit to The Abyss*

Flight PK 782 has taken off from Karachi. I recline my seat in an attempt to relax by closing my eyes, but it's in vain. My mind wanders despite my efforts to restrain it. I want to focus on the present, but it refuses to listen, as if it has a will of its own. It seems to be simultaneously in two lands—the past and the future. Like hundreds of thousands of refugees forced to flee their homes before me, my past is nothing but a collection of memories of hide and seek, and my future is yet to unfold. That is why I want my mind to focus only on the present, to rein it in, to no avail. In an effort to regain control, I pry open my eyes.

I think of starting a conversation with my daughter, Sahar, sitting next to me but then decide not to. Instead, the glossy airline magazine provides a diversion as I flip though it aimlessly. The plane has left Karachi far behind and is now travelling over the Arabian Sea. At night there's hardly anything to see outside except the carpet of fluffy multilayered clouds below. In the moonlight they appear like a collection of soft, giant cotton balls, their tips rising in places as if wanting to touch the aircraft, but they soon give up as the aircraft climbs higher. Due to light turbulence, the captain has kept the seatbelt sign on as the flight attendant dashes up the aisle to remind a lady passenger in the front of us to remain seated when she gets up to reach for her bag from the overhead compartment. Sarah (17) and Samia (16) appear engrossed in conversation while Sahar (13), sitting between her mom and me, reads *Harry Potter*. After the long day she has had, my wife, Fatma, is too tired to keep her eyes open and dozes off, relieved to be able to finally put her feet up. On the face of it, there is nothing unusual about a family travelling together, but this is hardly a holiday trip.

Soon my eyes become heavy too, and I start losing grip on the present. Once again, my impatient mind starts wandering aimlessly.

Where did it all begin? I ask myself as I try to revisit my first migration—the train journey that I made on my mother's lap back in 1953. I have no memory of it, yet I try to imagine what it would have been like. Excited about his first train journey, my elder brother, Iqbal, keeps looking out of the window, not complaining about being hungry, not demanding anything, just content to enjoy the scenery. Oblivious that he may never see his friends back in the village again, occasionally wiping his eyes with his shirt as the coal dust from the locomotive blows over his face, forcing him to pull away from the window. Then as darkness falls, he slowly crawls next to Mother to fall asleep.

Suddenly, the deafening shrill of the train's whistle jolts him out of his slumber, sending a chill down his spine. After a brief respite, the shrill returns, piercing the young boy's ears, forcing him to huddle ever closer to Mother. He grabs a corner of her sari to reassure himself that he would not lose her if he goes back to sleep again.

Tossed around in the ocean of humanity by the tides of history, a refugee for life, I begin to revisit all the migrations I have experienced. They start to flow in, one by one: 1971, 1972, 1977, 1989, and tonight, August 2002. This journey may be the one to end all those in the past, or it could turn out to be yet another episode in my never-ending quest for a home.

They say every word that hurts one in childhood leaves a deep imprint on one's mind. More so if that happens to be a contemptuous nickname given to a child by others. The words "Bihari" and "refugee" were etched on my heart early in life. Ever since they have been competing to replace the name my parents gave me. In school, a sense of insecurity would prompt me to hide my Bihari identity. Slowly but surely I would emulate the Bengalis and learn to speak their language fluently.

But despite all my precautions, frequently I would be found out and be embarrassed for no particular reason. Carrying the deep scars of the numerous migrations on my soul, I continue the unfinished journey of my life. Memories of childhood run wild in my unsettled mind. I hear the faint laughter of my brothers playing in the courtyard as I feel a creeping pain in the corner of my chest.

Then, in an instant, my mind switches back to the present. It tries to convince me that this is a new beginning. Unlike in the past, this migration of 2002 is planned, and I am in control of the events. It tries to reassure me that the penalty for failure will be less severe this time. But it still cannot tell me why I have to keep running.

As I try to imagine my new life in Canada, I am loaded with the luxury of hope and cushioned by my small savings to sustain my family until regular employment or business or something works out. I am not the least afraid to rough it in what will still be a five-star location with a welcome sign compared to the tribulations of the migration my parents faced, when unknown hardship lay ahead even as they were escaping from riots and bloodshed. They found respite and joy in their new home. For a while they even prospered. But in less than twenty years, it all caught up with them again. When their options ran out, surrounded by bloodthirsty vigilantes in 1971, my parents would have given their limbs to have their offspring transported to the safety of a place like Canada. Today the low probability of my own success in finding a suitable livelihood at age fifty is far outweighed by the prospect of a better life for my young daughters. They are being transported to a place where they can live and flourish without any fear of persecution.

Then I pause to think again. Human nature doesn't change, and in the post-9/11 world, the people from my part of the world may have to face new and unknown challenges even in Canada. Therefore, I cannot answer the one question that has been eluding me: how many times will the Ashrafs have to migrate before they settle down in one place? For how many generations will they remain refugees? Then it dawns on me that perhaps my final resting place will be the one that my children begin to call home; perhaps it will be Canada.

Over the past few weeks, I quietly watched every interaction my wife had with her mother. It felt like I was watching a replay of the conversations between my own mother and my grandmother almost fifty years earlier. Mother was migrating with my father from India to the newly independent Promised Land for Indian Muslims, East Pakistan. Different actors, different country, different time, but the same script.

Looking at Fatma, I try to visualize how my nervous mother must have felt when she was packing her few belongings in those tin boxes called "trunks" or in that big round cloth bag, aptly called a "hold-all" by the British travelers in the Indian railways. People used these sleeping bags cum luggage especially for long train journeys. I try to visualize how the fear of the unknown must have gripped her as the time to bid farewell approached. How my poor grandmother must have choked at every mention of her daughter's imminent departure. How she must have spent countless hours on the half-folded prayer mat that was gathering dust on her veranda. Every now and then, in an effort to hide her sorrow from her daughter, she must have wiped her streaming tears with her sari, looking this way or that. Bewildered and overwhelmed by the events, she would have sought to share her feelings with her God. Her prayers must have continued echoing in her daughter's ears long after she was gone.

BACK IN THE 1950S, LIFE was simple for the womenfolk, who could hardly comprehend the complexities of the changing political scenarios. They understood little about the redrawing of the map in the subcontinent or the reasons for ethnic riots following the partition of India. And they understood even less about the rape and murder of innocent people, the orgy of death and destruction being played out in the name of religion. Everything was seen then in the context of God's will or God's punishment for the wrongs committed by humans.

Half asleep, I recall how we almost missed the flight this evening, although we had arrived on time at the airport, somehow missing the boarding announcements. I do not know how long I was gone in the past.

"Last call for passengers leaving for Toronto by PK 782. Please proceed immediately to gate number 25." The monotonous voice kept rattling in the background. "Passengers for flight number PK782 . . ."

"Hurry up please, you are late," the anxious flight attendant at gate twenty-five sounded relieved to have found the missing passengers, all five of them.

Worn out and exhausted, Fatma took the window and quickly sank deep into her seat. Sahar sat next to her while I took the aisle. Sarah and Samia got seated in the row behind us, not looking too happy about sharing the row with a stranger. Fortunately, it was a lady, someone going to visit her son in Toronto for the first time. The lady wasted no time initiating a conversation with the girls, who were a quarter her age, speaking so knowledgeably about Canada and befriending them instantly.

The past few days have been like clockwork for Fatma. Vacating the house we had rented after selling our own, supervising the sale of the things we no longer needed, and shifting stuff that we decided to keep to her mother's house. Even though she has been running a slight fever for the past two days, this morning she got up early to visit her father's grave, something she had never done before. Born and brought up in Saudi Arabia in the Wahabi tradition, she didn't believe in visiting the dead. But this was only to say goodbye. Covering her head with her chador, she approached her father's grave on the slopes of the DHA graveyard. A beggar women from the gate followed her silently a few steps behind. She raised her hands to pray and then dropped them. She broke down and began to weep, as if she was asking her father to forgive her for leaving her recently widowed mother behind to mourn alone. Had he been alive today, he would have certainly tried to stop her.

"You all have everything going for you here," he told her last year when he found out about our plans. "Azmat has gone mad. It makes no sense to be ditching a good career that he has worked so hard to establish in Pakistan." Until his end he remained dead against our move to Canada, but he was not there to stop his daughter today.

I'm a seasoned refugee by now, but this decision to move to Canada was curiously the toughest for me to make. Unlike my parents, we are definitely not being forced to flee. In fact, my family is leaving behind a life of comparative comfort in Pakistan. For the past twelve years that we lived here, a lot went well for us despite the political upheavals in the country and the constant law-and-order problems in the city of Karachi, the city we love to hate. I had a successful career, the children were going to good schools, and we had a lovely house. Fatma had a retinue of servants to assist her around the house (one driver, one gardener, one cook, one maid, and one *chowkidar*). All for the husband, wife, and three kids, that is one servant for each family member. My brother, Shahid, had a modern furniture factory from which he earned enough to own a house next door to us and enjoy a good life. The two families decided to do away with the boundary wall between our properties, which allowed us to have a larger common garden where our children enjoyed a bigger space to play with each other and with their pets. In the evenings the two brothers and their spouses would meet regularly to have tea in the garden. Our children, who were in the same age group, spent even more time together. They went swimming at the Creek Club, had compatible hobbies, and lived as they pleased in each other's houses. Each weekend the men played bridge, and the ladies had their own dos. All that until we decided to pack up and head for Canada.

Everyone in our circle of friends thought it was crazy to abandon everything we had worked hard to build in Pakistan, literally from zero.

"What will you do there?" They wondered.

The odds stacked up on top of each other, starting with severe weather, low prospect for jobs at our age, limited savings, and no business experience in Canada.

"You have already failed in business here. That leaves you with only one option in Canada, a lot of bridge." That's how one bridge buddy who was truly going to miss us summarized it. He simply could not understand our haste to emigrate when everything seemed to be fine for us.

It was hard to tell everyone that none of the above mattered to me more than the prospect of a prejudice-free life in a country like Canada for my children. At 150, Canada is still a young country, but pretty much one where race or religion would never decide their fate, and where the reward for one's labour was assured. It is a country built largely by immigrants where the founding fathers painfully and patiently laid down a tradition of accommodation between various cultural, ethnic, and religious groups that laid the foundation of a safe and secure country. Early explorers, a collection of courageous men and women, started by building business alliances with the First Nations. Despite the daunting struggles to survive, the diverse group of early settlers managed to co-exist with the multitude of linguistic and religious groups. Nearly two centuries later, the same ethos defines the Canadian nationhood today, delivering one of the freest and most tolerant societies in the first world. Canada was among the earliest in the British Empire to abolish slavery and adopt self-rule heralding its democracy. Good intent brought good luck and good fortune. The lack propensity for armed conflicts, coupled with tolerance and good sense, meant that Canada managed to protect itself from major conflicts or invasions from the south.

My generation of survivors from East Pakistan had learned their lesson at enormous cost, which they were bound to pass on to their children. The newcomers have to do a lot to adapt, which means respecting the host culture and traditions and not standing out like sore thumbs.

For all their success in East Pakistan, the Bihari community failed miserably to embrace their new homeland. Instead of learning and respecting their hosts' way of life, they tried to impose their own, often making fun of the host community and identifying themselves with the West Pakistani culture, which was increasingly seen as foreign or hostile to the local Bengalis. Despite people like my father doing a lot of things right to fit into the society, on the whole, the community failed and paid a heavy price.

Why now? Why am I running away at this age? I ask myself. I am running away because I am afraid. Afraid of losing everything, including our lives, in a society threatening to disintegrate. Perhaps my judgment is heavily influenced by my parents' follies in the past. In East Pakistan, now known as Bangladesh, the success of my father's business led him to a false sense of security. When things changed, he did not have the courage to abandon the fruits of his labour. And when the storm clouds appeared on the horizon, he could not cut his losses. He was not prepared to accept the fact that not being a son of the soil, he had no roots and no natural claim on that land. His community (the Biharis) were despised by the locals for their comparative economic success as well as their collective failure to integrate with the host community. By the time the truth was staring him in the face, it was too late to do anything; his family was besieged by angry mobs, forced out of their homes and hunted down.

Thirty years since 1971, two of the surviving sons of the Ashrafs had come a long way in settling down in Karachi, the city situated in the part of Pakistan that their parents had died for but never got to see. Still haunted by their past, in some odd ways not much was different for the two sons of Hayat Ashraf in what remained of Pakistan. The descendants of Urdu-speaking émigrés from India were still called *muhajirs*, meaning refugees, nearly fifty-five years after Pakistan gained independence in 1947. The toxic politics of the day practiced by regional political parties who seemed bent upon playing their respective ethnic cards, was deeply fracturing the society.

People in Karachi saw each other as Panjabis, Pathans, Sindhis, Baluchis, or Muhajirs. One rarely met anyone who was only a Pakistani. There was no telling what would happen in that violence-prone society, where thousands of unemployed youth roamed the streets with a far greater number of lethal weapons in circulation than was the case in East Pakistan back in 1971. The self-serving elites were escalating the unmistakable drift toward anarchy and fundamentalism by pandering to party thugs and religious bigots. For the hapless mass caught up in the vicious circle of poverty and illiteracy, religion provided an escape. There was a longing for the elusive "glorious Islamic past" by "purifying" the society of all modern ills.

The Frankenstein's monster, the Taliban, in neighbouring Afghanistan, created largely by the US and Pakistan to fight the Russians, was casting a specter of doom on Pakistan itself. What may have been a true jihad in the 1980s lost all its meaning after the Soviets' departure from Afghanistan. Different factions soon broke up, fighting among themselves for the spoils of war, carving the unfortunate country into bits and pieces and extracting what they could from the wretched masses. The war-ravaged country with a lack of economic opportunities had been taken over by a handful of warlords who were ruthlessly engaged in a vicious free-for-all. Afghanistan's misfortunes were compounded by the confusion created by conflicting outside interests whose hegemonies knew no manners as they kept switching their horses.

By the time the Taliban took over in Afghanistan, bringing their medieval code of life in the early 1990s, the grounds were all but prepared for them. Their initial success in reigning in the warlords and bringing a modicum of peace by meting out brutal punishments won misplaced praise with the luckless masses next door in Pakistan.

The clergy in Pakistan joyfully greeted the medieval puritanical society run by the Taliban in Afghanistan as the realization of their own utopian dream. For the masses, reeling under high unemployment, poverty, illiteracy, and social injustice, conditions in Pakistan appeared rife for a Taliban-like phenomenon to take hold. The swelling ranks of the clerics and their fiefdom of *madrasahs* were visible across the country. Bearded men in green or white turbans and women in black burkhas had multiplied manifold on the streets and in the bazaars of Karachi, Lahore, Pindi, and Peshawar. Clerics of all sects in their respective seminaries were gaining hordes of followers, and the country looked set for some drastic journey to the past. Many in Pakistan believed the inevitable change appeared justified in the face of failing alternatives. "What if they are right?" kind of thinking was taking hold. The "silent majority," if there was one, had been cowed down, afraid to raise their voice, and had abdicated their rights.

I try to remember our own *maulvi sahib* (religious teacher) growing up back in the 1960s or the learned *ulemas* (Muslim scholars) I had met at the *Darul uloom* (seminary) Karachi in the early 1970s. Alas, they have long been lost, replaced by a new generation of fat-necked, pot-bellied, loud, and politically charged mullahs of the 1990s. Religion in Pakistan had undergone a transformation on the back of the failure of the state, which had allowed this new breed of mullahs to take over. The common targets of hatred for the mullahs were minority communities like the Qadianis, Shias, Hindus, and the Christians, who were regarded as western agents or enemies within. Even within the muslims, dwindling tolerance and growing hostility between various fanatic sects preaching and practicing violence were leading to targeted assassinations of moderate Pakistanis by sinister fascist groups in a disturbing trend toward the abyss.

The police protected only the powerful while the armed thugs went about their business even in broad daylight. Almost all the families we knew in the upper-class neighbourhoods of Defence and Clifton had fallen victim to rising robberies, kidnappings, and car snatching. If the statistics were anything to go by, the probability of something bad happening sooner or later to a family like ours seemed almost 100 percent.

In midst of all this, in 1998 came a chance meeting with a childhood friend, Zia, who lived in Canada. By pure luck while visiting Karachi, he met someone who mentioned our name, which rang a bell, and he was able to find us. Already terrified by the emerging scenario in Pakistan, within days of meeting Zia, my brother, Shahid, and I had decided to apply for Canadian immigration. Initially, we did it as a precaution, still hoping that through some miracle things would improve, and we would not have to go. But Zia had done his job. He had convinced us that Canada was a land of immigrants where no single community had a higher claim on the land than the others.

As luck also had it, our older brother, Hashmat, had moved from Miami to Buffalo, merely a two-hour drive from Toronto. Keen to see his brothers settle in a country where their lives would not involve playing hide-and-seek with violence, he had been urging us for a long time to leave Pakistan. Some years earlier, he had applied to have us join him in the US, and the approvals came through, but we were not ready then. Once we decided in favour of Canada, he was relieved. Unlike Shahid and me, he never made a second attempt to live in the subcontinent. After our studies when we left the UK for the Middle East, Hashmat had migrated to the US, where he had done well as a cardiac surgeon. It would be great for the three brothers to be near each other once again.

A series of events following our application to emigrate brought some urgency to our reasoning. In mid-1998 the stakes got higher when Pakistan, a poor country, stunned the international community and defied its western allies by testing a nuclear bomb. A few months later came the brief Kargill conflict with India in February 1999. The two incidents convinced us that things were unlikely to improve in a country where the priorities remained so lopsided. A curse of geography or the lack of vision on the part of the two neighbours, India and Pakistan, had condemned them to enmity since their independence in 1947. One didn't have to be an economist to know that the scarce resources in the desperately poor Pakistan were already diverted to the army, severely limiting its economic prospects.

Then came the final straw. In October 1999 Pakistan had its fourth military takeover in its fifty-five-year history. The coincidence of a family tie through Hashmat's marriage provided us a closer look beyond the unfolding drama. Except for the ardent optimists who cling to any hope in the midst of all confusion, the country was not ready for this potential Ataturk by any stretch of the imagination. Pervez Musharraf's pictures in the papers just after the coup, holding his two dogs, provided a glimpse of this little-known public figure, of his personal self, to the people of Pakistan. For those who knew him, also knew of his overly simplistic military logic, which guided his unshakeable belief that only the army could be trusted to save Pakistan. That fundamental handicap, we feared, would make it enormously difficult for this straightforward general to survive the intrigues of Pakistani politics. Taking the mullahs head on where the army itself was infested with fundamentalist elements was going to be a tricky business that could go badly wrong.

The military takeover was but a déjà vu for Shahid and me. It seemed as if we had travelled back in time to Bangladesh in the year 1969, when things around us had just begun to turn bleak after yet another takeover by General Yahya. Just like our father then, we were heavily invested in terms of time and effort to rebuild our lives in Pakistan. But if, like our father, we failed to cut our losses, we may come to regret it, as our family did in East Pakistan.

"It is decided; we are moving to Canada," I announced to my wife at the afternoon tea in the garden. The arguments and discussion it unleashed continued until dinner but remained inconclusive. Thirty years earlier my Uncle Ansari was making a similar argument to my father to leave East Pakistan but losing only because he was the younger of the two. This time though I was determined not to lose.

Over the next few weeks, our two families debated the matter almost daily after work when we sat in the garden for tea. Gradually, our children, some of whom were already in their teens, nearly as old as we were in East Pakistan, also got involved. Tired of the daily restrictions on their movements after school, our daughters were happy to go to a place where they could enjoy some freedom outside the high walls of their homes in Karachi. They were totally prepared to trade off the comfort and luxury of house servants for securing their freedom and their future. Finally, the landing papers arrived, and we began selling our properties at rock-bottom prices, the market having crashed two years earlier.

"What has happened to all of you?" my father-in-law protested from his deathbed.

"Don't worry, Shahid," he told my brother, "we will start a new business when I get better." The painful wait for him to die ended in October 2001 and with that any possibility of reversing our decision.

Leaving would still be a hard decision. Despite all the uncertainty, Karachi's riots might not ever dissolve into the kind of civil war we saw in East Pakistan, and the majority population might never turn on each other. President Musharraf might succeed in taming the fundamentalists, thus averting a Taliban-like takeover. Things were bad but not awful. We did not have to leave. But I had learned from experience that by the time one has to leave, it is always too late.

Finally on the move, I carry a strange feeling of sadness inside me. Is it because of a sense of failure that I am becoming a refugee again? Or is it because I see the shadow of my mother in Fatma? I see my mother's silent suffering half a century earlier in circumstances that were much tougher than those for Fatma today. The decision to migrate to East Pakistan was not my mother's; she had only gone along with her husband for the sake of a better life for her children, leaving all her folks behind. After that, outside events dictated her life and her death as her search for a better life was brought to a violent end a few years later.

I smell the heavy air laden with the odours of mango and lichi in our playground under those trees. Then I see the empty house that I visited in Thakurgaon, looking in vain for my dear ones. I hear the chatter of small children pulling and pushing each other, so much like my own daughters today.

The captain's announcement wakes me up as I find Fatma trying to fix my seatbelt.

"We shall soon be landing at Pearson International where the local time is 12:30 p.m., and the temperature on the ground is twenty-three degrees Celsius. Please fasten your seatbelts, bring your seatbacks to an upright position . . ."

A beautiful August day greets us as we arrive in our new homeland, Canada. My daughters take turns leaning to look out of the window as the city of Toronto appears. Sarah and Samia laugh as they pull the glasses from Sahar's nose.

"Can you see the city without your glasses?"

The plane loops and takes its final approach as a new world of shining multicoloured bright glass buildings appears on the horizon, their large colourful panes reflecting sunlight but not giving away much else from such a distance. Gold, green, silver buildings and the tall silver-gray tower are stacked neatly next to a large lake. Somewhere there awaits a home for the girls to replace the one they left behind in Karachi.

BIRTH OF A REFUGEE

We all came from refugees
Nobody simply just appeared,
Nobody is here without a struggle
And why should we live in fear
of the weather or the troubles?
We all came from somewhere.
—Benjamin Zephania

It's 1952. The industrial town of Jamshedpur is reeling under communal riots for the third night in a row. Hayat's (my father's) only daughter, Naushaba, has a high temperature, but they can't reach the hospital due to the curfew. There is no public transport on the roads. The riots have kept them confined indoors for the past three days. Hayat's wife, Bibi (my mother), is pregnant with her fourth child, and she looks frail and anemic. But her determination to cope with the difficult times that have befallen her family has not waned. The expression on her face shows her resolve. Quietly, she serves dinner for their two sons and puts them to bed as she sees Hayat walk home empty-handed in the dark. The only medical store in the vicinity is closed. Without speaking a word, dejected Hayat sits down next to his daughter. He touches Naushaba's forehead, then reaches for the thermometer next to her pillow. Wet cloths gently mopping the little girl's forehead have done little to bring down her temperature.

Late that night Naushaba's complications grow. She looks feeble and lifeless. Her congested chest groans as she struggles to breathe. Bibi's vigil continues through the longest night of her life. Afraid her child may choke, she keeps holding the baby upright in her lap, every now and then shaking and talking to her daughter, afraid she will die if she falls asleep. Too weak to cough anymore, little Naushaba keeps staring at her mother, as if looking to console her for the all the troubles she has brought upon her.

"She is not breathing," Bibi calls her husband "Sunay ji!" Her voice trembles as she lets out a cry. Hayat has just gone to the other room to catch some sleep when he hears his wife wailing in his dream. "I am coming, Bibi. Nothing will happen to our daughter. She will be alright." He jumps up and rushes back toward them.

The Hindu couple next door are awakened by the sound of Hayat trying to console his wife. They knock on the door.

"How is the baby?" the man asks Hayat when he opens the door. "What happened?" He hesitates, his voice trembling as he takes a look at Hayat's stone face, now visible in the light coming through the window of his apartment. The neighbour's wife draws closer to Bibi and tries to take the baby from her, but Bibi resists, not wanting to let go. Hayat intervenes, holding Bibi by her arm. "Please, Bibi, please let go," he begs his wife. "Her pain has ended. Where she's gone she will not suffer anymore."

The day after the burial, Bibi's brother arrives from his village.

"I have come to take you home," he says without formalities.

"This is my home; my daughter is buried here" she replies calmly without even looking at him.

"The situation in this town is not good. Your sons will be safe in the village"

"And you have to think of the coming child."

"I pray it's a girl," Hayat says, "just as beautiful as Naushaba."

Bibi utters no words as she begins preparing for her departure, gathering her belongings in a suitcase. She washes her husband's clothes, placing them neatly in the wardrobe where he will find them easily after she is gone.

Two months later in her village, Bibi delivers me, bringing another son of Hayat Ashraf into this world. Being the third surviving child in a middle-class family belonging to a minority community in one of the most populous countries in the world leaves one with slim odds of survival, let alone flourishing or prospering. The high birth rate and the high death rate combine to make my birth a non-event. To slap a final stamp of anonymity, no birth certificate is issued since I was delivered by a midwife at my grandma's house in the village of Kumhrauli in Bihar, India. As is the practice those days, the village pundit is called in to predict the future of the child.

"This boy is very lucky. He will travel the world," the pundit declares gleefully, seeing a hint of a mole on my right foot. No one present at the time would have known that within a year of birth, I was to embark on an epic journey that would continue for my entire life. My travel would never end; neither would my search for a place to call my own.

My father, Hayat Ashraf, was the only son of Qazi Abdus Shaheed, a descendant of Durvesh Husain, who had reportedly arrived from Baghdad during the eighteenth century as an emissary to the Mogul court. In the village of Baghaul, the descendants in my father's family to this day are called by the nickname "Iraqis." It is believed that Durvesh Husain had come to spread the message of Islam in the subcontinent. What is revealed from the family tree is that someone in the subsequent generation worked as a judge in the Mogul court. Three or four of the seven subsequent generations served as civil servants, yet for some reason the title "*Qazi*" (judge) stayed until my grandfather. Unfortunately, despite having worked in the Mogul courts and subsequently for the British Raj, the Qazis did not join the landed gentry, which may be attributed to their recurring failure to capitalize on their positions of authority.

The only daughter of Mehdi Hasan, my mother, Shakra (nicknamed Bibi), belonged to a small landowning family in the village of Kumhrauli in the district of Darbhanga in Bihar. Being *shaikhs*, they were considered somewhat lesser in stature compared to the syed community to which my father belonged.

Both my parents lost their fathers early in life. The circumstances that led to their marriage could only be described as part romance and part providence, since my father's family was totally against the wedding, and my mother's family was all but insulted out of it. I am, therefore, grateful to my parents for their steadfastness and owe my existence to their perseverance. They kept their vows through extremely volatile times and were blessed with seven sons and one daughter. They proved to be devoted parents and looked after their offspring in a manner that was the envy of their neighbours.

After the attack on Pearl Harbor, the theatre of World War II shifted to the eastern front. The British were fighting desperately with their backs against the wall after the humiliating setbacks in 1941 and 1942 when a large number of British troops surrendered to the Japanese in Burma and Singapore. By 1943 the Japanese were literally knocking at the doors of the empire, having pushed the British back to the Indian borders through Burma. Being a colony of the empire, India was obliged to join the war with the British by the viceroy back in 1939, supplying much-needed troops in East Asia, North Africa and beyond. With the debacle in the Eastern Front, the demand for Indian troops rose sharply. But the people of India were more interested in their own freedom movement, which was fast gaining ground. Popular heroes like Shubash Chandra Bose of Calcutta were urging the Indians to side with the Japanese. The economies of Bengal and Bihar benefited briefly from the war efforts as the port of Calcutta was once again thriving. Many young men from Bihar travelled to Calcutta in search of a livelihood. But Calcutta, politicizing fast, had also become the epicentre of anti-British movements. Many of my father's relatives and friends had moved to Calcutta for a host of reasons, including searching for employment, setting up small businesses, or joining the political movements. Hayat came to Calcutta to study in one of the English schools established there by the British . In short, it was in Calcutta where all the action belonged.

Repeated calls for strikes and boycotts had paralyzed the educational institutions, resulting in repeated cancellation of Hayat's matriculation exams. Eventually, when the date was finally fixed in 1942, he was determined to make the best attempt at it. His teacher and mentor from the village, Master Abu Saleh, as he was called, urged Hayat to return from Calcutta and live close to his old school in Kamtaul. That way Hayat would be closer to his own village of Baghaul some ten kilometers away and benefit from the coaching of Master Abu Saleh, who had a reputation for achieving a high degree of success with his students.

Having lost his father at age eleven, Hayat had no regular means to support himself. But he was an enterprising young man, and by the time he reached sixteen, he had already begun supporting himself by teaching students from junior grades in the same school. Hayat already had a noble host, his cousin Zaki Ashraf, ready to receive him in Kumhrauli, which was walking distance from the Kamtaul high school just outside the village by the railway station. Zaki, six years older than Hayat, had inherited properties at the main square in the district town of Darbhanga, which brought him good income, but he was no businessman. A bookshop that he ran himself was perennially struggling with bad receivables. He could never say no to credit, especially to students from his village, which eventually led to the collapse of the business. A man whose philanthropy was already known to be disproportionate to his means had even donated his ancestral home in Kumhrauli for setting up a *madrassah*. He believed the house was too big for his family while the village had no proper primary school. He moved to a smaller unit next door belonging to his stepmother, who he looked after until her death. Over the years, that little madrassah produced many able students, including my older brother, Hashmat, and other worthy students who, in time, spread over India, the Middle East, and North America as doctors, engineers, and lawyers.

Being a cousin to a respected figure like Zaki, Hayat had no difficulty in making friends in Kumhrauli. Among them were Zaki's neighbour Mahboob Alam, who belonged to a small landowning family in the village. Bored with life in the village, the young man from the city started visiting Mahboob's family next door frequently. Out of sympathy for the fatherless young man, and admiring his determination to succeed, Mahboob's mother developed a special fondness for young Hayat. She began sending him food whenever anything special was cooked, even inviting him over for dinner, making Hayat feel like a part of Mahboob's family. Occasionally, the lonely young man would spend evenings at his neighbour's house just to get over the monotony of the unfamiliar village.

Over the next few months, he came in contact with Mahboob's only sister, seventeen-year-old Shakra, who the family lovingly called Bibi. Tall and fair, Bibi was an extremely quiet person who kept to herself. Hayat was impressed by the demeanor of this shy village girl who was such a contrast to his own extroverted sisters back home. Bibi hardly ever spoke to strangers, and despite all the pampering she received from her brothers, being the only girl in the family, she was never demanding and never imposed her will. What may have exaggerated her timidity was the subtle scars of smallpox on her cheeks that she tried her best to hide with her *dupatta*. Before long, the simplicity and shyness of this village girl had all but won over young Hayat's heart.

But the budding romance soon encountered troubled waters. The good-looking Hayat belonged to a *syed* family while Bibi, the ordinary-looking village girl, was from a lesser-stature shaikh family. Together these added up to a firm "no" from Hayat's family, which was not prepared to compromise, least of all regarding the important matter of caste. Marriage with a shaikh girl looked like a nonstarter. While Hayat pondered his options. Bibi's family decided to appeal to their counterparts one last time when the reaction from Hayat's home filtered through.

Since Hayat's father was dead, the proposal for the marriage from the girl's family was sent to Hayat's oldest living uncle, Qazi Abdul Muneef, who turned it down without a second thought. Undeterred, the family approached Hayat's philanthropist cousin, Zaki, who also declined. Despite his high standing in the village, Zaki failed to rise above the caste barrier. Practically all doors for Bibi's family were closing, which merely fuelled Hayat's determination. In a last-ditch effort, Hayat turned to his elder sister, Husna, the family matriarch. She was a strong-willed lady who was extremely fond of her only brother. To make matters worse, by then everyone in Hayat's family firmly believed that someone had cast a spell on their boy. To support their theory they had found a ready scapegoat in the village, called Mangal Chahchi, who was known to practice witchcraft.

Very much in love, Hayat was not prepared to back out from his commitment to Bibi. So, he visited his sister for the last time, threatening to run away if no solution was found. Finally, Husna gave in, on the condition that no one from her family would attend the wedding. For Hayat a conditional "yes" was still better than a firm "no." He accepted his sister's terms knowing well that he was no longer interested in living in the village that had nothing more to offer him after his education. Soon he would look for a job in the city.

True to their word, no one from Hayat's family attended the wedding. When Bibi arrived at Hayat's family home in the village of Baghaul, Hayat's mother refused to receive her. After a prolonged wait, the nervous bride was eventually taken out of the *paalki* by Husna while the family continued their deliberations. By virtue of her marriage to a wealthy family, Husna wielded a lot of authority, particularly in the wake of her own family's declining fortunes in Baghaul. This act of charity was never forgotten by Bibi, who tried hard to befriend Husna all her life.

Still believing that Hayat had been duped by a lesser caste, the family's position remained unforgiving, even after the wedding. Husna herself appeared to sympathize with the family's contention, but she was too fond of Hayat to forsake him for this reason alone. Sixteen years his senior, she had brought up Hayat like her own child, breastfeeding him when her mother, having given birth to Hayat late in life, had failed to produce milk. Over a period of time, her affection for Hayat got the better of her, and she dropped her reservations to accommodate her brother.

The shy and timid Bibi struggled to maintain an aura of dignity about her. She avoided getting involved in squabbles between her sisters-in-laws, treading patiently and carefully for years until they began treating her with respect. But she never succeeded in winning over her mother-in-law, who passed away two years after the wedding, refusing any rapprochement until the very end.

Notwithstanding the immediate difficulties with her husband's family, she remained a devoted wife cluthching firmly the one straw she had. By the second year into her marriage, Bibi was pregnant with her first son and motherhood had bestowed her with a new poise and grace. As for Hayat, his affection for Bibi grew stronger and their marriage entered a phase of consolidation.

With nothing left for Hayat to do in his village, in 1946 he left for good and travelled to the industrial city of Muzaffarpur. Bibi's eldest brother, Mahmood, who worked there promised to help Hayat find a job. Fortunately, it did not take long to find one as a clerk at the training centre of the largest steel company in India, Tata Telco. Thanks to his personality and good looks, Hayat sped up the corporate ladder. He learned to play tennis and socialized with his bosses, becoming the envy of his Muslim colleagues, a small minority in that company.

Back in the village, Husna's marriage was not working out well. She was living away from her husband, which was affecting her sons' education. It was time for Hayat to return the favour when she asked Hayat to take her second son, Samee, to Muzaffarpur to see him through his matric exams. Samee Akhtar had shown potential at an early age, and Husna wanted to ensure he didn't drop out of school like her first son. Although Samee was an unusually intelligent boy, he did not show much interest in the school curriculum. The bright and mischievous young man had begun to show rebellious tendencies at an early age, part of which could have been prompted by the estranged relationship between his parents. He failed to appear at his all-important matriculation exams, which would have easily allowed him to move to higher education to Calcutta, where his father had built a successful career and opened doors for him. Instead, he plotted to run away and make his future in Bombay. The clock would turn a full circle many years later when Samee's daughter met Hayat's son in another country in a most unusual union.

By 1946 the Quit India movement against the British was gaining strength all over India. A series of strikes and lockouts paralyzed towns and cities across India. Muzaffarpur, which had remained relatively unscathed until then, was suddenly engulfed in anti-Muslim riots. Muslim shops were burned down, and their houses were attacked by Hindu mobs. Pitched battles took place in Muslim neighbourhoods where housewives joined their husbands in guarding their localities with chili powder-filled spray guns, a common defensive weapon those days. The same spray guns, filled with a multitude of bright colours, were used by the Hindus and even many Muslims to celebrate *hoili*, when people sprayed colours at each other. My parents' generation used to talk about the heroics of these housewives perched on the rooftops to keep a watch on their neighbourhoods, but no one questioned their effectiveness at the time.

In August 1947, the British finally granted independence to India and Pakistan, whereby the majority Muslim states became Pakistan and the majority Hindu states became India. Muzaffarpur remained part of India, as expected. As the dust settled in the aftermath of the riots, Hayat searched for a safe spot in the redrawn map of India where his offspring would not be a vulnerable minority. It took him five years, two more riots, and the death of his sick daughter, Naushaba, to implement his plan.

1947 – PARTITION OF INDIA AND THE GREAT MIGRATION

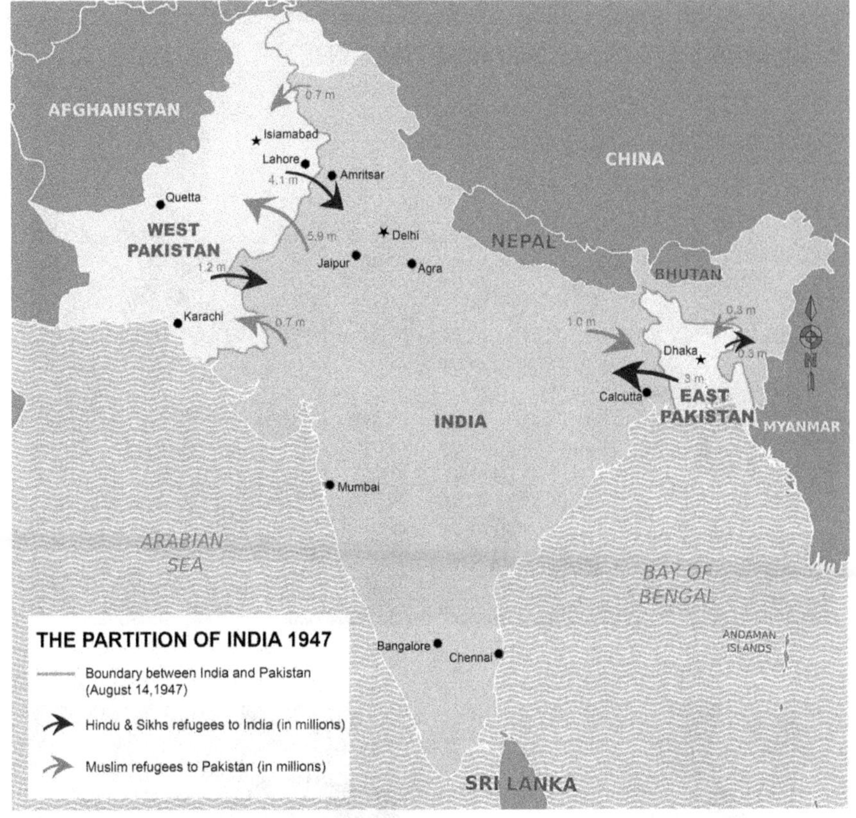

1947 – THE PARTITION OF INDIA UNLEASHED THE LARGEST MOVEMENT OF REFUGEES IN THE SUBCONTINENT. HINDUS AND SIKHS TRAVELLED TO INDIA; MUSLIMS TRAVELLED TO EAST AND WEST PAKISTAN

FIRST MIGRATION

To the Land of Opportunity

Where shall we go after the last border?
Where should birds fly after the last sky?
Where should plants sleep after the last breadth of air?
We write our names with crimson mist!
We end the hymn with our flesh
Here we would die. Here is the final passage
Here or there our blood would plant olive trees.

—Mahmood Darwaish

The year 1947 was extremely turbulent for the subcontinent, which had just won independence from the British. The celebrations were marred by large-scale violence, the aftershocks of which would be felt by Muslims and Hindus alike for a long time to come. One of the greatest migrations in human history was taking place across the subcontinent, uprooting and displacing Muslims, Hindus, and Sikhs from where they had coexisted for generations. To escape violence, millions of Muslims left India and crossed over to newly created Pakistan. In the opposite direction, hundreds of thousands of Hindus and Sikhs stranded in Pakistan were on the march toward India. The convoys of hapless refugees often travelled parallel to the railway lines in opposite directions carrying their wounded and sick. Often some would be overcome by the grief of their own community and attack the other side. Armed rioters on both sides were killing or plundering the already dispossessed with impunity. The Indian subcontinent had never seen such collective barbarism where young and old, women and children were being killed and maimed with knives and spears in an orgy of death and destruction that had descended upon the region.

The newly defined borders carved Pakistan in two parts, one on each side of erstwhile India. In their haste to leave India, the British had left behind a sea of human suffering with millions of miserable refugees fleeing for safety while carrying the deep scars of the partition in their souls that would continue to define future events in the region for years to come.

Life for the Muslims who remained behind in India hung in a precarious balance, the communal hatred showing no sign of abating. Since his arrival in Muzaffarpur in 1945, Hayat had done well career-wise and gotten his first promotion and had also become a proud father. Finally, anti-Muslim riots broke out in Muzaffarpur in 1949. For the first time Hayat began to worry about the future of his son in Hindu India. As things got tougher and tougher for Muslims in Bihar, Hayat decided he had had enough. He had been hearing about green and beautiful East Pakistan where many Muslims from Bihar had arrived, and those with skills and education were promptly finding employment. Civil servants were in short supply, and the new government was inviting Muslims from the Indian railways to man the newly carved out East Pakistan railways. Rumors were abound of Bengali leaders like Soharwardi and Fazlul Haq engineering Hindu-Muslim riots in the factories of Calcutta to force skilled jute mill workers and railway workers to flee to the safety of Muslim East Pakistan.

The riots returned to Muzaffarpur in 1952 just as many felt that conditions had begun to improve. It was during one of those riot-torn nights that Hayat lost his little daughter when the curfew prevented him from taking her to a hospital. The image of his wife holding her dying baby in her arms and the helplessness in her eyes that night tormented his mind. Hayat was convinced that his children would not be safe in India for a long time to come. He decided to leave India.

His cousin and mentor, Zaki, who had long been a father figure to Hayat, would have nothing to do with Hayat's move and remained opposed to his migration even after his departure. An ardent follower of Moulana Azad, Zaki opposed the very idea of the partition of India, whereby approximately half the Muslims in the subcontinent were left behind in Hindu India and would be paying the price of freedom of the other half that lived in Pakistan.

"I won't abandon my brothers here in India or weaken them," he told Hayat. "We will face the difficulties together." Such was his principled stand that he refused several subsequent invitations by his cousin to visit East Pakistan. He termed the creation of Pakistan a "disaster" for India's Muslims.

Even as Hayat prepared to leave, everyone in my mother's family kept hoping he would return to India when the Hindu-Muslim tensions subsided. His roots in India were deep, and even his only cousin had opposed the plan. They had done everything to dissuade Hayat and keep their only sister near them. But Hayat was an unusually strong-willed person, a leader and not a follower.

Finally, in April 1953 he boarded a train headed for the old East Bengal Railway (EBR), which remained linked with what was now the East Pakistan Railway (EPR). If one looked carefully, the engines and train cars on the other side of the border still carried the old mark of EBR. In places part of the B was rubbed off to make it look like a P. The instant rebranding of the railways on the other side of the border had been achieved without much fuss.

The plan was for Hayat to travel from Kathiar junction near the border by train toward the Birol border, where he with his wife and two little sons would board the EPR heading for Dinajpur in East Pakistan. It was decided that his eldest son, Hashmat, would be left behind with his maternal uncle. They would travel without passport or visas, as did many other refugees entering Pakistan. Given his education, he expected to be well received on the other side. Nevertheless, he was prepared to part with some cash at the border, if required. The protocol for visas and passports was yet to be fully established, even though trains had started crossing the border. For refugees, crossing the border in either direction often boiled down to how well they could negotiate the bribe with the guards at the border.

Our train was full of refugees or relatives of those who had already travelled to the Promised Land. Few possessed travel documents. As soon as the train reached the platform at Birol station, hungry border police asked all the passengers to get off. The search and questioning that followed panicked the passengers enough for them to succumb to offering whatever they could through individual negotiations. The rates for each family were set depending on the assessment of their means. Hayat, who looked less miserable, had to pay a bigger price. My mother took off her gold bangles and put them in my brother's pocket, where no one was likely to look. As expected, their luggage was searched so thoroughly that nothing of value was saved except for Hayat's wristwatch, his roliflex camera, and my mother's bangles.

While repacking the belongings, my feeder dropped on the floor and cracked. All hell broke loose, and I never stopped crying for the rest of the journey. At the next station, Mother begged for tea with lots of milk from a chaiwalla, probably making me the youngest refugee on that train to drink tea. That story was retold to everyone in the family for years to come.

Growing up with the story of that train journey, our young minds were filled with so much gratitude for our lucky escape. At the same time, it was also hard not to feel sad for those who were forced off the train for one reason or another. Some of these determined refugees completed the rest of their journey at night on bullock carts through treacherous trails full of small rivers and snake-infested bushes.

Left behind in India, our eldest brother, Hashmat, was in his fourth year in school studying in Urdu medium. His maternal uncles were happy with this arrangement, as if they held a hostage to lure back the family as soon as things improved or when Hayat tired of living in a land where he didn't even understand the local language. Hashmat spent another four years in India, first in Kumhrauli and then at a boarding school in Rampur. In 1957 while at the boarding school in Rampur, Hashmat met with an accident when a gas stove caught fire. He escaped relatively unscathed with only minor burns on his lips. When the news reached my mother, she became hysterical. "Either you bring my son here, or you send me back to India," she served her ultimatum. It was the first time Father had heard such a threat from his wife. He took it seriously and gave in. Hashmat's arrival in East Pakistan was one of the few battles my mother ever won against her husband.

For Hashmat it was not time for a homecoming yet. The only Urdu school in the district was some thirty-six miles away in Dinajpur, not even half as good as the one Hashmat had left behind in Rampur. So, Hashmat's life continued away from the rest of the family as he joined the Iqbal School in Dinajpur, living with some relatives there. Coming from a better school in India, his Urdu was good enough for class IX, although he was underage.

Hashmat's birthdate was amended without much difficulty to accommodate him in a higher class. Hardly two years later, he had to move again, this time to a college in Dhaka some 220 miles away. Hashmat, therefore, continued to live away from the rest of the family in the Promised Land. Except for vacations, he never got to live with his parents again.

The reasons for Hayat choosing Thakurgaon as his new home in East Pakistan were both practical and far sighted. First, it was the closest decent town to Darbhanga in India, where he had come from. Second, he found a job with the government's food supply department as an accounts clerk for a handsome monthly salary of 250 rupees, a respectable sum in the 1950s. Several educated Bengali Muslim families in Thakurgaon welcomed him into the community, along with several Bengali Muslims who had also freshly arrived from Murshidabad in West Bengal after the partition. The spirit of a new Muslim homeland ran strong in their hearts in that town, which had been dominated by the Hindus prior to independence, as the town's name suggested. It was a small, clean town of a few thousand residents with lots of lush, open, green playgrounds. It boasted a simple but effective storm drainage system that carried the rainwater quickly to the river that hugged the town from the west and southwest without flooding the town in the monsoon months. The British had built a small airstrip during World War II, which by the mid-1960s was repaired and rehabilitated for bi-weekly flights to the capital city Dhaka by small propeller-driven aircrafts. For a small town, Thakurgaon also had good schools, a college, *faujdari* courts, a central jail, and an officers' club built by the British.

Hayat was lucky to find a nice house next to the old British club with a large front yard and plenty of land around, providing enough playing space for his children. It was originally built in the 1920s by a Hindu doctor who abandoned it when his family fled to India at the time of partition in 1947. A plaque by the main entrance proudly displayed the owner's name, Dinesh Bhavan, meaning "Dinesh Lodge" and the year it was built, 1927. One family's loss had created an amazing opportunity for another. With so much open space and a courtyard inside, the house was ready to cater to the ever-growing Ashraf family, which was blessed with a child every other year, bringing the final tally to seven sons and one daughter by 1961.

Nature's bounty was abundant all around the house, which was surrounded by several fully-grown trees. Among them were mango, lichi, jackfruit, bokul, ber, jamun, and grapefruit trees. By the start of spring, these trees would flower for a few weeks, heralding a wondrous transformation of the flowers to fruits in nature's amazing gift of bounty. Not all the flowers turned into fruits. Each morning thousands would fall, forming a white carpet under the trees. Just as the fruits began to form, the month of *Chaitra* would bring its severe winds, tearing off thousands of the budding fruits. Each time the ominous thunderstorms gathered, we anxiously awaited their end only to assess the storm's cruelty once it was over. We prayed for the storms to go away, so more of the flowers could bear fruit. Then all our friends would be able to feast on this bounty, and we would still not be able to eat the rest. The trees made us many friends from school, who flocked to our house all summer. The daring amongst them showed off their skills by climbing the highest and farthest branches. The tricks were soon passed on to everyone else. No limbs broke, but often some returned home with bruises or a torn shirt. Complaints from their parents did little to stop anyone from taking those foolish risks.

The only addition Father made to his sprawling house was a guest house on one side under the large trees, which was to cater to a live-in *moulvi sahib,* and a separate room to house the frequent visitors who arrived from India in search of a better life and then moved on as they found a livelihood to support their respective families. Shops and small business run by immigrants from the neighbouring Indian provinces of West Bengal and Bihar sprang up all around. Hayat's good life remained a source of constant encouragement to the new refugees from India throughout the 1950s and 1960s.

A devoted father, Hayat's favourite pastime was playing with his children. From the moment he got home from work, he would engage his children in one activity or another. On holidays he would play twenty questions, carrom, badminton, and even cricket with them. Bibi adored this quality in her husband and happily took on the supporting role of a devoted wife and a committed mother. The unflinching dedication of these immigrant parents started to bear fruit in a decade or so. By the mid-1960s, each year two or three of their children began to win academic accolades, and almost all of them did well in sports. The annual sports day at the school would typically be a roll call for the Ashrafs. Most of the teachers in the government primary school and the high school knew the Ashrafs well. But for the Ashraf boys, their reputation had a flipside. They could never escape third-party vigilance. Anything and everything they did wrong was reported back to our father. Even when Father was out of town, one teacher or another would visit him when he returned, and the boys had nowhere to hide. The name "Ashraf" and the faces that bore that name were known to all who mattered in that small town.

Early in their lives, Hayat's sons were made to realize that their father set a high bar for them. There had to be a sense of purpose in everything they did, as if that was their mission in life. He dreamed of a dynasty, something previous generations had failed to do for lack of male heirs or lack of opportunity. For four generations, no more than one son had survived, until our grandfather was lucky enough to have a male sibling. Both brothers survived and went on to reproduce numerous daughters, but again they had only one son each. Finally, in the fifth generation of our family tree, Hayat hit the jackpot, being blessed with seven sons. His cousin, Zaki, back in India maintained the historic average with only one son. Hayat must have thought the jinx had finally been broken and saw it as ordained. He had to establish the Ashraf name in this newly created Muslim country where future generations would blossom and proudly carry the name forward.

To assimilate his family in his adopted homeland, he put all his children except the eldest, for whom it was too late, through Bengali medium schools. He himself learned to speak Bengali, becoming bilingual, in the tradition of many prominent Muslim Bengali families of West Bengal, who had also migrated to the newly created East Pakistan. Traditionally, many families of old Dhaka as well as those from Murshidabad in West Bengal spoke Urdu and Bengali equally well.

"It's easy, you add 'o' to every word and twist your tongue a bit, using the same Urdu word, just a slight change of pronunciation, and you can speak Bengali," he would say jokingly. With Sanskrit and Hindi forming the foundation of both languages, there were many common words, just pronounced differently. He soon became a living encouragement for other Bihari immigrants to overcome the language barrier and assimilate into their new country. He refused to donate to an Urdu medium school proposed to be built in

Thakurgaon, upsetting a few in his community. Without his backing, it never got established in that town. Within a few years of his arrival, thanks to a group of like-minded people in his community, most of the Bihari migrants in and around Thakurgaon, Panchagarh, Tetulia, Prannagar, and Birganj were speaking Bengali, and their children were going to Bengali schools.

Father's salary, which seemed adequate in the 1950s, had begun to feel less so with every addition to the family. To make up for the deficit, in his spare time he began selling life insurance. This brought him closer to the town's nascent business community, opening his eyes to the real opportunities in the new and growing country. He took that plunge in 1962, at age forty, leaving his accountant's job with the government to start his own business, a move none of the previous four generations had contemplated.

His first attempt as a government contractor failed before he got started, as he could not come up with the surety money. But his personality and his accounting background were about to pay dividends. A Swiss company, Brown Boveri, was building a power station and distribution towers in the area. They found Hayat to be one aspiring contractor whose inexperience was compensated by his ability to fill out contract documents and who could also speak English. With the project behind schedule, Hayat got his first contract to install prefabricated transmission towers and to paint them with special protective zinc coats. Hayat's authoritarian style of management worked well with the docile Bengali workforce, who toiled around the clock to complete the delayed project, much to the delight of his Swiss client. Soon he was awarded portions of unfinished work done by other contractors. The margins were good, and Hayat was on a roll.

A man of boundless energy, Hayat could not be content with small contracts; they were not enough for someone who was in a hurry to build a dynasty. His sons were growing up, and Hayat had plans for them too. He took on a haulage contract by purchasing two second-hand trucks. He also started investing his business profits in agricultural land next to the village of Prannagar, ten miles from Thakurgaon, where his sister Husna had settled down on a farm after arriving from India in the early 1960s.

Husna had returned from her pilgrimage and a long stint in Saudi Arabia with a retinue of other family members one night on two bullock carts carrying an extraordinary amount of luggage. Years later she boasted about how she managed to bring a handful of gold nuggets drilled into some wooden furniture. The farmland for Aunt Husna was purchased by her estranged husband, who, a few years earlier, had moved to Dhaka with his second wife. In the bargain, Husna got the farmland to settle down sufficiently away from her husband. Served by a small river and a few fishing ponds next to the only tarmac road connecting Thakurgaon with Dinajpur, the name Pran Nagar meant "Dwelling of Life." Aunt Husna settled down to a life of comparative comfort with her sons Jamal (16) and Kamal (20), her eldest daughter, Chanda, and her lovely granddaughter, Zareena. Chanda's marriage had also turned estranged as her husband never came to join her, preferring instead to remain in India. Jamal and Kamal were not going to school, since there was none nearby, but they had a lot to do on their farm. Yet, they quickly chose to adopt a sedentary life, preferring the servants to do all the work. Occasionally, Kamal travelled to Dhaka to demand money from his father. If he was refused, Kamal would cause his father's radio or gramophone to malfunction, then fix it and claim the cost of repair for the phantom mechanic. Kamal's elder brother, Shamim, was Husna's favourite and able son in Saudi Arabia, who regularly sent money to his mother. Money orders from Saudi Arabia would arrive each month through Hayat in Thakurgaon. For some reason Hayat made no attempt to induct Jamal or Kamal into his growing business, and Aunt Husna never asked, as if she expected her sons to live off their land without working themselves.

Less than a decade into business, through sheer hard work and some good luck, by the late 1960s Hayat had established himself as a prominent businessman in Thakurgaon. He had given up playing cards, one of his two known vices, the other being smoking, and allocated the precious time to his children like a football coach training his dream team.

With eldest son Hashmat kept away from home for schooling reasons, the second son, Iqbal, was dragged in to assist his father in business from an early age. By the time he was fifteen, Iqbal was already being driven against his will and abilities. Far from being a budding businessman, Iqbal was a romantic poet and artist in the making, often donning a chador and a kurta, trademarks of the revolutionary Bengali poet Nazrul Islam. With or without his heart in business, as his father's reluctant right-hand man, Iqbal was earmarked as the family patriarch in the making.

By the time he finished high school, Iqbal was already writing poetry and taking part in school plays. During his first year in college, the tall, lanky young man was cast as the lead in a play called *Tariq Bin-ziad*, where the young commander, Tariq, burns his boats after landing in Spain, so his men could never look back. The role won him the best actor award, but more notably, it made him a celebrity of sorts, whereby practically every young girl in the college wanted to talk to him. In true literary tradition, Iqbal, barely eighteen, received his first love letter from a girl two years junior to him, a girl from my class, as we found out later. When the secret was leaked to my mother, she could hardly contain her amusement, "Kaun nahi marta hai mere bachay par?" she boasted, meaning "Who can resist a crush on my son?"

Iqbal's business responsibilities kept encroaching upon his life of poetry and music, the former slowly gaining ground, especially when the first downturn in Father's business came in 1966. Facing completion delays, Father's financial resources were being stretched beyond his capacity. Iqbal would miss college for days while running around to attend to the crisis as the contract payments were not flowing due to delays in work, and the main contractor continued to put pressure on Father by withholding further payments that were badly needed to continue the work. The cash-flow crunch that followed put the project in the grip of a vicious circle. To make matters worse, one of his trucks met with a serious accident, killing a labourer. The ill-fated truck was not insured and was declared a total loss.

That year there were no new clothes for Eid, and for months we had no meat on the dinner table. My mother would cook omelets, cut them in small square pieces, and throw in some potatoes and onions to make curries to feed her large family. Some days it was rice and lentils only; occasionally just rice with onions and mustard oil or pickles or some green veggies. If there was any leftover rice, we ate that the next day. It was called *pantha bhat* or *baghara bhaat*, something we had only seen our servants eat in the past. Thanks to Mother's cooking, to us these preparations had so much novelty and tasted wonderful. For nutrition, our fruit trees came as a great blessing at that time. The good mangoes and even the particularly sour mangoes from the tree behind our kitchen were okay that season. None of us could stand the pungent jackfruits, but for active, hungry boys, everything on those trees was edible. Our maid taught Mother how to make curry out of the dried jackfruit seeds, an amazing discovery for all of us.

Through these testing times, Iqbal stood firmly by his father. He ran nonstop to remote villages on his motorbike trying to keep the work moving forward. At nearly six feet, he was much taller than an average Bengali those days, which made him look older than his age of eighteen and helped him handle his job better.

There were risks too. One evening while returning from a remote village on his motorbike, Iqbal was stopped by a group of *dacoits* who demanded money as well as the bike. While Iqbal was handing over the few hundred rupees he had on him, he recognized one of the dacoits, an ex-worker at one of his sites. Luckily, before he could open his mouth, the man asked his fellow dacoits to let Iqbal go, since they already had his money. An argument broke out between them, but the man who had worked for Iqbal did not relent as he stood firmly between Iqbal and his friends. Seizing the opportunity, Iqbal hit the gas and sped away. No one mentioned this to Father until after the project was completed, and Iqbal was no longer required to go to those sites.

Mother made sure the entire family rallied behind our father at a time when he was under tremendous stress. More than anything else, it was her nature of never complaining that must have saved Father from breaking down. Eventually, the project was completed. On the way out, the Swiss contractors sold their leftover furniture and equipment to Father at a nominal price to compensate him for his loss on the project. By early 1967 business was limping back to normal, and Father began to plan new projects again. Within a couple of years, his transport business had returned enough for him to set up a small rice mill not far from our house.

Iqbal scraped through his HSC exams, barely managing to pass, and joined the local college. Father wanted Iqbal to study law and run his business, but Iqbal's natural abilities lay elsewhere, in poetry and art. By then most of Iqbal's brothers were doing well academically: one in medical school, two in cadet college, the rest in Thakurgaon and doing well in their classes. The seeds of the family dynasty Hayat had so carefully been laying had begun to sprout, and people were noticing. At the opening of his rice mill, one of his friends remarked, "Hayat, you don't have one rice mill; you have seven, including those at your home"

It was not only the boys who gained the neighbours' attention. Even our little sister, Munni, was being sought after by families who wanted to get to know her brothers through her. Some of them began to dub us "Shaat Bhai Champa," based on the famous Bengali folktale, the story of seven brothers and one sister. In that story, the jealous enemies of the king bury the queen's newborn septuplet sons to deprive the king of a male heir and to make him weak. The last born, a daughter, somehow survives or is allowed to live. Seven trees with white flowers grew at the burial site of the seven sons in the forest. Many years later the daughter learns of the treachery and sets out in search of her brothers in the jungle, only to be told they are long dead. Heartbroken but not defeated, she is helped by some holy men. She sets out singing a famous song, "Shaat bhai champa jago re jago" ("Wake up, seven brothers, it's your sister calling, she misses you so much"). By some miracle seven flowers fall out of seven trees and turn into her brothers. That's how they come back to life, and they live happily ever after.

Little did those who called us "Shaat Bhai Champa" realize the famous folktale was about to be repeated for our unfortunate family, the only difference being that the real-life actors of the folktale would not see that happy ending. The evil eye had been cast, and the miracle of the folktale would elude the real Shaat Bhai Champa in the twentieth century.

The Innocent Sixties

Once we had a country and we thought it fair
Look in the atlas and you would find it there
We cannot go there now, my dear
We cannot go there
—W. H. Auden

"Run, run, don't look back!" Abu implored. The harder we ran, the deeper our feet sank in the soft sand on the riverbed. Soon they were too heavy to lift. Abu and I yelled at the top of our voice at the rest of our gang to wait for us. "Don't leave us behind!"

The two *chowkidars* (guards) suddenly gave up chasing Ranju and Dulal and turned toward us. They were now approaching from the front, trapping us on the riverbed on the small patches of sand dunes with water all around us. Behind us was the steep riverbank, from which we had just slid down after being chased out of the lichi orchard. In front of us were the stick-wielding chowkidars, who we had to cross to reach the other side of the river. Abu and I could see Ronju and Dulal still running in the distance, not stopping or looking back. Then we heard a faint splashing sound in the river as their small figures swam across and disappeared behind the bushes. Already in trouble with the chowkidars, the thought of our friends going back and informing my brothers, who could then tell our parents worried me no less than the stick wielding chowkidars.

"Tomar babar maal naki?" ("Are these your father's things?")

"Kaan Dhor, shalar beta, maare phelbo tomaake." ("Hold your ear, you sons of a . . . we will kill you.")

The man with the stick in his hand was standing firmly in front of us. The one carrying a spade stood next to him, looking set to bury us right there in the sand. They ordered us to empty our pockets and hand over our bags.

"Have we not seen you here before?" one asked.

"I am sure we have chased them before," the other confirmed, taking a good look at us.

We swore it was our first time. "You must be mistaken," we pleaded simultaneously.

The hot sand was burning our feet below while at the same time the sun was scorching our brains above. Sweat falling from Abu's forehead rolled down his cheeks and twinkled in the sun, making him look like he was already crying.

"Here, have them back," we said, spilling the lichis all around us. We had eaten enough lichi inside the orchard; we were not sorry to surrender the leftovers, which we were merely carrying as souvenirs.

As we entered our teens, our adventures varied from season to season, looking for bers, lichis, mangos, and kamrangas. Gradually, we also learned to keep our secrets which served to strengthen the bonds of our friendships. The carefree life continued as we moved from class VI to VII and VIII. Our favourite pastimes graduated to cricket, cinema, and hunting with air guns, and mischief was replaced by sports and outings. By class VII our group was skipping school for the matinee show at 3:00 p.m. at the local "Balaka Talkies." If caught coming out of the cinema by any of my brothers, it would cost me a few annas to buy a Lakri Mithai, the local candy, an adequate compensation in those days.

At the movies, the Hindi and Bengali melodramas made an immense impression on our teen minds. No one was ashamed to weep in the cinemas those days; my young friends and I were no exception to this group therapy. The trouble was that the reel broke down frequently, and the lights would come on, catching us in tears. Embarrassed, we would look around to see if anyone had recognized us. For a small town, the Balaka Talkies did good business, proudly displaying the "House Full" sign every time a new movie came to town. That sign invariably brought in more people the next day because no one wanted to miss out on a hit movie.

The money for my cinema tickets came from missed lunches or was stolen from my father's pocket. I was careful not to push my luck with my father too frequently, and he never found out. With or without the missed lunches, I had always been a sick child, frequently suffering from dysentery, diarrhea, or the flu. In winter my mother would cover me from head to toe at the slightest hint of a sneeze, massaging my neck and chest with warm mustard oil or Vicks VapoRub to protect me like a baby. She was always fearful of losing her weakest child. It nearly happened when, at age four, I was afflicted by an incurable dysentery. Had it not been for the *pir baba* of Dinajpur, who cured me with holy water, I would not have survived, my mother used to say.

Awareness of my small stature had already set in by the time I was twelve or thirteen. To compensate, I had little choice but to develop other faculties, not all directed toward positive ends. Thus began my search for risk taking and reaching out. Making friends and winning their trust by taking small risks in life became second nature for this extrovert in the making. With so many brothers, I had protection from potential bullies in the school. To prove our weight, we had our own cricket team with our own complete kit.

With all the distractions early in life, my academic performance was erratic at best, starting strongly with a direct admission in Class II, failing in Class IV, only to bounce back in Class V when I stood first in the class. I still remember the admiration in my mother's eyes when she saw my results. Father was more practical. He knew that after repeating a class I was only expected to improve. For me the real problem was the competition I faced from my siblings, who were showing a more consistent performance each year.

The 1960s was a period of tremendous progress and change in the lives of the people in East Pakistan. Things around us kept changing at a fast pace. Most of the roads in and around Thakurgaon got paved. A power station was built a few miles away, and an old World War II airstrip was restored for biweekly airplane service from Dhaka. In 1962 when electricity was connected to our house for the first time, our excitement was decidedly unfettered and liberating, Relieved that we would no longer have to bear the smell of the kerosene lanterns at night, Mother began the practice of keeping the zero lamps switched on all night. That helped reduce the perpetual nightmares I used to experience as a child, featuring Kali, the Hindu goddess of revenge. Every night before then, I would see her ghastly black statue, wearing a garland of human heads with her long bloodstained tongue sticking out. With that the sound of the horn and the bells of the nearby Kali temple would be ringing in my ears all night long.

Every night Mother would dutifully go around making sure the children were properly covered. She would adjust the fan or turn it off if it got cold. Whenever I was awakened by thunder or lightning, I found her doing her rounds, as if she never slept. And soon the magical sound of rain on the tin roof would hypnotize me back to sleep.

For the children in the neighbourhood, the monsoon months of June, July, and August brought so much joy and fun. The rains filled up the storm drains that ran next to our house, carrying water to the river two miles south. Tiny *putia* fish would appear from nowhere, filling those trenches; jumping all around the shrieking children wading in the water. They would spend all afternoon catching these tiny fish with their *gamchas* or makeshift nets, screaming with excitement and joy whenever they caught one. Even some grown up boys will be seen making various types of paper and cardboard boats to race in the water. Their boats tumbled downstream through the small mud barriers or went around the stones and bricks on the way or under the small bridges, quickly reappearing as the screaming children rushed to the other side.

In the winter months of December and January, a cool breeze would blow gently from the north, filling our neighbourhood with the lovely, faint smell of *Bokul.* The tiny white flowers shed by the bushy *Bokul* tree in our front yard each morning formed a white carpet. Young girls from the vicinity could be seen gathering them to make *jura* for their hair or *mala* and bracelets.

In the winter days, Mother sat on the sunny veranda on the west side of the house mending our clothes with her sewing machine or making dresses. The steel-plated "Singer" sign on that hand machine would reflect the sun's rays like a mirror, posting a round stamp on the opposite veranda in the east. One by one, her children would join her on the *charpai* next to the sewing machine to bask in the soothing sun. As the day progressed, they would shed their warm clothes and play in the courtyard. The dresses Mother made would invariably be for her only daughter, Munni, the "Champa" of the seven brothers in the Bengali folktale. Naturally, her brothers believed she was the luckiest girl in the world, not for simply having so many brothers to pamper and protect her but also for having a mother working full time for her. Even our stern father whom the sons dreaded so much, treated Munni ever so gently, allowing her to win most of the trivias he played on every festive occasion and passing it off as a mere coincidence. The brothers competed in spoiling her no less by risking their limbs to pick ripe lichis, guavas, or mangoes from the trees around the house. She would save them, only to share them with her brothers later.

Being a large family, we had to face a lot of rationing of pocket money. Our father allowed his sons a minimum sum, only enough for Munni to have her own piggy bank. But at times of special needs, it was Mother's black leather purse that came to her sons' rescue. She would quietly take it out from the steel almirah where she kept it and, without Father knowing it, hand us five or ten rupees. The magical purse was never empty, not even during the two difficult years when Father's business was doing poorly.

The Maghreb Rule

Late afternoon in the valley, the trees
Wear halos. The twilight steals the sun,
kitchen lights blink on like stars,
and coming home is a sigh
and the smile of someone waiting.
—Sarah Russel

A portrait of Father hanging on the wall in the living room kept a vigil over the boys when he was not around. Whenever we had done anything wrong, we would be afraid to even look at his picture. Such was the fear of the strict disciplinarian who ruled over the family like his personal fiefdom, commanding awe and respect from all. There was no question of anyone challenging his authority. A self-made man and a natural leader, clear headed and concise. He always seemed to know what he wanted, qualities I continued to aspire toward, years later in my practical life. Everyone in our extended clan was drawn to him for help and guidance. He would help, assist, get involved, and deal with everyone equally, appeasing no one.

The rules in the house were simple, firm, and non-negotiable. Retribution for breaching them was short and swift but quickly forgotten. Growing up with a mixture of fear and awe for our father, sometimes even hating his guts, was never easy. Yet from an early age, some of us aspired to copy his style. His towering personality contrasted with that of Mother, who must have been constantly intimidated by her husband, She never questioned his decisions or disobeyed him. Sometimes Mother's lack of say even in small matters made us feel sorry for her, and her fear of our father for no particular reason made us unhappy.

Aunt Husna used to tell us that in her younger days Mother suffered many excesses from her "tyrant" husband, who was the epitome of the male chauvinist that the society stood so firmly behind in those days. Thankfully, by the time we were old enough to understand, we never heard Mother complain of any abuse from him. With time he must have mellowed out, or his preoccupation with his business contributed to dividing his attention from things that didn't matter much. Yet the family's code of conduct remained clear for all to follow.

It was very important for Father to know and approve of our friends. We were not allowed to play with just anyone we chose lest we pick street language or other bad habits that were banned in our house. No matter where we went, every evening we had to be home by sunset. Father called this the "Maghreb rule," a reference to the Maghreb prayer at sunset. There was no compromise on the Maghreb rule. We would wash and often join Father in our only daily group prayer before we got down to our homework. When dinner was served, everyone had to be present at the dining table.

For the boys in the family, it seemed as if the bar was constantly being pushed higher. It was not enough to do well in our studies, which was necessary just to earn our daily meal. Participation in extra-curricular activities, such as debates, drama, and especially sports was important. Father's message to his children was clear and simple: "If you want a rightful place in this country, keep ahead of the locals. They will always have an advantage unless the difference is significant."

Living away from the family in Dhaka, Hashmat was preparing for his pre-medical examinations, the HSC. He had been the envy of his brothers to be enjoying the freedom away from the strict regime at home, but not for long. His freedom got the better of him when he sold his bike to pay off his gambling debts, something he always denied. Thereafter he started missing his classes, as the college was too far to walk. An above-average student until then, Hashmat had fallen into bad company, missing the supervision his siblings had back home. When the matter was reported back to Father, he was extremely distressed. To him if his first child went off track, the rest would follow those footsteps. That possibility threatened to destroy everything he had worked so hard to build. He was not prepared to see his dreams shattered by this one setback.

Hashmat was summoned home from Dhaka. During the three-month summer break that he spent with the family, he was made to undergo an unusual psychotherapy. His siblings were forbidden to talk to him or interact with him, and even Mother was not allowed to speak to him. Left out in the cold, Hashmat had no friends in Thakurgaon that he could call on. His banishment left him isolated in a house full of people.

The psychological toll of this social boycott was such that Hashmat stopped eating and withdrew totally. No one heard him utter a word even to the servants. Observing Hashmat's plight, Mother sobbed helplessly, which made Hashmat feel even worse. She was so helpless that even when Hashmat found an excuse to talk to her, she would not respond, lacking the courage to defy her husband. Eventually, the longest summer for Hashmat came to an end. He was summoned by Father in the presence of Mother just before the start of the next academic year.

"Do you want to continue your studies?" Father asked.

"Yes," Hashmat replied, mustering his courage. He could not utter another word; his voice was lost.

"Remember, this is your last chance. Go and start packing."

They were off to Dhaka the next morning. Mother did not even have time to say goodbye properly or to cook anything special for Hashmat. Arrangements were made to house him with some relatives in Dhaka, so he could get some home-cooked meals. In reality, it was more for better monitoring. As things turned out, Hashmat's grades improved soon, and within a year or so, to Father's relief, he was admitted to medical college.

Years later my mother used to weep just remembering Hashmat's banishment.

"What makes you think I enjoyed putting him through all that?" Father would ask.

"You have no emotions," she insisted. "You men are so cruel."

At that point Father would laugh and let her win the argument. It worked, as that only made her come around and concede it was the best thing to happen to Hashmat.

"Only because it worked."

"Precisely,"

"What if he had run away or given up?" she argued.

"You have to do what you think is best. You can't just shun a difficult choice only to regret it later when it's too late."

"In the end, it's still God's wish." As always, Mother would end the conversation by thanking God for His blessings.

The two-room annex to our house overlooked the old British officers' club and its beautiful green fields across the canal that divided it from our house. Our side of the canal was surrounded by fully grown lichi and mango trees, keeping the two rooms permanently in the shade and providing them with natural air conditioning in the heat of summer. The annex became a perennial guesthouse that saw a regular flow of guests. Relatives and friends from Dhaka and Pran Nagar or new immigrants from our ancestral village back in India would stay there until they found a place of their own and moved on. Choti Phuphi, Ehsan Bhai, Uncle Yaseen, Fakhre Alam, Afzal Mamu, one family after another came and left.

Not allowed to call our elders by name, it was our duty to address our guests as uncle, aunt, and so on and at the same time be at their service. We had to run their errands and fetch them water, food, anything they wanted. Unfortunately for us, some of our guests were busy keeping an eye on what the young boys were up to, assuming a caretaker role that was never part of the deal. The guest who stayed the longest, Ehsan Bhai, found it necessary to report to our father anything we did wrong, somehow always choosing the worst of times, when Father was not in a good mood. This would inflame Father's notorious temper, and the accused would get a beating often for no real fault of his own. This uncalled for interference into family matters or "spying" on her sons by our relatives bugged my mother no end. But whenever she summoned enough courage to protest, my father would dismiss her promptly, saying, "You must understand it is a part of their training," meaning they must not do anything to upset our guests which brings about a complaint.

Father was satisfied with the standards of the Bengali medium schools in Thakurgaon, which for a small town boasted a well-established high school and a degree college. The primary school was particularly known in the region and also served as a teachers' training centre, where new teachers from other towns came for training. The high school celebrated its golden jubilee in 1968 and had a record of matriculation results that were comparable to some of the best district schools those days, commonly known as Zila schools. Dedicated long-serving teachers who knew all the students and their families personally wielded the authority of guardians, a standard that has been lost to history. The only subjects the local schools did not cater to were the Quran and Urdu. So, Father began looking for a resident moulvi for his sons.

Our annex finally received a more permanent resident when Mr. Hadi, our *moulvi sahib,* arrived from Dinajpur in 1964. As was the tradition those days in many large families, the moulvi sahibs used to act as guardians to the children, and they were actively involved in the character building of their wards. Our moulvi sahib arrived with good references and an established track record of producing excellent students.

"Are you an aadmi or an insaan?" The first of his fun questions to his student was to challenge the young minds. To think of how they saw the difference between being children of Adam and possessing the qualities of a human. "Why do you exist?" or "What's the purpose of your existence?" That was his standard follow-up question.

"Look at your father. He has a dream for all of you. Do you know what it is?" he often asked. He made us aware early on as to how Father came to a new country, so we could all have a better future, leaving his birthplace, his friends, and his relatives behind. And he worked like crazy to provide for our needs, almost killing himself in the process.

Moulvi sahib's emphasis on basic human values was no less than his emphasis on reciting the Quran. Except for the Maghrib, which was already in practice in our house, there was no pressure on the young boys to pray at other times. The poems he would recite or the stories he would tell invariably carried some message. He took a keen interest in what was happening in our schools and, unlike a typical moulvi, he even encouraged us in sports. It was the kind of support in character building that my father was looking for, seeing as he had less and less time to give to his children as his business grew.

Within three years of his arrival, by 1967 two of moulvi sahib's worthy students, Shahid and I, were headed for an elite boarding school. After that he was able to concentrate exclusively on the youngest three, Zahid, Sajid, and Hamid. By then his students were eager and attentive, had learned to behave themselves without being subdued, and were the kind of students teachers pray for. The three siblings were not only competitive in their respective classes but also in sports. By then the Ashraf name was well recognized in the local schools. In addition, as if God sometimes gives certain chosen persons too much, all three were good-looking boys. Zahid was grey-eyed, tall for his age, and had a fair complexion. He also had a voice that used to win him *qirat* and elocution contests in school. Sajid was sharp-witted with an unusual twinkle in his eyes. Hamid, a fair and handsome young man, was sufficiently ahead of his class to complain of boredom and lack of competition by the time he was ten. With no concept of how to treat gifted children those days, he longed to go to an English school in Dhaka. The beloved Champa of the family, our only sister, Munni, remained the centre of attraction for all. The dark-eyed young lady with classic features, unassuming and quiet, was pampered but not spoiled. The 1960s saw all-round progress for our family when all the blessings of God seemed to follow one after another. The young boys and girl competed and excelled all around, popular with their teachers and their peers alike. Our parents or the Moulvi sahib could not have asked for more.

The First True Friend

When under kindred shape, like loves and hates
And a kindered nature,
Proclaims us mates,
Exposed to equal fates
Eternally.
—Henry David Thoreau

Saifullah, a Bengali boy, joined our school in Thakurgaon in Class VI in early 1964. He had to commute nearly three miles from out of town, which seemed so far away those days that I felt sorry for him. Chubby and slightly big for a Bengali boy, Saif, as he was called, had yet to qualify to be a member of our gang, all aged between eleven and twelve. Each day after school he had to hurry home, making him unavailable for the gang's activities.

One day someone in the class told me that Saif was the grandson of the famous controversial holy man known as the 'Kuchia Pir'. I learned much later that the Pir was very enlightened and progressive, which was why he was so controversial. The Pir had issued a fatwa or ruling that a certain type of fish called Kutchia was *halal,* and the starving poor need not be choosey about what to eat as long as it was edible. Instead of earning appreciation for his wisdom, the people chose instead to bestow on him the derogatory title *kutchia.*

"Kutchia," I teased Saif in my first interaction with him.

"Hey, Bihari, watch your words." He had found out about me too. "I will fix you, shala Bihari." His sharp rebuke embarrassed and angered me. Capitulating to his offensive manner was difficult for me in front of my other mates. So, my provocations continued. "Kutchia, Kutchia," I kept chanting while Saif grew even more furious. Then in a fit of rage he pushed me to the ground and started punching me. Our friends watching the spectacle made it impossible for me to yield so easily. "Kutchia, kuchia," I persisted, some of my friends by then had joined the chorus.

Whatever punches I threw at Saif had little effect. Then God intervened. The class teacher appeared from nowhere. "What's going on with you boys?" We heard his shout. Both of us quickly withdrew and stood up, trying to look normal. I thanked my luck but learned a lesson that I forgot only one more time in my future life.

The next day, quite unexpectedly, Saif walked up to me and apologized. Sufficiently embarrassed by my own behavior, I apologized in return. That was the start of a friendship that survived the test of time in a manner we could have not imagined back then. Few people are fortunate to experience a true friendship the way we did.

He was an average student but way ahead in literature, something Saif had inherited from his father, who was the head teacher in a local primary school and a poet. Within weeks we were exchanging class notes, studying together, and visiting each other's homes. Always struggling with my Bengali literature, soon my marks in that subject got a lift.

Saif's father, a thin, soft-spoken figure in a white kurta and pajamas and a white cap with a goat-like beard, was the epitome of a schoolteacher with perfect manners. As I got to know the rest of the family, it wasn't difficult to see that Saif's family was devoid of ethnic prejudices and my being Urdu-speaking was no hindrance to our friendship. Saif's father spoke good Urdu, as most educated families from Murshidabad did in those days. In no time I began to feel so welcome and comfortable with his family, who also got used to Saif's new Bihari friend.

Two years later, in early 1966, our fathers, who had never met until then, coincidentally and simultaneously applied for our admission in a newly established boarding school 200 kilometers away. Ayub Cadet College in Rajshahi was a new elite school named after the president. Neither of us did well in the admission test, which was conducted in English. My younger brother, Shahid, also took the admission test and passed comfortably. Somehow Saif and I got accepted for class IX, and

Shahid was to study in class VII. Thus we began our preparations to leave our hometown and move to a boarding school.

Mother didn't like the idea one bit and for days before we were due to leave never stopped sobbing. "They are doing fine in the school here. Besides, they are too young to be living without their mother," she complained.

"Rajshahi is less than two hundred kilometres away," my father reassured her time and again. "You can visit them whenever you want." She paid little attention to Father's assurances that we would be coming home at least twice a year.

The day arrived soon. The photograph taken with her on the afternoon of our departure remains one of the few souvenirs that survived the subsequent upheavals in our lives.

The journey to Rajshahi, still preserved vividly in my mind, began the afternoon before. Hashmat took Shahid and me on his motorbike to Dinajpur while our suitcases went with Father on the bus. The three of us laughed and joked as we balanced on the small seat meant for two passengers. In Dinajpur, we spent the night at the house of Dr. Saba, a family friend and, incidentally, one of the first Biharis to marry a Bengali girl. His example was cited often in our family whenever a prospect for inter-ethnic marriage appeared in the community. Early the next morning, we boarded the train for Rajshahi. Since Saifullah's father was travelling with him, our father, who had business to attend to, entrusted Shahid and me to him.

About five hours later, we reached the small town of Shardah, one station short of Rajshahi and the nearest to our destination. The cadet college was another three miles from the station in the countryside. Coming out in the mild afternoon sun in February was a relief from the second-class compartment, where we had been braving cold air gushing from the open windows for the past few hours. Dozens of other young boys we had noticed earlier on the train also got off with their parents, headed for the same destination. Our group was soon mobbed by a noisy lot of *tomtom wallas*, who offered the only transport available, their horse-drawn tomtoms. I had never seen so many of them before, and watching them take off in a horde was a treat. In a rush to get back in time for the next train, the tomtom drivers converted the three-mile journey into an exciting Ben Hur-style chase. As the drivers raced each other on the uneven dirt track, any one of them could have easily tipped over and spilled its passengers onto the road or into the shallow ditches. Oblivious of any safety standards at the time, the young boys shouted and backed their chariots in an instant rush of zeal. By the time we reached the front gate of the cadet college, our clothes were all but covered in dust.

Life at Cadet College

We are all meant to shine,
As children do.
We were born to make manifest
The glory of God that is within us.
It is not just in some of us;
It's in everyone.
—Emily Dickinson

As our tomtoms raced toward the cadet college, a sprawling compound of smart new buildings spread over one hundred plus acres of lush green lawns emerged before our eyes. The grand academic block formed the centrepiece. Behind it stood a number of new buildings, the student houses, the workshop, the dining hall, the staff quarters, the infirmary, the principal's bungalow, and the tall, proud water tank. All this was set on the banks of the majestic Padma River. One couldn't have found a better place to build a school. Our excitement was beyond containment.

As we settled down in our dormitory that evening, we had little idea how tough life in that semi-military school would be. Unlike West Pakistan where the elite culture had reportedly taken root, education in East Pakistan was, by and large, egalitarian. A few English medium convent schools in Dhaka and Chittagong, operating since the British times, were not considered that exclusive, since they mostly followed the curriculum of the local boards of education. But by the early 1960s, the government itself encouraged the setting up of English medium elite schools, such as the cadet colleges, ostensibly to train future leadership in that new country. By the mid-1960s, four cadet colleges were operating in East Pakistan with roughly 250 students per college, an expensive proposition for a poor country. The tuition fee, starting at 150 rupees per month, was also beyond the reach of many families those days. That meant only the students from the upper income groups could be selected, with a few exceptions aimed at providing scholarships and top-ups.

A typical day at cadet college started at 5:45 a.m., when everyone was hounded out of bed with the sound of a bugle. Still rubbing their eyes, boys would rush to the common toilets at the end of each corridor to wash and dress for PT, which was to start in fifteen minutes. This was followed by breakfast and academic classes. A one-hour respite after lunch was followed by a self-study hour until 4:30 p.m., when everyone was required to be on the sports ground playing one sport or another. No one was allowed to loiter in the dorms. At six we returned to the dorms for a shower and to report for Maghreb prayers, the only compulsory daily prayer. After prayers we would stay back in the academic block for one hour of self-study or extra classes for those needing help in any subject. At 8:30 p.m., we would all line up one last time heading toward the dining hall for dinner, ending the day's activities.

Having drained off all our energy, at 9:00 p.m. we would finally be allowed back in the dormitory, which meant we had one hour of free time until lights out at 10:00 p.m. No one was allowed out or to even to chat in the rooms after the house captain's whistle announcing lights out. Once lights were out, the only sound we heard until we fell asleep was from the housemaster's shoes walking past on the dormitory's long veranda as he did his nightly vigil. Those caught straying out or even whispering in their beds would be promptly awarded an extra drill, usually to be administered the following day during the afternoon rest hour. For those unlucky few, that was bound to ruin their evening as well as the next day.

Everyone was known by their cadet numbers instead of their given names. I was number 34, Saif was 32, Shahid was 120, Mustafeez was 12, Taneem was 18, Hamid was 1, Sadek was 17, and so on. Some even had nicknames that permanently replaced the names their parents had so lovingly chosen for them. These included Kodu, Potka, Baansh, Goda, Portia, and Lamda, adjectives that either described the recipient's physical appearance or demeanor. Not all nicknames stuck, but for any that did, there was no escape. The person's original name was all but forgotten.

A few amongst us made an immediate impact in the college and competed hard in studies, sports, and extra-curricular activities. Saif and I remained on the sidelines, to be noticed much later.

Like me, Saif had not seen electricity at home until only a few years earlier. He was particularly pleased to have his own ceiling fan hanging above his bed. One night when the housemaster, Mr. Singha, was on his rounds, he found Saifullah playing with the fan's regulator, reducing the speed and then increasing it again.

"Where are you from?" Mr. Singha asked.

"Yes, sir. From Thakurgaon, sir"

"That is in Dinajpur, isn't it? Do you have electricity there?" To rub it in, Mr. Singha calmly proceeded to inform Saif that he—and, for that matter, most of the students from that area—were there simply because the cadet college's governing body had decided to admit students from backward areas too. Most of these students had not passed the entrance test or, at best, were borderline cases. Saif should therefore consider himself fortunate and make the best of the opportunity so provided. Those who did not know Saif well, laughed and teased him about that incident for days.

Saif's admonition by Mr. Singha hurt me no less. I too was from the backwaters of north Bengal, hadn't done well in the entry test, and was probably allowed in only on special consideration. I never stopped hating Mr. Singha for his cruel candor and his sharp rebuke of Saif stung me for no particular reason. Oddly, I tried my best to do well in his class, geography, but he was hard to please. It wasn't until the matriculation results came two years later that Mr. Singha was ready to accept me as an okay student. Yet somehow he made me feel that my grades could still have been a mere fluke.

Among the young teaching staff, the college was fortunate to have a group of dashing, smartly dressed young bachelors. Three of them were our housemasters, who lived on the top floors of the respective student houses, so they could keep constant vigil. In so many ways they were role models for the young cadets, well educated and proficient in the subjects they taught. Some stood out for flair and style, like Mr. Khalid, Mr. Farhad, and Mr. Maroof. Among the married teachers, Mr. Shuja Hyder, who wore thick glasses, taught us arts and crafts and introduced us to his cubist collages on cut-out cardboard, mimicking Picasso. His works were proudly displayed on large frames in the main auditorium. His pretty wife wore colourful saris—bright yellow, green, and red—that made her look like a model of her own Picasso. Another well-dressed person in the compound was the principal's wife, who we used to simply call "Madam." She had so many saris that we never saw her in the same one twice. The kind and gracious lady was quite unlike her stern, dry husband from the air force, Wing Commander Syed.

Unlike any was our math teacher, Mr. Habib. Brilliant in math but appeared to possess much more interest in music and literature. Whenever he was in a good mood, he would finish his class early and tell us short stories. A master storyteller with a penchant for creating special effects, he narrated the best of Chekhov, Maupassant, and Andre Guide, his audience gasped for more. Mr. Habib's popularity must have been the envy of many teachers, some of whom regarded him as a real-life Romeo. As if to malign him, someone let out bits of his personal life to us, but it had the opposite effect. Like the Bollywood movies, the story went that he was in love with a girl he wanted to marry, but the girl's family was totally against it. They tried to dissuade Mr. Habib, but sensing his determination, they threatened him with dire consequences if he didn't stop seeing the girl. When that didn't succeed, the girl's family hired some thugs to rough him up, which landed him in the hospital. The couple's resolve was not broken; they ran away from home and got married. The family permanently disowned them which was why no folks of theirs were ever seen visiting them at the college. Mr. Habib's students could not have found a better real-life inspiration.

Like others, I was busy making new friends in my first year at the cadet college. In our teens, this was the perfect age for friendships to be forged. Some of these friends, particularly Taneem and Mustafiz, helped me get into various sports activities. Our trio also enjoyed many adventures together as we gained confidence, and a small gang formed around us, including Byron, Alauddin, and others. After dinner some nights, we would slip across the barbed-wire fence and smuggle in sweets from Basheer's restaurant. We would easily finish off a kilo of *rosogolla* or *chamcham* in one night. We stole bananas growing in the principal's backyard and even went to movies in the nearby town of Rajshahi, slipping away on our hiking trips.

My friend from Thakurgaon, Saifullah, hardly played any sports or attempted to make friends. Keeping to himself, he was growing bigger and bulkier by not participating in any sports. It took him two years to be noticed, first by his roommates, then by his literature teacher. A picture of Tagore hung inside his cupboard, to which he used to say *pranaam* each morning. Some regarded him as an eccentric, others grudgingly acknowledged his propensity for literature and his Marxist ideals.

With barely six weeks to go, everyone was preparing for the matriculation exams—except Saif, who was found loitering in the field in the middle of the night. Something seemed to have possessed him. Behaving strangely, he kept reciting some of the verses he had recently written, like: "Oh, Mr. GOC, stop Chapati at the ACC" and "Oh, Syed, my Syed, come down and be counted."

The incompetent campus doctor quickly declared Saif mentally deranged. His father was summoned and asked to take Saif home. Fortunately, he refused to accept the doctor's verdict. Before he took Saif away for treatment, he got the principal to agree to take Saif back if the mental hospital in Pabna cleared him. To our great relief, Saif was back within a month or so, just in time for exams. Saif's roommates had made up all kinds of stories of how he was strapped and administered electric shocks at the mental asylum. Once by mistake Saif entered another room walking back from dinner which was quickly interpreted as if he no longer remembered his room number. There was also a joke about a part of his brain being taken out, causing him to convert from a mere socialist to a confirmed atheist.

Within two years, the fun part of boarding school had slowly begun to outweigh the harshness of the military discipline. During the three-month summer vacation that followed exams, I realized how much I had started missing the cadet college life. I especially missed Taneem and Mustafiz, my housemates and two of the best friends I made there. While at home, after only two years of my absence, my old schoolmates in Thakurgaon seemed to be drifting away.

All summer Iqbal and I went hunting almost every other day on his motorbike with our air gun and some days, when Father was away, with the shotgun, which Iqbal was not allowed to carry until then. We ventured farther and farther than we had ever been to nearby villages and swamps looking for ducks, *boglas* (egrets), and a kind of green dove called *harials*.

Our matriculation results arrived just as the summer was coming to an end. Saif and I had done quite well in the exams. Never used to so much attention from Father, who was increasingly having to ration his precious time between his business and his eight children, I was almost embarrassed by his affection. Inside, I always wished to outdo my siblings, so I could get close to him, to learn his extraordinary ways of commanding respect from people. I could never decide which of my emotions was greater: the awe and fear he inflicted on me or the love and affection I felt for him. But that day for the first time I thought I saw his eyes well up when he spotted my roll number in the newspaper from behind his glasses. His smile of approval as he stood up to carry the paper to Mother inside was the first sign of an easing up in our relationship.

Upon our return from summer break, we learned that a new principal was to replace the tough disciplinarian, Mr. Syed, soon. Almost answering the prayers of some of us, Wg. Cdr. Keyani, our next principal, began to change a lot of things as soon as he arrived. Good looking, well dressed, and a suave gentleman of around fifty, Keyani spoke perfect English. He had excellent command over world affairs and possessed a sense of humour that quickly won over students and teachers alike.

The first thing he proceeded to change was the elite culture, allowing a lot of new faces to be tried for everything and providing leadership training to all the students, not just a select few. Mr. Keyani's arrival gradually began to change the lives of many cadets for the better. He approved additional budget for us to go on geographical tours to various parts of the country and for our football and cricket teams to visit other cadet colleges. There was much less emphasis on PT and parades and more on sports, debates, plays, and workshops. Every parents' day became a colourful and festive occasion, and every sports day ended with a joyful musical evening. Important personalities from the district and beyond were invited to these functions.

Keyani's reputation for having a sharp wit and a keen sense of humor spread through other cadet colleges too. On a visit to another Cadet College, Kayani was being introduced to the wing under officers, prefects, and house captains by the host principal, who began introducing them as "this is so and so, son of so and so" until he came to one whose father's name he could not remember, so he paused, searching for words.

"And he stands for himself," Keyani helped out.

Such incidents made him immensely popular with students and teachers alike at our college. Deeply inspired by Keyani's knowledge of history and world affairs, his students, including me, wanted to understand things the way he did. We wanted to have his knowledge, to be able to talk confidently about world affairs and to one day emulate his flair and style. For me it started with extra time in the library reading magazines and books I had never picked up before. For the first time I would open those thick volumes about the great wars, world history, biographies of people who made history, and great books of quotations. Each week I would also await the beautiful glossy magazines to arrive at the library from the nearby British council, titles like *Life* , *Punch* and *London.* The last two have sadly ceased publication since then. By 1969 I found myself playing a lot of sports and growing in confidence, particularly in academics. While my life and that of my family back home was looking up, we all failed to notice the black clouds on the horizon.

Mr. Keyani allowed us to have cross-country hiking trips that would end in the town of Rajshahi. We would watch movies in the local theatre and eat kacha golla at the local sweet shops before returning to our hostels. Our principal guide in Rajshahi was Talibul Maula, nick-named Rumi, who was one class junior to us; a tall, handsome young man with the personality of a child. His father was the commissioner of Rajshahi, which effectively made him the prince of that town. On one of our cross-country trips to Rajshahi, we were late returning because the group led by Rumi had purposefully strayed off course, pretending they had lost their way and conveniently ended up in Rajshahi. With the day's plan all upset, the group decided to go to the movies before returning to campus late that evening. The newly arrived adjutant, Capt. Tariq, was so mad that as soon as we arrived back at the college, around ten in the evening, we were lined up for an extra drill. After hours on the road, this would have killed us. Rumi stood up, took all the blame, and completed the extra drill, forever earning the respect of his peers.

There were other kinds of heroics too for those who had scores to settle with fellow students but could not, fearing punishment. Such feelings ran high in the class immediately junior to us, the class of Rumi, Arshad Jamal, and Moni Bhai. Even the seniors used to call him Moni Bhai (bhai means brother, a term of respect). The advantage of the physical size of some of them was of no avail at the cadet college where, being their seniors, we could still punish them as per the college discipline by subjecting them to extra drills under any pretext.

Returning from vacations, we would frequently hear about schoolmates being beaten up in their hometown. Those who could not wait to settle their scores until they got home opted for a quick boxing match or verbal abuse even on the train on the way home. This tradition was catching up in Arshad's class. Unknown to me, Arshad had a score to settle with me too.

For the next vacation, we were on our way home on the same train. Arshad's hometown, Shantahar, was on the way. I had never taken the threats seriously and had forgotten all about the incidents back at college. At the Shantahar junction, the train used to stop for at least an hour or so. I was sitting with Shahid and some others in one compartment while Arshad and his friends were in the next one. Saif inexplicably had chosen to remain with Arshad. But as soon as the train reached Shantahar, Saif came back to our compartment and sat down next to me, not telling me what was going on. Minutes later Arshad entered our compartment along with a few friends from his old school. Most of them looked older than him, somewhat rough and tough.

"How come you changed so soon?" I asked Arshad, looking at his civilian dress, which had replaced his uniform.

Arshad was taken aback by this direct friendly conversation. Not knowing how to respond, he began looking around, scratching his head. In a few seconds, he left the compartment, taking his friends with him without uttering a word.

"Do you know what he was here for?" Saif asked

"No idea," I said. "Wait, you must be joking." It couldn't be true; I could hardly believe what he was about to say.

Saif told me how he had tried to dissuade Arshad from his plan to rough me up. He had tried that throughout the journey from Sharda to Shantahar, but Arshad was adamant and wanted his revenge.

"It will ruin your life," Saif warned, trying talk some sense into him. "He is your senior, don't forget. This will surely get reported back at the college, and you will be expelled."

When Arshad entered our compartment, seeing both Saif and Shahid next to me, he must have realized we would have been at least three against his four.

Years later when Arshad and I had become business partners a thousand miles away in Karachi, I reminded him of the incident on the train. Conveniently for him, he had no recollection of what happened that day.

Keyani's beautiful daughter, Humaira, came to visit him from Lahore during her college break. All the bachelor teachers began taking extra care to dress up and look presentable whenever she was around. A liberated college girl, Humaira would drive around in Keyani's car with her large black Alsatian, Zangi, beside her or play table tennis with her friends in the gym. Just as she had become the fantasy of teachers and students alike, some relatives of Keyani came visiting. Among them was a handsome young CSP officer who was totally taken in by Humaira's charm. Strolling in the garden one evening, the young suitor plucked a flower but hesitated before making an advance.

"Do you mind giving this to Humaira from me, sir?" the shy young man asked, approaching Keyani instead.

"Why don't you give it yourself?" Keyani asked.

"Sir, if I give it myself, she might misunderstand," he replied.

"No, you give, and she will understand. If I give , she will misunderstand." Keyani's sense of humor always matched his presence of mind.

The colourful period of Keyani was short. After spending just under two years at the college, Keyani was transferred to another cadet college, Momenshahi. Concerned by the emerging political scenario, the British principal at Momenshahi had decided to cut short his tenure. Keyani wanted to go there, given his history of heart problems, he preferred to be closer to the military hospital at Dhaka.

He received a memorable farewell. His speech, the final march past, and the salute by the cadets followed by the farewell tune on the bugle ripped our hearts out. Many, including the teachers and the office staff, had tears in their eyes.

"All good things come to an end," Keyani wrote in my autograph book.

Over the years I came to realize the true significance of this phrase as I experienced this fundamental truth again and again in my life.

For our batch, the final year at cadet college passed quickly, mainly because we were having a good time enjoying the privileges of the senior class. By June 1970 everyone was focused on the HSC board exams before going home for good. Some were to join the army, and some were headed for different universities, forever leaving behind the protected life of the boarding school. The frogs from the well were going into the river. Life would not be the same again.

The Writing on the Wall

I am told I have no country now
I am told I am a lie
I am told that modern history books
May forget my name
—Benjamin Zephania

We were too young to see the writing on the wall but old enough to understand the flaws in the creation of East Pakistan, a thousand miles away from West Pakistan, having little in common with the other province. Defying the logic of history and geography, East Bengal became a part of Pakistan in 1947, the second country after Israel to be established on the basis of religion alone. Growing up in East Pakistan, even as teenagers some could sense that to become part of Pakistan, the Bengali body had been separated from its soul. The centre of Bengali culture, its music and its literature, was left behind in West Bengal, which had become part of India. The sensitive Bengali intellectuals soon began to miss all that they cherished. Invariably, many felt suffocated by the imported *askari* culture of West Pakistan.

It was hard to understand the wisdom of this unnatural union. But not for my father, whose generation believed in the new dawn from the Muslims in India. Their generation had fought hard for a Muslim homeland and were committed to its success. By contrast his cousin, Ansari, who had lived in Calcutta before the partition, understood why many Bengalis lamented the gradual loss of their identity. Even though he had a good job at one of the local banks, he didn't like what he was seeing and almost regretted his move to East Pakistan.

Islam had arrived in East Bengal in the eleventh century when Muhammad bin Tughlaq conquered it with only twenty-eight or so followers. The Moguls arrived nearly a century and a half later in ad 1202 when Bakhtiar Khilji, a commander of Sultan Qutubuddin Aiybak, conquered Bengal. Except for what happened at the top for the next five centuries in that part of the world, Hindus and Muslims continued to coexist in peace. Perhaps it was the absence of conflict in the region that gradually weakened the military prowess of the local Nawab Sirajuddaula, who was defeated by the British in the Battle of Plassey in 1756, heralding British rule. British colonization affected the Muslim community in Bengal much more than their Hindu counterparts. Being the previous rulers, the Muslims were seen as bigger threats to the British authority, leading to a concerted effort by the British to suppress Muslims economically.

The educated Muslims of East Bengal were not irked by the Hindu culture, which was deep rooted through centuries of coexistence, but they were troubled by the economic domination of the 13 percent or so Hindus in East Bengal. The prominent Muslim families of Dhaka and Murshidabad, the Nawabs of Dhaka, the Suharwardies, and the Fazlul Haqs emerged as the proponents of economic freedom of Muslim Bengal. Their struggle initially delivered East Bengal as a separate province out of the province of British Bengal and, half a century later, East Pakistan as a part of independent Pakistan.

Mr. Jinnah, the creator of Pakistan, was not even on the radar screen when the Muslims of Bengal formed the All India Muslim League in 1905. The Bengalis' aspirations were harnessed well by the Muslim leaders of the subcontinent in their struggle for a separate homeland. But the logical second step of letting the Bengalis be truly independent was forgotten. Just as the Bengali leaders at the time failed to define their true objectives within the struggle for Pakistan, Pakistan's founding fathers showed little wisdom to accommodate that logic into their ideology. Carried away by the initial euphoria of their movement, they refused to listen to the warning bells being sounded by other Muslim leaders of the time. The historic errors of the subsequent Pakistani leadership after independence were no less responsible for the Bengalis' alienation. No one foresaw in 1947 that East Pakistan's freedom, won after so much sacrifice, would require so much more blood to achieve the same goal twenty-five years later.

East Pakistan was an experiment that did little to improve the lives of the poor masses. The decisions about their lives were once again being made far away, this time in West Pakistan instead of Westminister. The people were even being told that their language would not be the language of the state of Pakistan, a mistake only corrected after creating martyrs of the Bengali language movement. These martyrs in due course provided the Bengalis with a symbol of discord, one that laid the seeds of mistrust between the two provinces within five years of independence.

When the countrywide popular discontent against President Ayub Khan's regime began in 1968, the sons of the Bengali elites at the cadet college were in a state of disbelief. Oblivious to the world outside, the young cadets revered Ayub as their hero and a symbol of the federation of Pakistan. Before the young men at cadet college could grasp the reasons for discontent against Ayub, he was gone.

Outside of cadet college, in the real world, the Bengali nation was undergoing a transformation. They had become politically aware. Even the rickshaw pullers understood the logic of the nationalist Mujib and began to respond to his repeated calls for strikes or lockdowns.

On March 25, 1969, President Ayub handed over power to General Yahya Khan. The founder of our college and our hero had been finally humbled, and many of us could not hold back our tears. But our students and teachers hardly represented the masses. They were the Bengali elite who had benefited tremendously as Pakistanis. Outside the gates of the cadet college, the Bengali nationalist sentiment was taking root in colleges and universities around East Pakistan. When it got closer, it was merely seen as a one-off tragedy or an unfortunate event. A professor at Rajshahi University who was related to one of our teachers was killed taking part in a procession. At the cadet college, the gloom lasted all of one or two days. Matters like the break-up of the Beatles, pictures of the moon landing, and the latest movies had more airtime in our discussions than the nationalist movements sweeping through the colleges and universities outside. Everyone appeared committed to staying within the framework of Pakistan. Unfortunately, the new military regime's successive actions eventually alienated even this constituency of the Bengali population against Pakistan.

As for my own community, the Urdu-speaking residents of the province, generically called the Biharis (since the majority of them were immigrants from the Indian state of Bihar), a feeling of uneasiness had already set in by 1969. They began to worry that the foundations of a united Pakistan were being weakened by the growing popularity of Shaikh Mujib, whose six-point agenda was seen by many Biharis as a prelude to total independence. There were basically two groups of Biharis within the half million so (roughly 1 percent of the population of East Pakistan). One group had not made much effort to become part of the local population in the host country. The other, like my own family, had done everything to assimilate.

Those who had failed to assimilate typically lived in big towns where Urdu medium schools had sprung up or in railway colonies where a lot of Biharis were employed. Those who did assimilate spoke Bengali, married into Bengali families, and mainly lived in small towns all over East Pakistan. They felt less threatened, had higher stakes in the community, and could not easily extricate themselves from their adopted homes.

Having staked their future squarely on East Pakistan, the Ashraf family belonged to the latter category. They hoped the dark clouds on the horizon were but a passing phase. Within the family, they would debate and discuss the murky political scenario without ever reaching a conclusion. The only devil's advocate in the family happened to be Uncle Ansari, who had narrowly escaped death in the communal riots in Calcutta in 1947. He would never fail to ring the alarm bells and exhort my father to move to West Pakistan.

"Let's move while there's still time. Mark my words, things are not going to improve here," he would assert.

"Let us wait for the situation to settle down," Father would reply, occasionally conceding under pressure that he may consider selling some assets once the opportunity arose. The contradiction in that argument was that such an option seemed possible only after the situation improved. In other words, when such action was no longer required.

"You cannot throw away years of labour," Father argued.

The disagreements and squabbles continued through weeks and months while the ground beneath their feet kept shifting.

The elections were to be held in December 1970 after an unusually long period of campaigning. With his highly popular six-point manifesto, which promised complete provincial autonomy, Shaikh Mujib's Awami League was emerging as the clear favourite. His emotive speeches were drawing large crowds, and he was increasingly seen as the only Bengali leader willing to challenge the status quo.

Somehow no one in my privileged cadet college believed this was the end of the federation. By the time my batch was graduating in 1970, many in our class still went ahead and joined the Pakistani army in October that year.

The Summer of Our Lives

The birds they sang, at the break of day
Start again, I heard them say
Don't dwell on what has passed away
Or what is yet to be
—Leonard Cohen

Back home from cadet college, our summer vacation in Thakurgaon in 1970 was a time of great celebration for the Ashraf family with a bumper crop of graduations. Shahid passed his matric, Iqbal his bachelor of commerce, and Hashmat had become a doctor, passing his MBBS. The result of my own HSC exams was yet to arrive, and my anxious wait continued until the end of summer. One person who expected me to do well was Hashmat. When asked by a friend how his brother had done, he confidently replied, "You would see his photograph in the papers."

Hashmat's own picture was published in the papers earlier that summer when he secured first position in his MBBS exams at Dhaka University. The young men in the Ashraf family were now being noticed by girls in the circle of friends. Iqbal and Hashmat joined the ranks of the most eligible bachelors in town.

Each time the phone rang, I picked up the receiver. "Hello! Hello!" A brief pause, then the line would drop. Watching Iqbal sitting uneasily nearby with Mother, it was not difficult to guess who the calls were for. If Iqbal was losing patience, he had yet to show it until the phone rang one more time. "You idiot, it's not for you" Iqbal finally spoke before I could pick up the phone again.

"I know, my dear. I also know who it may be for," I teased.

I had lost touch with Paru years earlier when she left school after her father was transferred out of Thakurgaon. She was back now in the same college as Iqbal, two years his junior. Ever since she saw the play *Tariq bin Ziad,* in which Iqbal played the lead role, she had fallen for him. First she began writing anonymous letters to him, which were no longer anonymous once he found out who was writing them. Soon Iqbal was reciprocating in the most literary style. A little embarrassed and suspicious, Iqbal knew that Paru used to be in his younger brother's class some years earlier.

I had not seen Paru in years but was definitely looking forward to meeting her, courtesy Iqbal. I wasn't jealous, just happy for him. When the phone rang again, Paru decided to speak. I quickly introduced myself to avoid any trouble,

"So you can speak," I teased.

"I knew it must be you. Your manners haven't changed in all these years," she replied quickly. I relented and surrendered the phone to Iqbal.

When Iqbal hung up, he gave me a sheepish look. "I know what you're thinking, but don't look so concerned," he said.

"Why should I be concerned? Are you in love with her?"

"Of course not," he said. "Stop making things up."

"And those letters?"

"Shut up," he said, hiding his embarrassment in front of Mother.

When we finally met within the next few days at a friend's house, I hardly recognized her. Paru was wearing a brightly coloured *shalwar qameez.* Her dupatta was hardly able to contain her well-endowed bossom, my first realization that girls change faster than boys. Unable to take my eyes off her beautiful figure, I felt embarrassed when our eyes met. The shy petite Paru of a few years earlier had grown up so fast into a confident, gorgeous young woman, like a wife or a mother, I thought. The only thing that hadn't changed was her boldness and her sharp wit. Her smile had a tinge of wickedness about it, and her eyes lit up whenever she spoke. She kept asking me about life in cadet college, which I had left behind, and about my future plans. Did I still paint? She gave me little opportunity to ask her much but allowed me all the time to look at her.

"I talk too much," she said, realizing that Mother was watching her too. "Tell me to stop." She laughed.

"No, no carry on," I said. "There's no need to stop. It's your friend's house." I couldn't have found a better opportunity to tease my future sister-in-law.

"How did you like your would-be daughter-in-law?" I asked Mother on the way back, tongue planted firmly in cheek. "It's the same girl who has been calling Iqbal and writing to him."

"I know," she said. "Not so soon. Let Hashmat get married first." She was not ready to commit yet, but she was not opposed to the idea. It mattered little to her that Paru was Bengali.

Tall, smart, and talkative, Paru seemed to be in love with Iqbal, considering the way she was taking care of her future mother-in-law and how she managed to instantly befriend her. At least on the basis of her height and personality, Mother must have thought Paru would be a good match for her tall, lanky son.

A telegram from our new principal, Mr. Bokiatullah, arrived, breaking the news that I had secured second position in the HSC board exams. I had waited for this day anxiously all summer and almost tore the envelop to pieces trying to open it. I had never seen tears in my father's eyes except once back in 1960 when our second sister, who was only six months old, died of dysentery. He never forgave himself for his perceived negligence in not taking her to the doctor sooner. I had grown up hungry for my father's acknowledgement of my worth. Not since my SSC results two years earlier had I felt like a worthy son to an extremely demanding father. The previous time it was only a hint of moisture in his eyes. This time a drop or two of tears squeezed out from behind his glasses, and he gave me a hug, patting me on the back.

Apart from Mr. Bokiatullah, Hashmat also sent a telegram from Dhaka. He always had high expectations of his brother, who had come a long way from his initial years at cadet college when I was struggling to cope with the harsh regimen there. After the first official warning from the school, Father was sufficiently alarmed to ask Hashmat to look for a technical training school for me in Dhaka where I could be sent after I was thrown out of cadet college. It was Hashmat who kept reassuring him, "Don't worry. He will do better than you think. He's just unpredictable."

Paru was quick to congratulate me when my result arrived, as if she was waiting for it just as anxiously. "Your brother was right," she said. "But you were just an okay student as far as I can remember, never that good." " If you don't mind me saying that," she hastened to add. It was hard to ascertain if she was pulling my leg or complimenting me.

"I don't know what my brother told you, but things change when you are in the right company." I wasted no time paying her back. It was almost an expected ritual to pull one's sister-in-law's leg in those days, and I needed practice.

My HSC results made me bit of a celebrity overnight in the small town of Thakurgaon. No one in recent years had secured second position in the board exams. My ex-teacher, Mr Yusuf, visited our home to congratulate us. The newspaper vendor, who was also the local reporter of the Morning News, came to take my photograph and had it printed the following week. Zahid and Hamid, still studying in Thakurgaon high school, told me their teachers remembered me and felt truly proud of their worthy student.

Each weekend that summer, we would go to our farm, which had begun to fill up with choicest guava and mango trees reaching maturity. We planted a fine variety of lemon trees, called *kagzi* and *shahtut*, on the parcel of land next to the main road where Father was planning to build a hut for his retirement, not too far from my Aunt Husna's house. In the afternoons we would wander away on the riverbed behind the farm looking for *boglas* to hunt with our air gun and regroup at Aunt Husna's before sunset for dinner.

While my summer still had a couple of weeks to run, others began preparing to return to school. My younger brother, Sajid, a bright, promising young man, had passed his entrance test for cadet college. The third of the Ashrafs left for cadet college along with Shahid, who was returning there to start his class XI and to enjoy his new status as a college senior. Iqbal and I prepared to join Hashmat in Dhaka, where we were to attend university starting in late September. The house in Thakurgaon was suddenly going to look too big for those left behind: Zahid, Hamid, and our sister, Munni.

As the most memorable summer of our lives drew to a close, our parents seemed mighty pleased with their sons' achievements. Dr. Hashmat, as he was now called, had started his job at Holy Family Hospital in Dhaka. He had higher ambitions and was already applying for jobs in the United Kingdom, expecting to leave in a few months. The only condition Father put on him was that he should get married before leaving. Father didn't want him to bring a *mamesahib* from London, as the parents used to say in those days. Mother already knew all about the Bengali lady doctor in Hashmat's life.

Elections and the Black Eid

People have been trying to kill me since I was born
A man tells his son, trying to explain
The wisdom of learning a second tongue.
—Li-Young Lee from "Immigrant Blues"

Iqbal and I arrived in Dhaka around mid-September 1970 to start our academic year at Dhaka University, where I was going to study economics and Iqbal was to study law. We lived with Hashmat in his apartment at Sobhan Bagh near Dhanmondi. By then Dhaka had taken centre stage for the country's political drama, and election fever was reaching its peak. The house of Shaikh Mujeeb, leader of the Awami League, whose movement within the next few months would turn our lives upside down, was only a stone's throw from our apartment.

A brief pause in the election fervour was provided by nature. On the night of November 13, hardly a month before the scheduled elections, the country's focus shifted south. One of the worst natural disasters of the century had struck the southern coastal areas. Twenty-foot waves from the Bay of Bengal crashed against the bamboo huts of hundreds of small villages and towns, washing them away. Winds of around 125 mph lashed the little islands and the delta region of Patuakhali, Chittagong, Noakhali, and Feni. The full impact of the disaster only began to unfold over the next couple of days.

The worst cyclone in living memory and one of the greatest natural disasters of the century in terms of human casualties stunned the nation. The death toll from it kept rising until it reached the staggering figure of 300,000. Some put it as high as half a million. Noakhali, Bhola, Hatya, Sandwip, and dozens of small islands were all under water. Two hundred square miles of densely populated territory lay battered and obliterated.

As the nation mourned the death and destruction, many Bengali politicians, including Bhashani, asked for a postponement of the elections, which most people thought was becoming inevitable. But the Awami League would not relinquish their advantageous position. Bent on capitalizing on every opportunity, it denounced and condemned the government's relief efforts. The climate of estrangement and alienation had reached a point where even a tragedy of biblical proportion was being exploited for political ends.

In the midst of all the destruction and suffering, the month of Ramadan arrived, and we headed north for what turned out to be our last Eid in our hometown of Thakurgaon. Winter had arrived early there, heralding a depressing time across the country. The devastating cyclone that had taken so many lives in the south, the political uncertainty, and the fear of a nationalist uprising combined to cast a spectre of gloom never witnessed before.

Out of nowhere the Awami League had found new scapegoats. The Urdu-speaking minority that had prospered economically thus far was suddenly being dubbed as economic exploiters. Ominously for them with the political situation on a knife's edge, the Biharis, as they were called, began to be branded as collaborators with the Pakistani political masters.

Ramadan passed without festivity, and Eid had arrived without even the usual controversy of whether the moon had been sighted. Nothing had happened since that morning that would tell us it was Eid, a day of celebration marking the end of Ramadan. As per the Gregorian calendar, it was December 1, 1970. According to the Awami League, it was yet another black day, ostensibly to protest against the poor relief efforts in the aftermath of the cyclone. There was no chatter of small children playing in the streets, no distribution of sweets, and no children in bright new dresses visible anywhere. Instead, we saw small groups of young Awami League volunteers asking people to wear black armbands to mark their "black day." Missing the smell of the traditional perfume *itar* or the aroma of *sewaiyan*, the air was filled with an uneasy stillness on that unusually cold, damp morning.

The morning mist, so common at that time of year, hung heavily over the town, hiding the sun behind it and casting a gloom over the horizon. At around 7:30 a.m. we were walking to the nearby football field, which served as the venue for the annual Eid congregation. Father and Uncle Ansari were in front, their sons following quietly behind them. The Eidgah was in full view, and we could hear the *khutba* of Moulvi Tameezuddin, his familiar voice on the loudspeaker echoing all around. Suddenly, half a dozen students coming from the opposite direction surrounded Uncle Ansari.

"Put on the armband," one of them commanded as he held out a black armband toward him. The rest of us were already wearing the black bands.

"Why?" he asked, without showing any sign of nervousness.

"Do you not know this is a black day?" One student approached him as if to forcibly tie it on his arm, standing less than a foot from him. "Put it on," he ordered.

"This is Eid day, my friend. Wearing this on Eid day is not permissible in my religion. I presume you are Muslims too." Uncle Ansari was unmoved by the threatening posture of these students. He had seen many such close calls as a teenager during the Hindu-Muslim riots in Calcutta.

"What if we force you to wear it?" One who looked like the group leader pushed Uncle Ansari lightly on his chest and moved menacingly closer. At that point Father intervened.

"My son, let me talk to him. Let's just calm down for a minute." He tried to pacify the students, putting his arm on the shoulder of one amicable looking young man he thought he recognized.

"Don't bother, *Bhaia,*" said Uncle Ansari said, looking defiantly at Father. "I will not wear the black band on Eid day. No one can make me do it." With that he had managed to destroy whatever goodwill Father had momentarily gained.

A few tense seconds followed, everyone expecting the students to react. Perhaps one of them was going to manhandle Uncle Ansari.

"Allah-o-Akbar!" we heard the call for the start of the *jamaat* reverberating on the loudspeaker, and everyone rushed forward toward the congregation. We were literally saved by the bell as the young men also decided to rush toward the prayers.

"We will see you after the prayers, mister," one of them muttered. The young man kept staring at Uncle Ansari as he walked toward the congregation.

It was hard to concentrate on the prayer. All I could think was what was going to happen later. For once I kept hoping for the moulvi to prolong his *doa* so much that the students would lose interest and move on.

As soon as the prayers ended, without the traditional embraces or exchange of greetings with the people we knew, Father asked us to head home straight away. On the way back, the students were nowhere to be seen. Upon reaching home, everyone breathed a huge sigh of relief.

In the eyes of our brothers, Uncle Ansari was a hero. But in Father's opinion, he was clearly being foolhardy. Worse, his confrontational attitude was doing a disservice to the Urdu-speaking community. Shaken by that morning's events, we spent the rest of the day indoors. Father did not allow Uncle Ansari to go back home until late that evening. It was the only Eid in our life when no one came to visit us. The phone kept ringing all day as almost all our relatives and friends phoned to inquire about what had happened that morning. They were surprised to miss us all at the Eid ground after the prayers. There were no Eid greeting, and those who chose to say "Eid mubarak" did so thanking God that it was a day without a serious incident and that we were still safe. None of the children asked for the traditional "Eidi," as if they had accepted this was not Eid. After lunch on the sunny side of the veranda in the courtyard, we spent the entire afternoon discussing the alarming situation surrounding us.

"Things will settle down when Shaikh Mujib becomes prime minister," Father said, ever the optimist.

"You are wrong," Uncle Ansari countered. "You are living in fool's paradise. Things will only get worse. Read the six-point demand Mujeeb has made. The days are numbered for the Urdu-speaking people here." The more he spoke, the worse it felt to all of us.

He had never been so dejected and so utterly disrespectful of our father. We watched helplessly as he continued to defy Father, afraid their relationship was in jeopardy. They were not real brothers, but I could not imagine anyone respecting his elder cousin more than Uncle Ansari did, at least until that day.

"Don't be a stubborn fool"

"Forget what I'm saying. Why don't you tell me what you can do to improve your own chances of survival here?"

"What plans you have for yourself?" Father asked, holding back his anger.

For all his brilliance, our hero had no answer. Except for his long-pending request with his regional manager for a transfer to West Pakistan, we were aware of. All he knew was that there was no time to wait, if one was going to act at all.

"As a minority community, it's important for us not to be seen opposing Bengali nationalism," Father said,once the arguments had subsided. "You must watch your words; sentiments are running high."

Father had put all his faith on his contacts in the Awami League. From that day onwards it was all about not doing anything to antagonize them and not giving them an excuse to vent their anger at the Bihari community.

Before leaving that evening, Uncle Ansari repeated his onerous warning to the boys, some of whom were now grown up enough to understand. Even if the Biharis supported the Awami League or tried to appease them, as our father was doing, we wouldn't be safe. "They won't spare anyone when the crunch comes. I can see the hatred in their eyes. It is no different than what I saw in Calcutta. Our time here is up."

According to him, they were fully capable of killing him when things got rough there, but they would not spare the Ashraf family just because Father had been playing his cards right. Even though some of us dreaded he could be right, we didn't like how he was making our father look stupid and naïve.

In bed that night, I kept thinking about what had happened that day, replaying the days depressing arguments in my mind. Uncle Ansari's ominous warning bells kept ringing in my ears. The ominous storm clouds gathering over our heads were now all around us. Closing my eyes I dreamt that Father had been stabbed by someone and was lying in a pool of blood. I woke up almost screaming. *Thank God it was a dream*, I said to myself. *But where is Father?* I couldn't hear his snoring in the next room. Mother used to keep the door connecting our bedroom with hers open for her nightly vigil. I listened closely, moments later, his snoring was audible again. Reassured, I slipped back into my dream.

The image of the first violent death I had seen a few years earlier reappeared before me. A mad rickshaw puller had stabbed Sadhu, who owned a sweet shop not too far from our house. The intestines from his large belly had spilled out as he lay dying in a pool of blood, right in front of us, on the roadside. Going back to sleep, I saw the continuation of the same dream with my father in place of Sadhu. Then the dreaded Kali maa with that garland of human heads around her neck appeared again. This time I thought I recognized some of the heads in her garland, but I was too terrified to look closely, lest they turned out to be people I knew. I heard some shooting and someone cry. I woke up again and cursed the devil to go away, saying, "*Astaghfarullah!*"

I tried one more time to go back to sleep.

A few days after Eid, I left for Dhaka, following Iqbal, who had left a few days earlier, arriving by train on the night of December 4. As I rode in a rickshaw from the railway station to Subhan Bagh, the unusually deserted roads took me aback. I glanced at my watch. It was 10 p.m., not that late.

"What has happened here?" I asked the rickshaw puller as he turned from the airport road toward Mohammadpur through Farm Gate, headed for the Subhanbagh doctors' hostel, where Hashmat and Iqbal were staying.

"There is so much tension in the city," he replied. He informed that a prominent student leader *khokon* was murdered at Dhaka University that morning, and the university had been closed. A *hartal* had been called for the following day. My immediate regret was that I would have stayed a few more days with the family in Thakurgaon had this happened a day or two earlier.

The lights on the stairs were switched off, and the entire building bore an eerie silence. I struggled in the dark to walk up the stairs, watching each step carefully, and knocked lightly on the door. No one answered, so I knocked again.

Am I on the right floor? I wondered. To confirm, I looked up at the apartment number, which was barely visible in the light from the single bulb at one end of the corridor. So I tried to peek through the window. There was no light inside either, and the curtains were drawn. Even if Hashmat was on call, Iqbal had to be home at that hour. Just as I began to worry, I thought I heard some movement inside. I knocked again, taking care not to disturb the neighbours or draw unnecessary attention. Still in utter confusion, I sensed someone peeking from behind the curtains. Suddenly, the door opened, and I was pulled inside.

"Shush . . . it's me, it's me," Iqbal whispered. I almost hit the side table as I fell on the floor next to Hashmat, who was sitting on the bed.

"What's going on?" I whispered back.

"Do you know what's happening in Dhaka?" Iqbal asked.

"And Enam hasn't returned since last night," Hashmat added.

Until the previous year, when Dr. Enam was a medical student, he had been an activist for the pro-government National Student Federation (NSF). Set up by the thugs of ex-governor Monem Khan, the NSF was a feared force when Monem was in power, disrupting opposition meetings and beating up rival groups. Their ex-patrons were on the run now. The tide had changed, and the NSF leadership was being hunted down. Only the previous month its general secretary, Saeedur Rahman, a.k.a. "Pashpattu," was lynched, his body left hanging outside the university. The incident that the rickshaw puller told me about was apparently about another top NSF leader, Khokon, whose body was found on the race course ground.

"You think something has happened to Enam Bhai?" I asked. The gravity of the situation began to sink in. Inside I was still cursing myself for hurrying back to Dhaka. Perhaps it was time that my brothers left Dhaka for Thakurgaon for their own safety.

"For all you know, he may be hiding somewhere," I offered a suggestion, when no one answered.

"The trouble is that everyone here thinks we're related to Enam." Hashmat was working on the possibilities, but his tone suggested he was fearing the worst.

"Did you ask the Bengali doctor on the second floor?"

"He denies seeing him today." Hashmat's tone was telling how little he believed that doctor. The previous week the doctor had a heated argument with Enam over whose responsibility it was to clean the veranda outside their rooms. It was clear to the three of us that if anyone came looking for Enam there, we would all be in trouble. But there was not much to gain by panicking. We would just have to act normal and tell them he had gone to his sister's house in Mirpur.

To defend themselves in case anyone mistaking them for Enam's relatives attacked them, Hashmat and Iqbal had taken the wooden legs from the mosquito stands to use as weapons. I wanted to laugh but could not. We sat quietly, pondering whether we should shift to another place in the morning. The incident with Uncle Ansari on Eid day in Thakurgaon was still fresh in our minds. We did not agree with Uncle Ansari's dire predictions, who viewed everything with the lenses of what he had experienced during the riots in Calcutta in 1947. No such calamity could happen in Thakurgaon. If there was a political showdown between the government and the Awami League, it would play out in Dhaka. We continued to talk in low voice, taking care to keep our ears open, looking at table clock every few minutes.

"*Chalein hai dil waley road to swat*," we heard someone singing on the stairs. The voice got louder and nearer.

"Shush . . . is that Enam?"

It could only have been him. Iqbal and I rushed to open the door when we heard the first knock.

Dr. Enam had been to the movies to see the new hit, *Road to Swat*, probably with some nurses, which he would not admit. It was the last thing anyone would have guessed. Besides, it was hard to believe that any movie theatre could be running the second show with the city on a knife's edge.

"How could you do this? Don't you know what's happening in the city?" Hashmat asked angrily.

"Relax, Hashmat Bhai," Enam replied. "If something is destined to happen, we will never be able to stop it. So, why not at least enjoy the time we have left?" He smiled wryly. "One day in the life of a lion is worth a hundred years in the life of a fox," he said, repeating his favourite silly phrase, which we had heard from him so many times before.

Then he proceeded to casually tell us how some students near the medical college had waylaid the ambulance that he and some other doctors were commuting in that morning.

"Are there any Biharis here?" the students demanded to know.

Straight-faced, Enam kept looking at the Bengali doctor he had quarreled with the previous week. "Thank God he did not speak. He is not as bad as I thought." He made the incident sound like a joke; that's how Dr. Enam always was, brave and foolhardy.

The elections were to be held within days of my arrival in Dhaka. Since most schools, colleges, and shopping centres were closed, we had little choice but to spend our time talking about whether Mujib was going to win a landslide and what would happen after that. Most notably, if things would ever get back to normal after the expected Mujib win. One of our father's friends, Motiul Islam, a successful businessman in Dhaka, knew someone in the intelligence agencies. According to him, Shaikh Mujib was expected to get a slim majority at best. The agency was filing reports to Islamabad that the religious parties, especially Jamaat Islami, were gaining ground in East Pakistan. Whether such reports were ever filed or how much the reports had anything to do with the series of miscalculations and blunders Islamabad committed, we would never know. Whether such reports had anything to do with the conspiracy theories that abound to this day in Pakistan also remains a question no one will ever be able to answer.

To us, the residents of East Pakistan, predictions of Islamic parties gaining ground were farcical or wishful thinking at best. It was easy to see that the tide was in Mujib's favour. His campaign of Bengali nationalism was carefully crafted and he had galvanized the university students to shut things down at will. The Awami League did not need to use the word "independence"; they just espoused every cause that weakened the federation of Pakistan. Mujib's six-point program seeking complete provincial autonomy was expected to win the day at the ballot box. It was difficult to imagine how Pakistan could stay in its present shape after the elections.

Election day, December 7, passed peacefully, to everyones relief. Yahya was being hailed as the champion of democracy after the free and fair election with no hidden agenda of his own. Contrary to the expectations of the government's intelligence agencies, but not to the surprise of the majority of residents in East Pakistan, Mujib won a landslide in East Pakistan. His party won 160 of the 162 seats in the national assembly. In West Pakistan Bhutto won 81 of the 120 seats, making his People's Party the largest in that province. Neither the Awami League nor the People's Party won any representation in the other province. With the two potential neutralizing factors, the Muslim League and the Jamaat Islami, out in the cold, the election results polarized the country.

Mujib's party was now in a position to draft a new constitution on the basis of his six-point program. This made Bhutto suspicious of Mujib, and he kept telling Yahya Khan not to allow Mujib to become the PM, i.e., not to transfer power to him. He did everything to convince Yahya that Mujib would weaken the federation with his insistence on a six-point plan that would be inducted into the constitution by virtue of his party's strength in the new assembly. Bhutto began to create conditions that would push Mujib to the wall, leaving him few options in the face of a rising wave of Bengali nationalism that he could no longer contain.

The inordinate delay in Yahya's decision to convene the national assembly after Mujib won the elections served to convince many Bengalis that they would never get their legitimate rights. They were becoming restless and furious at the delay tactics being adopted by the army regime at Bhutto's behest. Perhaps the military junta feared that Mujib would relegate Kashmir to the back burner and show a conciliatory attitude toward archenemy India. Bhutto utilized the top army brass's fear of becoming redundant to his full advantage. Bhutto and Mujib's brinkmanship was risking the very integrity of Pakistan. At the same time, they could not have been oblivious to the fact that they were also playing with the lives of the minority Urdu-speaking community, who were bound to become collateral damage as the country threatened to pull itself apart. The political tussle and behind-the-scenes conspiracies continued while the people in East Pakistan were getting increasingly restless.

That restlessness was on full display at the mammoth public meeting at the Dhaka race course on January 3, 1971. Mujib declared that if he was not made prime minister, the Bengalis would have no choice but to seek an alternative course. It was the largest gathering we had ever seen. Iqbal, Hashmat, and I parked our bike behind the Radio Pakistan building and climbed the walls of a house next door to reach the edge of the crowd to witness an unforgettable spectacle. A sea of humanity lay before our eyes as far as we could see. Hundreds of thousands of people in their white kurta pajamas, the dress that had become the symbol of Bengali nationalism, popularized by Mujib.

"This is how the Day of Judgment will look like," Iqbal whispered, "when we are all raised from our graves in our white *kaffans*."[1]

Only Mujib's commanding oratory could contain the charged crowd as they cheered every word the leader spoke. Iqbal said something in Urdu, quickly realizing what he had done when a couple of people from the crowd began to size us up. The threatening manner in which they looked at us suggested we must be Pakistani spies, enemies of the people.

"Let's move," Hashmat said.

Without another word, the three of us moved out swiftly from the crowd, not looking back even once. Mujib's voice was still reverberating in our ears

1 Muslims are buried in white robes, which they call "kaffan."

all the way back. For the first time we had come face to face with the ominous side of Bengali nationalism; something in those eyes told us that.

We learned later that night that Mujib had made the elected members of the assembly in that rally take their oath of allegiance for the cause of an autonomous East Pakistan. The crowd went wild with each pledge Mujib made for them. Each time he paused, there was total silence, as if they were listening to a messiah. The passion at the rally was like the videos we had seen of Hitler's rally at Nuremburg in 1939.

Back in the safety of Hashmat's apartment, we spent the rest of that evening contemplating what might be coming next.

"You must leave for Karachi at once," Iqbal told me firmly, a move he had opposed only two months earlier when he first learned that I had applied for a scholarship to study in Karachi.

"Regardless of whether you get the inter-wing scholarship or not, we will manage the expense somehow."

The three of us talked about how, after my departure, we could gradually transfer Shahid and Sajid to cadet colleges in West Pakistan. "I will convince Abbu of that." For the first time, Iqbal, the 20 year old guardian of the family, was conceding that our days in East Pakistan were numbered.

In those days the government of Pakistan used to award scholarships to five or six position holders in the HSC board exams to study in the other province under a student exchange program. Having stood second in the Rajshahi board exams, I was qualified to apply. When the scholarship was finally confirmed at the end of January, everyone in the family appeared relieved. Iqbal and Hashmat were going to miss me in Dhaka, but they were happy that not only would I be away from that increasingly volatile city, my departure could also be the catalyst for taking others out gradually. Feeling a mixture of guilt for leaving my brothers behind at such a difficult time and relief that my move may prove helpful to the family, I prepared to leave for Karachi.

Father and Mother came to Dhaka, along with my sister, Munni, and my youngest brother, Hamid, to see me off. It was hard to say goodbye to them as the time approached for the train to depart, taking them back to Thakurgaon. The guard had blown his whistle and was waving the green flag. Tears squeezed out of Mother's eyes as we stood up to leave her compartment.

"I wouldn't let you go so far if it was not for your own good," she said.

Hamid and Munni looked on admiringly at their brother, who had grown up enough to go away literally to another country. One day they might follow in my footsteps, they must have thought.

We had no idea when we would see each other again. I freed myself from Mother's hug. She let go only when Father intervened by saying the train had started to move.

"Watch your step," Father warned as Hashmat and I jumped out.

We stood there on the platform waving at them until the train disappeared in the distance.

A couple of days later, on January 31, 1971, the day I was to fly to Karachi, several of my Bengali friends from Dhaka University came to the airport to see me off. Also at the airport was Abdul Hamid, my dear friend from cadet college, who I had become particularly attached to during the past few months in Dhaka. My departure would be missed by everyone in Hamid's family since they had come to rely on me for taking care of him when he had a bout of sickness. His father had refused to accompany him to the clinic because he thought Hamid was old enough to go by himself.

Saying goodbye to me in Urdu, Iqbal managed to surprise some of my new friends from the university, who until then were unaware that I was not Bengali. His eyes unashamedly wet, Iqbal hugged me and held me tightly in his arm, somewhat embarrassing me in front of my friends. Relieved to see his brother heading for safety, he kept waving from the visitors' gallery. In a small airport like Dhaka in those days, he was in full view from my seat on the plane, although he could no longer see me. Had I looked closer, I would have read in his eyes that he believed this was our last meeting. He did not move from the gallery until the plane had begun to taxi towards the runway.

XXXXX

IN CONTRAST TO THE TENSIONS in the eastern wing of Pakistan, the city of Karachi struck me as even livelier and more vibrant than I had heard. It seemed no one was affected by what was happening in the other part of Pakistan. Even the newspapers appeared to treat the standoff between Mujib and Bhutto as if that was just more political jockeying between two adversaries.

Yahya finally yielded to pressures from every quarter by convening the national assembly in Dhaka's newly built second capital on March 2, 1971, nearly three months after the election results had been announced. But in a land of conspiracies, somehow the back-door intrigues continued to convince Yahya to call off the assembly. He was being told that Mujib must first agree to the terms of his premiership and spell out the extent of constitutional reforms. Otherwise, with the majority in his hand, he could secede from the federation or do anything to harm the country's integrity.

The political seesaw continued as Mujib and Bhutto hardened their stands. Bhutto demanded two national assemblies and two prime ministers, one for each province. "Idhar ham udhar tum," he was famously quoted as saying. Adamant that he would not attend the national assembly session in Dhaka, he even threatened to break the legs of West Pakistani politicians who dared go to Dhaka to attend the assembly.

Whether it was under pressure from Bhutto or under the advice of his generals or under the influence of excessive alcohol he was known to consume, General Yahya finally cancelled the assembly session planned for March 2 in Dhaka. Thereafter events began to take their own course, and the government lost its grip on East Pakistan. The beginning of the end of Pakistan as we knew it, had arrived. A cycle of violence was about to unleash itself in East Pakistan.

1971 – SHAIKH MUJIB DELIVERS A STERN WARNING TO THE FEDERATION OF PAKISTAN. THE ECSTATIC CROWD CHEERING "JOY BANGLA" SENDS A CHILL DOWN THE SPINE OF THE NON-BENGALI POPULATION.

Death of the Federation and Genocide of the Biharis

The dead man was no one,
just a man in tattered clothes,
no shoes . . .
a no one, a nobody
who clenched his hand before he died.
When they pried open his fingers,
this nobody,
they found a whole country.
—Hama Tuma from "Just a nobody"

After the postponement of the national assembly session planned for March 2, 1971, all hell broke loose. The Bengali population had given up hope that the Pakistani establishment would ever allow their undisputed leader, Mujib, who had won the elections, to become prime minister. The hardliners in the Awami League began to see independence as the only course of action left to them. The people appeared ready to back Mujib's call, and the word "Bangladesh" was on everyone's lips except for the lips of the Urdu-speaking minority, whose hearts sank every time they heard the chant "Joy Bangla," ("Long live Bangladesh"). The economic resentment against the small Urdu-speaking minority had already been simmering under the surface for some time. Collectively called the Biharis, they were seen by vast majority of the Bengalis as fifth columnists and the symbol of Pakistani nationhood that could only be an obstacle to achieving their goal of independence.

Within hours of the postponement of the assembly session, angry mobs took to the streets in town after town around East Pakistan, brandishing bamboo sticks and iron rods, and burning and looting houses and shops mainly belonging to the Biharis. Mujib called a *hartaal* (lockdown) for March 2 in Dhaka and a province-wide shut down on March 3. He gave the government a three-day ultimatum promising to spell out his next course of action after the expiry of the ultimatum at a public meeting on March 7.

With the province plunged into chaos, the soft-spoken governor, Admiral Ahson, pleaded with President Yahya to fix a fresh date for the assembly without wasting any more time. Ahson was fired and asked to hand over power to the martial law administrator, General Yaqoob. Glued to their radios, the unfortunate Biharis held their breath as their death sentence was being reviewed. Their nervous wait continued through every twist and turn. Days seemed like weeks and weeks like months. None of the predictions favoured even the downright optimists like my father back in Thakurgaon. The ideology of the "two-nation theory" that carved out the Muslim homeland Pakistan in 1947 on the basis of their religion was meeting a dead end. The Bihari Muslim community was being branded as collaborators and traitors by their Bengali Muslim neighbours. The great fervour of the independence movement in which my father's generation participated was all but forgotten and replaced with the anger and frustration of the Bengali population, which was consuming them.

Iqbal returned one evening to Hashmat's hostel bringing news of the fresh arrival of troops at the Dhaka airport from West Pakistan. He had heard that on the BBC. After being confined to the doctors' hostel in Subhanbagh for nearly two weeks, the two brothers sighed in relief thinking that the army action might calm things down even if temporarily. But that temporary reprieve was nothing more than the calm before the storm, because the countdown for the independence of Bangladesh had already begun.

Not surprisingly, when news of the troop movement reached Mujib, he set out on the warpath by launching his non-cooperation movement, demanding the troops return to the barracks immediately. As the de facto ruler of the province, Mujib himself undertook to maintain order using his Awami League volunteers. To the horror of the Urdu-speaking people, the troops were sent back to the barracks, whereby the government effectively surrendered the province to the league's volunteers. A collection of young men with bamboo sticks, knifes, a few guns, badges, and party flags took over the streets. An almost non-stop procession of these people were on the move everywhere shouting, "Joy Bangla!"at the top of their voice. The Bihari population watched in horror and disbelief as they braced for the full fury of the vigilantes. They knew the league's anger would be directed toward them sooner or later. The defenseless Biharis were in a state of disbelief, seeing how they were being sacrificed by the Pakistani politicians using tactics of backtracking and procrastination. No one understood why the winner of the elections, Sheikh Mujib, was not being allowed to become prime minister.

Many Urdu speaking people fled their homes and took refuge near the cantonment areas. Houses in those localities were flooded with dozens of relatives and friends from other parts of the city squatting on the verandas, backyards, and in the servant quarters. The lucky few who could afford to buy a ticket to safety fled to West Pakistan. With only one flight per day, the price of a one-way ticket to Karachi, normally 250 rupees, shot up to several thousand in the black market. A mile-long queue had built up outside Dhaka airport, and people slept on the pavement to stay in the queue. News began to trickle in from various corners of the province of widespread burning and looting of properties belonging to the Urdu-speaking community.

Stranded in volatile Dhaka, Iqbal could only watch the anarchy take hold in the city and hear about the killing of Biharis in other towns. Sensing the mood in Dhaka, his Bengali colleg mate, Mustafa, persuaded him to go to the nearby town of Chandpur where Mustafa's parents lived, a suggestion Hashmat immediately endorsed. But Iqbal found no peace in the relative safety of his friend's house, listening to the same depressing news on the radio all day long.

He made several attempts to call home, but no one picked up. Calls to different friends in the town yielded no clues as to where the family had gone. Iqbal's unease became acute. Iqbal told his friend that he must return to Thakurgaon. His father was alone and needed him.

A land known for its docile and peace-loving people who had surrendered to the miniscule army of Muhammad bin Tughlaq a few centuries earlier had no history of violent uprising. But they had been so galvanized by the league's leadership that they would stop at nothing to achieve independence. That "nothing" was the sinister side to their plan and their best-kept secret: the ethnic cleansing of the Biharis.

Among the first massacres was Pahartali in Chittagong, where 102 Biharis were killed on March 3. Bengali martial law administrator Brigadier Mozumdar apparently did nothing to prevent the butchery. Sporadic news of killings followed from towns across the province.

The day Mujib was to address the all-important public rally arrived on March 7. Dhaka was rife with rumours of a unilateral declaration of independence by Mujib.

Wearing their signature black armbands and their white pajamas, the young volunteers kept their vigil trapping Biharis in the confines of their homes. No one was allowed to leave. In our hometown of Thakurgaon, one Urdu-speaking businessman, Pir Mohammad, a kerosene dealer, was caught trying to flee to India. He was brought back near his own home and hacked to death by a mob. Perhaps the mob believed the fleeing Biharis would somehow take the wealth of Bangladesh with them. Conversely, if they stayed and were allowed to live, they would continue to dominate economically while at the same time remain fifth columnists amongst them.

"Bloody Pakistani agents." The Bengalis had not forgotten that only a few months earlier, the previous August, these Biharis were proudly flying the Pakistani flag on Independence Day. The Awami Leaguers believed the Biharis had always supported the federation and would continue to sympathize with Pakistan. As such, they would always be against the independence of Bangladesh. That suspicion continued to feed their hatred against them. With the local media in total control and mobs ready to act, the Awami League's leadership prepared to conduct the final act of ethnic cleansing of the abandoned, defenseless people, taking out their anger on those who symbolized Pakistan for them.

As East Pakistan simmered in anger, General Yaqoob made one last effort to persuade Yahya to come to Dhaka and find a political solution. But he gave up and resigned. His replacement, General Tikka Khan, a man with a ruthless reputation, in stark contrast to his two predecessors, arrived on March 8 to take charge. The fact that East Pakistan was already under Mujib's rule did not require further proof when the general could not find a judge to swear him in as governor.

The Awami League continued to consolidate its grip on the province, issuing a series of edicts and directives to government departments, commercial organizations, banks, schools, and so on. Except for the military cantonment areas in the major cities, Mujib ruled everywhere. He issued orders to his countrymen to block all supplies to the cantonments and not to assist in the movement of the Pakistani armed forces.

The Pakistani government deliberately suppressed the news of violence against the Urdu-speaking people, probably intending to avoid a backlash against the small Bengali population in the western province, mostly in Karachi. More importantly, the ideology of Pakistan was under threat as they feared the fatal blow it would give to the "two-nation theory," the very basis of Pakistan's existence. The ideology that led to the carving out of a separate homeland for the Muslims from British India less than a quarter century earlier was being tested on the streets.

When Yahya arrived again in Dhaka on March 15, he was warned by his own generals that any military solution could cost thousands of innocent lives, and a political solution to the impasse must be found. Over a week of discussions with Mujib yielded nothing, and Tikka Khan was ordered to prepare for restoration of the writ of the government in East Pakistan.

Preparations had also started by Mujib's de facto commander in chief, Col. Osmani, who had secretly begun contacting Bengali troops in the Pakistani army. His plans reportedly included the capture of Dhaka airport and Chittagong seaport to cut off the supply lines with Pakistan. Then the defecting soldiers and police officers of East Pakistan were to storm the cantonment and occupy them. It was now a question of who was going to strike first.

The "Joy Bangla" slogan was reverberating on the loudspeakers on every street corner throughout the province where the Bengali youth had already begun to celebrate their independence. The Awami League declared March 23 as Resistance Day. Pakistani flags were burnt and the portrait of the nation's founder, Jinnah, was replaced with that of the "Bongo Bandhu," Sheikh Mujib, at government offices and public places. The red, green, and gold Bangladesh flag, which later became red and green, could be seen fluttering on every building, including the rooftop of Mujib's own house in Dhanmondi. President Yahya left unannounced on the evening of March 25, having approved the military crackdown that was to begin that same night.

Around midnight on March 25, army tanks rolled out and headed toward Dhaka University. The military column was greeted by large tree trunks and broken-down vehicles blocking the roads in the direction of the city and toward the second capital where the elected assembly was supposed to meet and install Shaikh Mujib as the new prime minister. Several thousand protesters chanting "Joy Bangla" were on the vigil. As the army column pushed forward, those pickets were met with the fire of light machine guns. It wasn't long before the resistance collapsed in front of this onslaught. A few miles into the city, the fiercest battle of the night took place at the university, which had been the home of the Awami League's student wing. The university hostels were torn down by machine gun and artillery fire and their occupants killed. Large trenches were hurriedly dug the next morning to bury the dead. The government of Pakistan accepted one hundred dead. The Awami League claimed several thousand were massacred. Mujib was arrested at his home the same night and whisked away.

That same night Mujib's pre-recorded message was aired by local radio stations proclaiming the creation of the Peoples Republic of Bangladesh. He called upon his people to resist the army occupation until the last Pakistani soldier was expelled from the soil of Bangladesh.

From their apartment in Subhan Bagh, Hashmat could hear the gunfire for the better part of that night. By morning, the ever-present large crowd around Shaikh Mujib's house on Road #32 Dhanmondi, visible in the distance from the roof of their building, had disappeared. Dhaka woke up to an eerie silence on the morning of March 26, its streets appeared calm again. The airport had been taken over by the Pakistani army, and additional troops began to arrive from West Pakistan by the planeloads. The empty planes on the way back were lifting to safety the families of Pakistani army officials and a lucky few civilians. Some businessmen paid for a one-way ticket with their cars, gold, or cash as the civilian passes for the journey began to trade at an enormous premium.

Pakistan was now at war with itself. The ill-planned military solution aimed at forcibly keeping the people of Bangladesh within the union began to wreak havoc on the Bengali population. To restore order, widespread arrests and killing of political activists were taking place. That only fuelled their hatred against Pakistan and against all those who stood for the federation, namely the Urdu-speaking people. A province-wide reaction to the show of massive force in Dhaka began to unfold over the next few days. In the army garrisons spread over the other towns and cities, the Pakistani troops were far outnumbered by their Bengali counterparts. The Bengali soldiers of the EPR (East Pakistan Rifles) and the local police refused to obey their old masters. In camp after camp they began to rebel and run away with their guns to join the *mukti bahini*. As a first step, the rebels killed the heavily outnumbered Pakistani soldiers and their families in their respective garrisons and then fled to join the Awami League *Sacha Sebok,* volunteers setting off with their guns and ammunition to eliminate the Urdu-speaking Bihari population.

By the time the Pakistani army was able to advance against the rebels with fresh reinforcements, the intense retribution had unleashed an unprecedented wave of killing of Urdu-speaking civilians. The well-organized *sacha seboks* were aiding the Bengali soldiers' rebellion by helping them hunt down the Biharis in their neighbourhoods.

By March 27, 1971, within two days of the army action, the local administration in the hands of the *sacha sebok* volunteers had rounded up the prominent heads of Bihari families. This volunteer force had been managing the "peace committees" set up ostensibly to maintain law and order. They quickly began taking away any arms and ammunition in the hands of Bihari families. Then the heads of prominent Bihari families were taken to what they called "safe" places, promising to protect them against the angry mobs. A few days later, the volunteers handed them over to either the rebel police or EPR soldiers, who escorted them out to a nearby riverbank or under a designated bridge, where they were executed in cold blood.

Almost immediately after killing the family heads, women and children were rounded up and taken away in jeeps and trucks outside the towns. Those refusing to be taken away were shot and killed at their homes without much fuss. In northern towns, these families were driven to a riverbank or a bridge earmarked for the purpose, where they were lined up and shot by a firing squad. Those not killed immediately would be hacked to death if any sign of life was seen after the shooting. The consistent pattern of killing in those smaller towns and villages only served to confirm that the massacre of the Biharis could not have been a spontaneous outburst of Bengalis angered by the army action. To the victims and their families who witnessed it, it had the hallmark of an organized genocide that could only have been conceived well in advance.

Survivors mention how their captors pointing their guns at them would ask, "Where are the rest of your folks? Where is your brother? Your father? Your uncle?"

The attackers were so organized and meticulous that it seemed as if they had the census survey in their hands. Wherever their tally did not match the dead, they would come back to look for more. For nearly two weeks, the Biharis remained sitting ducks in their own homes or hiding here and there, exhausted, hungry, or wounded. No one was prepared to own even those poor folks who had totally assimilated in the society, spoke the language, married into Bengali families, and had Bengali children. The Haiders, the Shobratis, and the Ashrafs were all to be dealt with. In towns like Thakurgaon and Dinajpur, the carnage was so extensive that no one was spared, not even women and children, newborns, the old, or the infirm.

Those who carried out the killings may have been a small fraction of the Bengali population, but none of the survivors I met believed that a small number of people could carry out a systematic extermination on such a scale. They had seen the *sacha sebok* informers and guides working with the rebel soldiers. Without any planning or without the complicity of the political leadership, which was in total command over the province, the scale of the massacre is inexplicable. The killing of the Biharis intensified after the military action on March 25, but the fact remains that it started weeks before the military action. Years later some Bengali friends revealed to me what they had heard at the time. The fleeing EPR soldiers wanted to ensure that no one was left to side with the Pakistani army when they returned to fight for the independence of Bangladesh. The handful of survivors of the tragedy corroborated that by early March the Awami League volunteers were already surrounding Bihari homes to disarm anyone who had any weapons.

It took nearly three weeks for the Pakistani army to "liberate" the towns and cities one by one. Saidpur, Dinajpur, Thakurgaon, Isherdi, Parbatipur, and Shantahar, were reached one by one. When the army reached these towns, they were stunned by the brutality and the scale of the massacre. All they could do then was bury the dead, with the help of the few who had survived.

Within four months of the black Eid, Uncle Ansari's premonitions came true. The Awami League vigilantes were looking for him everywhere as he kept changing his hiding place. Finally, one morning they waylaid him when he was visiting his family. They ordered him to go with them. He refused, knowing the end had arrived. Along with his two small sons, ages eight and six, and his wife, he was butchered in the courtyard of his own house a few blocks from our house. During the riots in Calcutta in 1947, he had taken shelter in a Hindu's house and survived. Now in a Muslim country, there was no one to protect him or his little children.

By the time the army arrived in Thakurgaon, only a dozen or so small children and five or six adults were found alive, either hiding among the dead or hiding in their neighbourhood without food or water for days. No one compiled any statistics, but by the account of these survivors, the total killed in Thakurgaon and adjoining settlements was in the thousands. Almost all of my relatives and friends who lived in that town were killed. We counted around 200 dead among the people who were either related to us or who we knew closely. After so many years, their names and faces still remain imprinted in our minds.

Thirty-six miles away in our beautiful district town Dinajpur, we also had many friends and relatives. The massacre there was extensive too. Two hundred and fifty bodies of women and children lay butchered on the premises of Iqbal School, from which Hashmat had graduated. In the neighbourhood of Balubari, where Father had bought our second house for his family's future needs, rows of houses owned by Urdu-speaking people lay empty, their doors wide open. Most of the womenfolk and their children were killed in their homes, while their men had been taken to the banks of Kanchan River next to the railway bridge and executed.

In Chittagong around 150 women and children were hacked to death in the clubhouse at the Ispahani jute mills, where they had taken shelter. At the Karnafully paper mills, the Urdu-speaking people's families were bundled into the rest house and massacred there. In Sirajganj 350 women and children were locked in a hall, which was then set on fire.

In Mymensingh the entire colony of Urdu-speaking people was exterminated. Another badly hit town was the railway junction of Shantahar, where Arshad Jamal, our friend from cadet college, lost his brother, sister, and parents, all of whom lived in the railway compound. In the same compound, Qamar's elder brother was abducted, never to be seen again. When his father refused to go, they stabbed him in front of his wife and daughters.

Pockets of resistance proved Uncle Ansari's theory of non-appeasement and self-defence as the only way for survival. In Dinajpur, only one area, sector five of the satellite town, which was built for Bihari immigrants, remained largely unscathed, simply because a handful of young men put up a brave resistance. Their youth had refused to surrender their weapons and even managed to secure some guns from the Pakistani soldiers in the nearby EPR camp by the time the rebellion happened. In the three-week siege, some died in the crossfire and a few weak ones due to hunger, but they managed to keep the attackers at bay. Sadly, those who put their lives in the hands of their Bengali friends were the ones who perished in Thakurgaon and in Dinajpur.

The Bihari community estimated that between 150,000 and 200,000 perished across East Pakistan in what would have been the first major ethnic cleansing the world had witnessed since World War II. The dead cannot speak, but the survivors who lived through those harrowing weeks and months saw what happened, and those images would haunt them as long as they lived.

Pakistan's inept military leadership initially played down the havoc being wrought by the Awami Leaguers. It did not want to give the impression to the outside world that the majority of the Bengalis were up in arms against Pakistan. And the hatred against the West Pakistanis had reached a point that those branded as Pakistanis were being killed by the Bengali mobs in every town. The dilemma facing Pakistan was the basis of its ideology and existence, the 'two-nation theory', the theory that formed the basis of the argument that Hindus and Muslims were two distinct nations requiring two homelands at the time of independence of India from the British in 1947. The rationale for the creation of a homeland based on religion was being discredited and refuted by this uprising, and the two-nation theory had all but met its end in East Pakistan.

The outside world knew little of what was going on; there was no appeal to Mujib or his party to end all this. No attempt was made after the massacre either in Pakistan or newborn Bangladesh to find the perpetrators who were responsible for the deaths of so many thousands of innocent unarmed linguistic minority. The world's attention was focused only on the political fallout of the Bangladesh movement and the excesses committed by the Pakistani army against the Bengalis.

Had the Bengalis not been so brutal in their struggle for independence toward the defenceless Biharis, it is possible that the Pakistani army's response might have been more measured. Many Pakistani soldiers and their families were killed in the initial days of the uprising. Wherever reinforcements finally arrived, they encountered thousands of mutilated bodies, among them their own colleagues and their families, who were killed by the Bengali soldiers in every garrison. The spectre of brutality against their compatriots as well as against the Urdu-speaking civilians would have shaken even the bravest of hearts.

Ironically, it was the brutalities against the Urdu-speaking Biharis that put Bangladesh on the fast track to freedom. The organizers and perpetrators of the massacre fled across the border to India . The Pakistani army ended up subjecting the innocent Bengalis to all kinds of excesses in their wild goose chase, causing a bigger exodus. The attention of the world press was drawn by the plight of the millions of Bengali civilians who fled across the border to India, flooding the refugee camps there. By successfully publicizing the vicious crackdown of the Pakistani army and the sufferings of the Bangladeshis, the Indians were winning the propaganda war.

The second irony in this tragedy was that with Pakistan suppressing the news of the massacre of Urdu-speaking civilians, they lost the only plausible *raison d'etre* of a foolish military action. After that the world paid little attention when the massacre of the Urdu-speaking people or the Biharis began to filter through. By then a bigger human tragedy, the indiscriminate killing of Bengali civilians, was hitting the front pages of the world press and unfolding on television screens around the world.

The End of a Dream

No one leaves home unless
home is the mouth of a shark
No one leaves home until home is sweaty
voice in your ear
saying—leave, run away from me now . . .
—Warsan Shire

As East Pakistan descended into chaos, by early March 1971, the Ashrafs, like other Urdu-speaking families around the province, found themselves surrounded by an increasingly hostile and restless Bengali population. Schools and colleges across the country were being forced to close down. Fearing for the safety of the students and teachers, the cadet college in Rajshahi closed its doors. Shahid and Sajid had no choice but to return home to Thakurgaon.

Ten days before the army action, around March 16, Iqbal was persuaded by a Bengali friend to get away to his village to escape the daily disturbances in Dhaka. But Iqbal failed to find peace in Chandpur. Listening to news on the radio every day, he was becoming desperate to join the family in Thakurgaon. Amidst all the turmoil, Iqbal returned to Dhaka, making most of his journey by boat and on foot. There he met Hashmat for the last time.

"Abbu is alone; he needs me to be with him at this time," Iqbal told Hashmat. This was going to be Iqbal's final act of standing firmly behind his father in his hour of greatest need.

"You will be better off there than in Dhaka." Hashmat was happy, thinking Iqbal would not only be safe in the small town of Thakurgaon but also provide the family with much-needed moral support. Iqbal looked more Bengali than anyone else in the family, and he had so many friends in

Thakurgaon who he could draw upon to provide reassurance that the family needed in these turbulent times. Partly by train and partly by bus, Iqbal managed to hitch his way back to Thakurgaon around March 18. How he made that perilous journey, we will never know.

By the time Iqbal arrived in Thakurgaon, the small town had been transformed into a battle zone. Processions of Awami League volunteers were marching every day on the streets chanting "Joy Bangla." Most of the shops were closed, and public transport had all but disappeared. It was not the beautiful and peaceful town that he had left only a few months earlier. None of his friends wanted to know him anymore. Then came his real heartbreak. One of his Bengali friends from the local college advised him to leave the country.

"It's no longer safe for you Biharis to be here," he put it bluntly.

"What do you mean?" Iqbal asked, stunned by the suggestion. "Where can we go?"

"Tell your family to leave as soon as you can. It's just not safe for you to be here. Cross the border; go to India or Pakistan."

"I was born here; everything we have is here," Iqbal protested. "We would be shot crossing the border. It's impossible for us to go to India. My father fled India for the safety of our family."

A member of the Awami League's youth wing, Iqbal's friend probably knew more than what he was sharing. He would have been aware of the party's game plan in terms of inciting rebellion in the nearby EPR camp and the plans to expel or kill the Biharis who they could no longer trust. The Biharis, they feared, were likely to side with the Pakistani army when the liberation war begins. How those steps would unfold was known only to the party's high commands, but Iqbal's friend sensed the worst. Devastated, Iqbal could hardly believe what he was hearing.

The clock was ticking fast; it was time to make some impossible choices. For everyone to travel together to Dhaka or Chittagong and escape to Pakistan was one option. But with riots around the country and extremely limited public transport, it was dangerous to consider the 200-mile journey with so many people. Two months earlier they had considered a gradual move to Karachi in West Pakistan, but it was too late for that now. The 1,200-mile trek through hostile India, which was on the verge of war against Pakistan, was just as absurd. Praying for things to improve was the only thing the family could do, and that's what they settled for in the end.

Saving as many lives in the family as possible was all that Father and Iqbal could now think of. It was no longer safe to stay in their own house with armed Bengali mobs roaming the streets, looking for one pretext or another to attack the Biharis. Hiding five brothers, one sister, and two parents or moving anywhere in a group without being noticed would not be easy.

Sensing a complete change in the Bengalis' mood toward their community, the Biharis in Thakurgaon had thus far showed some foresight by contacting the local Awami League leadership directly for protection. Unlike the rest of the province, the Bihari community assured the Awami Leaguers of all cooperation in their struggle to have their demands met by the central government in Pakistan. By the time the Awami League announced the non-cooperation movement, the Urdu-speaking people of Thakurgaon had already started participating in the street corner meetings and rallies organized by the Awami League to show solidarity with their Bengali brothers.

"Be ready with whatever you have, start training, and brace for difficult times ahead," Shaikh Mujib had declared in his March 7 speech, effectively declaring Bangladesh independent even though he did not use the word "independence" in that speech.

"We live here, and we will die here. We are with you, Bongo Bondhu." That's how the Bihari speakers responded at rallies in Thakurgaon, publicly paying tribute to Bongo Bondhu in various street corner meetings.

With their backs toward the wall, it was a last-ditch effort to convince the Awami Leaguers of the Urdu-speaking people's support or at the least to assure them that the community will not stand in the way of their Bengali brothers' struggle for autonomy. To save their own lives, they chanted "Joy Bangla" along with the crowd, even though their hearts sank with every utterance of these words. Some Urdu-speaking people hailed this show of solidarity, but many remained skeptical of its ability to secure their lives and property. The Awami League leadership in the town outwardly welcomed it but did nothing to provide any assurance of security to the Bihari community.

Despite this show of solidarity, the Awami League volunteers began demanding that any weapons in the hands of Biharis be surrendered. Ostensibly, these were required by the league volunteers to defend everyone against the Pakistani army. Virtually cut off from the capital, Dhaka, the Pakistani army was nowhere to be seen around the district. When the league volunteers came asking people to surrender their weapons, it was not difficult for the Biharis to work out that they had good information. They knew who amongst the Urdu-speaking people had weapons (how many and what type) when they went about the business of collecting them.

"Joy Bangla," the chants in the daily processions in Thakurgaon continued. "Bongo Bondhu-jindabad, Pakistan-murdabad."

By the third week of March, the local Awami League demanded that Urdu-speaking families participate in all the rallies to show solidarity. What was volunteered by the community only a week earlier had been mandated by the party. On the morning of March 21, Iqbal, Zahid, and Sajid were in one such rally. Hamid was too young to matter. A mob of a thousand or so chanting slogans passed by our house. Suddenly, the mob stopped right infront of the house.

Father peeked through the window, trying to figure out why they had stopped there and instinctively started looking for his sons.

Where are my boys? He was nervously scanning the crowd. Just as Mother was about to lose her mind, the young son of our Hundu neighbour, Bhavani Babu, walked straight into their bedroom. "Uncle, let's go to our house. Abba is calling you. Come on, auntie, this way," he insisted.

Before they could say anything, he ushered them through the little opening at the rear perimeter wall to their house, Mother clutching Munni and Hamid's hands. The four of them swiftly negotiated the narrow storm drain between the two houses into our neighbour's house.

"Hurry up, Ashraf Bhai," they heard Bhavani Babu call from inside his house. Once inside, Mother and Munni joined the anxious ladies squatting on the veranda. Bhavani Babu, Hamid, and Father carefully climbed the unfinished rough stairs to the roof of the recently completed two-floor house, almost tripping over a small heap of gravel that had not been removed from the landing of the staircase.

"Joy Bangla," the crowd continued to chant while they waited outside our house. By then a small section of the noisy crowd had entered the gate to our front yard. They thumped on the front door, threatening to break it open.

"What do they want, master sahib?" Father asked Sadequl, the young Bengali tutor to Hamid and Munni, who had joined them on the roof.

"Ashraf sahib, they want your guns," he replied.

Father explained to Sadequl where to find the shotgun and the rifle and asked him to go and hand them over.

Sadequl went in, took the guns from under the mattress in Father's room, and opened the front door; the crown burst out in chants of "Joy Bangla."

From Bhawani Babu's roof the men watched the crowd move out of the front yard. For the first time they noticed a lot of new faces in the crowd, almost a new leadership guiding them.

"Where are these people from?" Father asked. No one replied as they watched the procession move out of the front yard and head east toward the EPR camp, their chants slowly receding in the distance. Everyone in town had heard of some impending mutiny or plans by *sacha seboks* to attack the nearby EPR camp. Maybe the time had come. Rumour had it that volunteers from India had joined the league's youth wing in that district.

The procession disappeared behind the high walls of the girls' school east of our house almost halfway to the EPR camp. After a few minutes, the crowd decided to turn back, and re-emerged from behind the school's perimeter wall, their chanting audible once again.

After handing them the guns, Sadequl had slowly moved toward the back of the procession. "Go home," he whispered to Zahid and Sajid. "Your father is getting worried."

Bhawani Babu and Father were still watching the procession from the rooftop, both praying to their respective gods for the best. Suddenly, they heard a gunshot and then another one. Some EPR soldiers on patrol coming from the opposite direction had fired at the crowd. People screamed and fled in all directions. Then someone fell right in the middle of the road while the crowd ran helter skelter. A bullet must have hit the man, who was lying motionless. By then Zahid and Sajid had joined Father on the roof. In a few minutes, the crowd appeared to be regrouping again. The firing had gotten them extremely agitated. Their slogans resumed as they picked up the body, and carried it away. It was a small miracle that the rest of the day passed without further incident. The first martyr in the independence movement in

Thakurgaon had fallen, a victim of a sniper shooting it seemed or a shot from one of the EPR soldiers.

Strangely, the incident brought a respite of a couple days as a precarious peace hung over Thakurgaon. But news of Bengali mobs looting and burning the properties of Urdu-speaking people continued to trickle in from the rest of East Pakistan. The violence was becoming less sporadic and more intense as the reports of casualties indicated. Telephone and postal services were no longer operating, but grim news was dripping in bit by bit on the radio or from Biharis fleeing from one part to another. Large-scale murders of Biharis were being reported from Chittagong, Khulna, and Mymensingh.

In Thakurgaon the fate of the Bihari community still rested on a thin wedge thanks to the correct political steps taken earlier by the community, declaring their allegiance to the Awami League. Yet everyone believed it was only a matter of time before the first blow was struck. When it finally happened, the news of the first Bihari casualty in Thakurgaon was received with less disbelief and more with a sense of urgency to hide and flee no matter the risks. Saif's neighbour, Pirbhai, a petroleum dealer, was hacked to death for trying to flee the town. No one believed any longer that Thakurgaon would be spared. Whatever was happening in the rest of the country was bound to come there.

"The situation is extremely volatile here. We may finally have to flee but only if the opportunity ever comes," Iqbal wrote in a letter on March 22, which was hand-carried by a family friend who survived the massacre and reached me in Karachi after Iqbal's death. The trouble was that the faces of all the Ashrafs were well known in that small town, which made it impossible for them to flee. Iqbal ended the letter saying, "The rest—if we live to tell the tale."

Given the growing popular anger against the Bihari community, any offer of safety, however slim, could not be overlooked. Four days after the procession, on March 27, the local administration in Thakurgaon—by then in the hands of the Awami League—ordered the prominent Bihari family heads to be temporarily shifted to a "safe place" under the "protection" of their armed young volunteers. Only after these people agreed, they were told that the designated safe place was, in fact, the local jail, which had been vacated because all the inmates had escaped or were allowed to escape. Whatever immediate suspicion this move may have raised in everyone's mind mattered little since this captive community no longer had a choice.

There was no time to waste, and the family had to divide the risk. The night before he was taken away, Father decided to split the family, which was to take refuge with the most trusted Bengali friends he had. That he deemed was the only way to increase the odds of survival for at least a few. Mother, Munni, and Hamid went to live with Dr. Yusuf, our family doctor and a long-time friend of the family, at his village home. Two of my brothers, Zahid and Sajid, went to live with the family of Mr. Nurul Huda, one of my father's ex-colleagues; we called him "Head Clerk Chacha." One of Mr. Huda's sons was going to school with Sajid. Iqbal went to live with his school friend and Shahid with the family of his school friend Shubro, whose father we called "Lal Chacha" due to his fair complexion.

"These are our most trusted friends who will look after you," Father assured everyone. "You must leave tonight. Do not stay here after they take me away." He handed each some cash and went on to forbid everyone from returning to the house until things settled down or until Iqbal came looking for them. While making his plans, Father hadn't thought much about his twelve-year-old niece, Firoza. She was Husna's stepdaughter, who had recently joined the family from Pran Nagar and, as such, was now his responsibility. Almost as an afterthought, she was sent to stay with our Hindu neighbour, Bhavani Babu. Perhaps Father couldn't bring himself to trust his neighbour with any of his own children because Bhavani Babu was Hindu. Ironically, choosing his Muslim friends for his own children and the Hindu neighbour for his niece turned out to be another grave error of judgement that Father made in those desperate times.

Everyone in the family was keenly aware that regardless of what happened, Iqbal was already a target, and people were looking for him. The hunting rifle he had managed to hide would be his friend and companion, his only defence against the overwhelming odds he faced. A few days earlier, when Sadequl had handed over the shotgun and the air gun to the mob, they left satisfied, their count of two guns from our house was complete.

The designated "safe place" for the fifteen or so family heads where Father was taken had been placed under the responsibility of the local police and the sub-divisional officer (SDO). Since the SDO's son was my classmate,

Father must have drawn some comfort that he would not be harmed. But as the duration of the confinement lingered on for several days, his confidence began to wane. All day the so-called community leaders, the heads of the most successful Bihari families in that town, would either pray or sit on the floor of the jail to deliberate over their options, knowing well that they had none. With each passing day, they received news from their visitors as well as their captors about more violence across the country. Finally, the killings started in their own town, and fewer and fewer visitors came to meet them. Between March 30 and April 4, only one or two servants or visitors came with food or medicine as well as terrible news of their near and dear ones. After that no one visited them. The only source of news from the outside world was the guards or their radios.

In captivity Father received the news about the massacre of Uncle Ansari and his family. That increased his desperation to see his own family at least one last time. A suspected angina attack brought him some relief and some special treatment. He was admitted to the ill-equipped government hospital close to the jail premises, where a guard kept watch over him. Somehow Iqbal got the news and was able to visit Father at the hospital. One evening, after bribing the guard, Iqbal slipped Father out of the hospital, and Father managed to reach Dr. Yusuf's village a few miles away.

There he met Mother, Munni, and Hamid for the last time. The four of them sat on a mat in the thatched room, dimly lit by a small kerosene lamp, overcome by the joy of their reunion. After dinner they lay on the makeshift bed not knowing where to begin. Mother, Hamid, and Munni had so many futile questions to ask, to which Father had no answers. They held back, not wanting to cause him further pain. Somehow they still had not lost confidence that Father would be able to find a way out, just as he had managed to make this perilous and impossible visit. Their faith may have been shaken, but it was not completely lost.

"I am sorry, Bibi, but I am unable to do anything," Father began.

"Where have you sent Iqbal, Zahid, and Sajid?" she demanded quietly, not happy to be separated from them. "How are they?" She was still questioning her husband's decision to break up the family.

"I met them today, and they are fine," he lied. "Don't worry; things will get better." He looked away as he uttered those words, unable to look her in the eyes anymore. He also decided to hide the news about Uncle Ansari from her. His informer at the jail had found it futile to say much about our other relatives, who had been killed. Especially about the families of Afzal Mamu, the pregnant Jhanna Baji who lived next door to Uncle Ansari, and our other family friends, like the Pathan tea shop owner near the bus stop, along with his infant son and two wives. In the most gruesome of all murders, we learned later that our cousin Jhana Baji's belly was cut open, and even her unborn baby was killed. All the other Biharis we knew in town had been killed too. Until then the only known survivors outside our own family were Hashim Chacha and two of his three sons, who managed to hide in the bushes behind the wapda colony for days without food or water.

"How much longer can we live like this?" Mother asked, fighting back tears. "The children stay awake all night; they have never slept on the floor. They are used to so much comfort, and now?" She paused to stare at her husband, who had lost so much weight since she last saw him. He seemed to have aged years since the unrest began barely two months earlier. "You look so weak. Do you still have your medicines?"

"Sure." He took out the little bottle to show her his blood-pressure tablets. Smiling, he held it out toward Munni and Hamid. "See?" He gave them a nudge, bringing smiles on their faces.

"Do you have electric fans at the hospital?" Mother asked.

"Yes."

She only knew about the hospital because she was never told Father was being detained at the central jail. Father was not going to make her life more unbearable than it already was by saying any more.

"It's because of me that you all find yourselves in this dreadful mess," he said, then paused to reflect.

"Perhaps we should all have stayed back in India," Mother replied.

"You would not be going through all this today,"

"Yes, he admitted," wiping her tears with his *kurta*. Hamid and Munni looked on in silence.

"Don't say that. It is because of you that I have these wonderful children" she protested, gently stroking her husband's hair with her fingers as if to comb it back. She noticed his hair had gone gray and had not been washed or combed for days.

"Just make sure you don't let my absence—" Before Father could finish, she covered his lips with her hand.

"Talk about something else," she pleaded.

Finding nothing else to talk about, they remained quiet for a while, huddled together with the two children, relishing every moment, fearing it may never return. After a while they started to talk again. Like the old days, once again planning wishfully what they would do when the Pakistani army finally arrived and they were able to come out of hiding. Munni and Hamid listened intently, their eyes lighting up. They wanted to believe their father.

"Zahid and Sajid must be dispatched to Dhaka immediately," Father said. "From there they should proceed to Karachi to join Azmat." He also told Mother that he didn't mind if she wanted to go back to her village in India. "They will be so happy to see you; I will go with you too."

He kept talking aimlessly until he fell asleep unashamedly in his Bibi's (mother) arms with the two children huddled next to them.

The next morning as Father was getting ready to leave, Mother protested. "Why can't you stay with us here? We will face the same fate together; I don't mind dying with you."

"No! It will endanger everyone if I stay here. There is no place for me to hide; everyone knows me. They will find me whenever they decide to kill me. I don't want to risk the lives of my children."

He explained why they were holding the men hostage as if he accepted what they were doing. So many in the community relied on him to protect them; and there was safety in numbers. "Trust me, things will change," he struggled to convince her.

Events had moved so quickly that he had lost touch with the outside world. He still believed the SDO was in charge of the town. He also trusted the personal assurances from Awami League MPA elect Fazlul Karim Mukhtar. They said that if the detained family heads listened to them and cooperated, their families would not be touched.

"If only Ansari had listened to me, he would still be with us today," he lamented.

"What happened to him?" Mother asked.

"Nothing! We just don't know where or how he is," he lied again. He paused to collect his thoughts, his voice trembling. "Promise me . . . if anything happens to me, you will not give up hope. You will take care of our children the way you have all your life. I know I could not have found a better mother for them or a better wife for me in a hundred years."

He kissed the children before leaving. For the first time he also kissed his wife in their presence. Then he left quietly through the back of the house. Long after he was gone, Mother kept looking that way. Maybe he would return to collect something he forgot. Maybe he would decide to stay one more day with her.

After meeting the family in that remote village, Father must have satisfied himself that they were safe. He did not know that he had been spotted leaving the village by someone who was not going to keep quiet.

Upon his return, he was told that the hospital no longer had any ability to look after patients. They were being turned away, and all medicines had run out. He was escorted back to the central jail. Back in detention, Father began to lose hope for his own freedom. The prominent Biharis were clearly the prisoners of the Awami League volunteers, who insisted they stay there for their own safety. They were no longer allowed to meet anyone, and if anyone from their families dared to visit them, even to bring them food, they were sternly warned and turned away. The wolves were now guarding the sheep.

Everyone knew that after the March 25 crackdown, the Pakistani army was advancing to retake the towns from the hands of the rebels, one by one. But it was taking far too long to reach the northern towns of Thakurgaon and Dinajpur. Father told his fellow prisoners not to inform his family if he died in captivity. Not until the Pakistani army liberated everyone.

"Tell them later where I am buried, so they can visit me to offer fateha," he said, making his last wish known to them. One day later, on April 8, he suffered a stroke that left him so weak that he didn't think he had the strength to pull through. The only prayer he kept repeating over and over again was for the safety of his wife and children. That was the last favour he asked of his God. He stopped listening to the news on the radio, just stared at his friends huddled around that device and praying for a miracle. Lying on the mattress on the jail floor, he reminisced about his childhood back in the village of Baghaul, about his mother and his father, who he could hardly recall. He thought about his wife, the time he got married, the night of his wedding, how beautiful Bibi looked, how lucky he was to have married a girl like her. She never asked for anything all her life. Even when she was saying goodbye three days earlier, the tears in her eyes were only for her husband. For his part, he had always stood by her from the time his family objected to their marriage. But now when she needed him more than ever, he was totally helpless.

"Who will take care of her when I'm gone?" he muttered to himself as he lay on the floor. She had given him seven worthy sons and the most beautiful daughter in the world. Hashmat was already a doctor, and the others were doing so well. They all had a bright future, maybe not there anymore but in Karachi or someplace else. He imagined Mother in a white sari praying at his grave with her sons standing next to her. Too tired to think, he fell asleep on the dirty mattress, pulling the unwashed bedsheet over himself.

On the morning of April 9, Father and the other Bihari prisoners were taken to the bank of the Tangon River, a short walk from the jail. They were lined up and shot by a group of EPR soldiers. Their bodies were left there for days until the army arrived on April 14.

The person who had seen Father coming out of the village informed other villagers, who got angry with Dr. Yusuf for taking such a risk by sheltering a Bihari family. A weak person by nature, Dr. Yusuf panicked and decided to send Mother with her two children back to Thakurgaon to hide in his house there, which was virtually empty by then. In no position to object, Mother had to abide by those instructions.

She was asked to stay indoors and to make sure no one went near the front windows. The doctor assured them that no one would think of searching an abandoned Bengali home. He was also kind enough to arrange for a Bengali cook to live with them. No one would ever know if that was a grave mistake that Dr. Yusuf made in his half-hearted stand to save his friend's family or if it was just horrible luck that a neighbour spotted them and decided to inform the EPR. Munni's close friend and classmate, Lipi, Dr. Yusuf's daughter, hugged Munni with a look of guilt and helplessness on her face. At the tender age of twelve, time had already taught the two young girls to have unusual control over their emotions.

Unknown to the rest of the family, Zahid (14) and Sajid (13) were facing constant nagging from the lady of the house, the wife of the head clerk uncle.

She kept telling her husband that he was inviting trouble by sheltering the boys in their home.

“They must leave,” she insisted each time they sat down for a meal. She had nothing against the boys, but she was not prepared to risk her own family's safety. Her constant nagging deeply hurt the boys, who could not bear to see her fight her husband over them every day. The head clerk uncle's own children were of the same age group, went to the same school, and had grown up together with Zahid and Sajid. They were embarrassed by their mother's behavior but were too young to prevail.

“How can I ask them to leave?” Uncle pleaded with her in vain. “What face would I have left to show Ashraf Bhai if anything happened to them?”

Tired of the daily bickering, the two brothers decided to leave. Ignoring their father's command, they decided to go look for the rest of the family. On the evening of April 9, they left under the cover of darkness and arrived at Dr. Yusuf's house to join Mother and their two siblings. How they found out where Mother was, we will never know.

Shahid and Iqbal had been sneaking out at night to rendezvous in the yard behind the empty shops near our home. They would exchange information and try to bolster each other's morale. On the night of April 11, they met for the last time behind those shops. Iqbal told Shahid that he preferred to die with his family. Sick and tired of being on the run and fed up of hiding alone, Iqbal had begun to lose all hope once he found out that Father had been killed.

“There is only one end for me,” he said calmly. “Everybody is looking for me, and I know they would not rest until they find me. Maybe if they find me, they will stop looking for you all. Maybe their thirst will be quenched with my blood.”

Although he did not say anything about Father's death, Shahid could read that all over Iqbal's face. Defiant and no longer afraid of anything, Iqbal had lost his will to live. He urged Shahid to go back to Lal Chacha's house. “They are honourable people, and they will do anything to protect you. For God's sake, stay with them until the army reaches Thakurgaon. They are already in Saidpur, barely forty miles from here. I heard that on the radio today.”

They hugged each other tightly. Then Iqbal turned and disappeared into the dark. As Shahid walked back toward Lal Chacha's house, he knew Iqbal was hiding something from him, but he shuddered to think any further. Had something terrible happened to Father? What was next for the rest of the family? He also knew that Iqbal, due in part to his reputation as being good with a gun, had always been a prime target. His own college mates from the Awami League were now looking for him. He could no longer trust anyone to protect him and had nowhere to run. Sooner or later they would find him. Suddenly, Shahid had the urge to turn back and run toward his brother, to hug him one more time. He stopped to look back but couldn't see anything in the dark. Iqbal had melted away.

Like Zahid and Sajid, Iqbal had also learned that Mother had returned to Thakurgaon and was hiding at Dr. Yusuf's house. He decided to join them the same night he met Shahid. Under the cover of darkness, he entered Dr. Yusuf's house by scaling the boundary wall at the back. To his utter surprise, he found Zahid and Sajid sitting quietly by Mother's side.

"Why are you here?" he asked in disbelief as they reached out simultaneously to hug him.

"Don't be mad at us; we just couldn't stay there any longer." Zahid explained how they were being constantly reminded that they were endangering the lives of their hosts.

"Never mind; if we are going to die, it is better we die together," Mother said resolutely clutching the hands of her two sons, no longer showing any fear or emotion.

Together again, Iqbal tried to console everyone and raise their morale. Zahid and Sajid also supported his efforts, still feeling guilty about returning. Together they coaxed Hamid, who had refused to speak at all, to play X's and O's, so they could kill time in the dim candlelight in the small storeroom, which had no windows. The electricity had been disconnected ever since their return to town. Then they played Twenty Questions and Find the Word until the lack of competition started to bore them. For years they had played such games with their father as the referee, but he was not there to join them that night. His absence was all everyone thought about, but they avoided discussing it in front of Mother. Instead they chose to talk about the good days gone by or teased Hamid and then Munni to force a response. A faint attempt to laugh was immediately followed by a total silence. Without a word from anyone, the guilty party would leave, pretending to go to the washroom and wipe their tears there. They huddled around on the mat to eat what the cook had prepared that afternoon, which had lain untouched thus far.

"Tea, anyone?" Munni asked as she got up to go to the kitchen. For once it was her intending to restart the conversation that had ended a while earlier. She acted as if her brothers were her guests, visiting from out of town.

"No! No! You are not going anywhere. Sit here; let me do your hair." Mother found a bottle of hair oil to put in Munni's hair and began to comb it, though it was not the usual time she did her hair. It had been weeks since Munni had spent an evening with the four brothers and at least a week since anyone had combed her hair. At just over twelve years of age, Munni already looked like a lovely maid. When Mother pulled back her hair to tie it, she revealed her beautiful forehead and deep black eyes, which sparkled in the candlelight. Mother imagined how Munni might feel when her brothers came to visit her after she was married off to the prince of her dreams. How she would welcome them or look after them as her mind wandered off to some distant land.

Until that night Iqbal had never disobeyed his father; neither had Zahid or Sajid. Perhaps he was there that night to persuade Zahid and Sajid to go back. They might have even planned to split up again the next morning as Father had commanded. They had to stay in separate places to improve the chances of survival for at least a few. But the second opportunity never came. They all slept in one room on the first floor facing the back of the house to ensure that no one passing by on the road in front of the house saw any sign of life there.

Late at night Iqbal tiptoed through the living room in the front portion of the house to take stock of things. The road in front was deserted; not a soul anywhere. Chokha Mia's house next door was empty. Their family, like everyone else, had fled to their village. Moharrir's house, on the other side, looked deserted too. There was no sign of life in that town. Where had they all disappeared? Then he recalled he had seen some movement in Muharrir's house earlier in the evening. From the window of the empty living room, Iqbal could see a portion of his own house less than 300 meters away. The annex on the right side of the lawn was clearly visible along with the lichi tree and the mango trees behind it. Would they ever live in that house again? Would he ever be able to play with his brothers again under those trees? He asked no one, and no one had the answer. Except for the howling of the stray dogs far away, he heard nothing. No one seemed to live in that town anymore.

"Go back to sleep, beta." Iqbal did not know how long his mother had been there with him.

"Remember Ammi? Before that annex was built, we used to cross that ditch to go to the club grounds. Father would be so angry at us crossing over the barbed-wire fence, but we always did that in search of a shortcut."

"Forever you boys were in such a hurry. Remember how many times you all came home with bruised knees?" She smiled, squeezing her son's arm.

They talked about the time spent at that house in past tense, as if they already knew they would never return. In the dark Iqbal hid his tears as he continued to engage his mother.

"Did you hear something?" Mother asked. "She has woken up. She must be looking for me." Thinking she heard Munni call out, she went back to her room. Munni had been especially quiet lately. Her looks were beginning to worry Mother, and her silence had begun to hurt her.

Iqbal stood by the window thinking about his mother and her desperate prayers for her husband. How would she cope when she found out that Father was no more? He was angry with the head clerk uncle for turning out Zahid and Sajid despite his promise to protect them. But there was no one he could complain to. Lifelong ties had been broken and friendships betrayed. Iqbal's faith in everything was shaken beyond repair.

For many nights that April, Iqbal must have felt like he had been sleeping in trenches with his ammunition, exhausted, while the war raged above. He was surrounded on all sides, and vultures were flying overhead looking for human flesh. He could choose to die early by merely lifting his head or wait in the trenches for his turn to die. Or he might have held a belief that no one could die until his time came; faith provides that hope to many.

Back in the room Iqbal joined Mother who seemed like she was wiping the tears from Munni's face. A child so pampered by all reduced to a life of hiding to save her from being killed. Not so concerned about her own predicament, she was just angry that no one was telling her anything about her father. All attempts by Iqbal and her brothers to make her smile failed. All she did was clutch Iqbal's arm and ask, "Where is Abbu? When is he joining us?"

THE TOWN WORE A TOTALLY deserted look by April 12 as the news of the Pakistani army's imminent arrival spread through Thakurgaon. The bloodthirsty EPR soldiers roaming the town had begun to flee. Few volunteers of the *Sacha Sebok Bahini* were visible on the streets during that day. The killings had more or less stopped because there were hardly any Bihari left to kill. The morning was so calm that it must have seemed to Iqbal and the others that they were going to survive after all, and their life of hiding would end soon.

BASED ON THE EYEWITNESS ACCOUNT of their final journey, I tried to piece together the last few days of their lives above and the last few minutes below. What thoughts were going through their minds when the end arrived? I can only imagine, knowing them so well, as if I was there myself.

The Bengali Islamiat teacher (we called moulvi sahib) from Hamid's school who lived nearby happened to be outside Dr. Yusuf's house witnessing what happened on the fateful morning of April 12.

At approximately 9 a.m., Dr. Yusuf's house was surrounded by a dozen or so EPR soldiers and some Awami League *sacha sebok* volunteers. Their van pulled in and stopped just inside the gate. Mother was preparing breakfast; the Bengali cook was nowhere to be seen. Suddenly, they heard someone call Iqbal by name. Then other voices joined in, getting louder and louder.

"We know you are hiding there!" one of them shouted. One voice threatened to break the door and kill him right there if he refused to come out. After a few seconds, the front door opened. Iqbal came out alone, probably hoping the soldiers did not know who else was inside or perhaps thinking that if he surrendered, the others would be spared. He must have asked everyone to stay inside and keep quiet since no one came out with him. With his hands in the air, like a prisoner of war facing his captors, Iqbal came out on the veranda. The soldiers' rumblings were followed by a sudden silence as Iqbal paused to look at his captors, who were a few feet away, one pointing a gun at him. Iqbal knew the end had arrived. As he took one more step toward the stairs at the end of the veranda, the sharp sound of a gunshot echoed under the carport. The bullet hit Iqbal in his neck. Clutching his neck with one hand, he fell down the stairs. A soldier rushed forward with his rifle as if he was going to attack him again, this time with his bayonet. Iqbal was bleeding profusely. Trying to cover his neck with his hands, he rolled over, falling two steps down the stairs and landing in the carport.

Hearing the gunshot from inside, the family could not hold back any longer. Everyone rushed out. Mother took Iqbal's head in her lap, staining her white sari red.

"Mera laal!" she shrieked. Zahid, Hamid, Sajid, and Munni sat down motionless next to their mother.

"You heartless bastards!" she yelled with all the strength she could muster. "What has he done to you? You will all burn in hell, hear me? It would be much worse for you all." She wasn't holding back anymore.

Iqbal was still breathing when the soldiers commanded everyone to board the van. One of them struggled to pull Mother away from Iqbal, dragging her toward the waiting vehicle. "Chalo, chalo," they commanded, pointing their guns at them. Mother did not resist. Holding Munni's hand, she proceeded to board the open jeep.

The Islamiat teacher watching all this by the gate fell on his knees in front of the men and pleaded for mercy. "Please, for God's sake, spare them. They are good people. I know them; they are my students, my own children." " Please, at least let the youngest one go," clutching Hamid tightly in his arms, he begged them, not letting go. His pleas stopped when one of the soldiers pushed him hard, and he fell to the ground.

"Shut up, you collaborator." One of the soldiers lifted his gun and pointed it at the moulvi sahib and threatened to kill him right there if he did not stop.

The family was driven north about two kilometers past our rice mill, where Zahid and Sajid often used to come with their father on the days their school was closed. The gate was wide open. No chowkidars or workers were in sight who could intervene on behalf of their young masters. They had all disappeared days before the mill was looted and vandalized. The jeep stopped near a small bridge not far from the mill, and everyone was asked to get out and follow the soldiers. All obeyed silently. With no will to live, they would have preferred to be killed with Iqbal back at Dr. Yusuf's house.

A Bengali boy who witnessed the final moments described how they were made to stand in line under the bridge and shot one by one. The first bullet hit Mother, who seemed to be instinctively reaching for her daughter Munni, who was hit next. Clutching each other, the two fell to the ground, lying there motionless until they stopped breathing. The three brothers, Zahid, Sajid, and Hamid, stood silently awaiting their turn as they were shot one by one.

"None of them uttered a word or begged for mercy," the boy told us.

For months and years after that day, I saw those moments in my dream. There was a dignity in their silence that would have made our father proud.

By the time Lal Chacha found out what happened, he had already reached the Indian border. The rebel EPR soldiers, aided by the *Sacha Sebok* volunteers, were still hunting down any Biharis hiding here and there. At the same time, they were fleeing from the advancing Pakistani army. It seemed like the entire Bengali population had joined the exodus headed for India. Tall and fair, Lal Chacha did not look Bengali. At one of the border villages, the residents attacked him, thinking he was a Pakistani. Fortunately for him, his own wife and children were the living proof that saved him from his attackers. Bleeding from his forehead, they continued their journey toward India.

Determined to save Hayat's only remaining son, Lal Chacha would not let Shahid out of his sight even for a minute. They stopped at their ancestral village not far from the Ruhia border. Sensing danger, that night he insisted that Shahid sleep with his son, Shubhro, Lal Chahcha, and Chachi, all in the same room. Despite the precaution, someone on the prowl that night threw a spear through the window in an attempt to kill Shahid. The spear landed a few inches from him. Realizing that such attempts would be repeated, on April 15, Lal Chacha finally found someone he could trust to take Shahid across the border to India. He gave Shahid some money and asked him to head straight for his grandma's village in Bihar by train once his escorts took him over the border. Lal Chacha and his wife had been discussing this option for Shahid for several days.

Having lost everything except his determination to live, Shahid was in no position to argue; he just obeyed his benefactor. While saying goodbye, Lal Chacha broke the news of the final tragedy to Shahid. He told him there was nothing left in Thakurgaon for him to go back to. By then Shahid was prepared for that news; he had been listening to the constant whispering between Lal Chacha and his wife about who was going to speak to him. The tears in Chachi's eyes whenever she looked at him had all but confirmed his worst fears.

As the jeep roared down the dusty, bumpy road toward the Indian border, a million questions rushed through his head. Shahid wondered what would happen to the family of Lal Chacha and his dear friend, Shubhro. Would he see them again? Would he ever return to this country? Would he ever be able to repay his benefactors, who had risked their lives to save him?

Shahid had only visited his grandma's village, Kumhrauli, when he was around age four. He had no recollection of how he had travelled there then. He knew Mamu and Nani's faces only through photographs he had seen at home. Now that old lady who walked with a stick and her bearded middle-aged son were supposed to take care of him. But he did not want to stay there with them, and he had already begun to plan his next step. He wanted to go to Karachi, where I lived, but he had no idea how to cross the border on the western side.

His thoughts were interrupted when the Bengali driver of the jeep started humming a Tagore song. Here is an English translation.

> When you don't see my footsteps here
> And I no longer row this place
> All our transactions would have been settled
> And all our give and take ended.
> No more would I frequent this place
> You may no longer remember me
> Looking at the starts, you may no longer call me.

Tears gushed out of his eyes, providing him with a strange sense of relief. The other Bengali passengers in the jeep who were also fleeing to India were discussing and savoring their recollections of how they had dodged the army when it arrived in Thakurgaon. They had succeeded in running away with this jeep, which did not belong to them. Since the driver had been paid well by Lal Chacha to take Shahid across, they seemed least concerned that he was a Bihari boy. The driver knew Shahid spoke fluent Bengali and posed no danger to them if they were stopped by anyone looking for Biharis. No one in the jeep attempted a conversation with him. Since the other four passengers had already occupied the bench seats on each side of the vintage World War II jeep, Shahid sat on two jute sacks in the middle, uncomfortably adjusting and balancing himself each time the jeep went over a bump on the dirt road.

From the conversation of the four passengers, he was able to make out that the jute sacks contained money looted from a local bank by the same people he was travelling with.

On the morning of April 16, Shahid reached the Indian border town of Islampur and parted ways with the other travellers. Now he was all alone and began to figure out how to get to Kumhrauli as he walked a couple of miles toward the railway station the jeep driver had pointed out. Hungry, exhausted, and hardly able to move, he found a small wooden bench by a tailor's shop next to the railway station, where he sat and waited. Someone at the station master's office told him a train would be going west toward Darbhanga that evening, but there was no definite time.

At a nearby intersection, the town's only paved road crossed a dirt road. A dozen or so tin-roofed shops, some with brick walls and paved floors, others with bamboo partitions and clay floors, lined both sides of each road. The locality seemed to slowly come alive with activity as the evening approached. As the sun faded on the horizon, some of the shop owners lit their lanterns. Others were busy cleaning the glass or pumping air in their gas lamps, which would soon flood the intersection with more light and be ready to receive more shoppers or visitors to the nearby teashop. Misery was written all over his face as he pondered the future, barely able to move and barely awake, deep inside, Shahid still felt grateful to be breathing the air of freedom after a long time.

"Hello, son. What are you doing here? Are you waiting for someone?" the tailor master repeated the same to catch the boy's attention.

I have left everyone behind, Shahid thought. *Who could be talking to me here?*

"Are you running away from home? Have you eaten anything, *beta*? Don't be afraid, son, talk to me." The tailor master gently nudged Shahid's shoulder and informed him that he was about to close his shop and leave for the evening. Weighed down by fatigue and wretchedness, Shahid began to sob at the first touch of a friendly human hand. The tailor knew instinctively that the young man must have been separated from his family, probably an Urdu-speaking boy from across the border. He had heard of the massacre of the Biharis taking place there.

"I speak Urdu too," he tried to reassure him. "You look like you are from a good family. Where are your folks, son?"

Hundreds of destitute people from across the border were pouring in every day, travelling through that border town, bringing with them heart-rending tales of misery and misfortune. Many from those silent processions had stopped at that intersection to ask for directions to the refugee camps set up by the Indian government, to ask for water, or to buy food.

"Are there trains going to Darbhanga from here?" Shahid spoke finally in Urdu.

"There is one train in the afternoon and one in the morning."

"Afternoon?" Disappointed at having missed it, Shahid started working out in his mind the number of hours he will have to wait until the next morning.

"You can still catch it; it's a few hours late today."

Hearing that made Shahid almost jump up. It was the first thing that had gone right for him in a long time.

"But that's after you come home with me and have something to eat. I live 'round the corner," the kind-hearted tailor insisted.

As promised, the tailor brought him back to the station in good time. Since Shahid had no Indian money, the tailor bought him the ticket and put him on the train to Darbhanga. Shahid was now going to the same house as a refugee that his mother had left to become one in East Pakistan some seventeen years earlier.

XXXXX

STRANDED IN DHAKA AND DESPERATE for news from the family in Thakurgaon, Hashmat continued to fulfill his emergency duties at Holy Family Hospital. The last news he had received three weeks earlier was that Iqbal had reached home. The telephone at home had stopped working when the small exchange in Thakurgaon had ceased operation, probably because there was no one to man the exchange anymore, or the rebels had severed the lines. Last time they spoke, Father had hinted that the family might break up and try to cross the border in smaller groups. He didn't say more, fearing someone may be listening.

Three weeks since that call, everything had changed. Whatever news was travelling back to Dhaka from the north of the country came through the wireless messages at the army control rooms in Dhaka. Hashmat had little direct access to anyone at the cantonment, but what he was hearing was not good. As the army advanced to regain control in the north, each day brought eyewitness accounts of widespread atrocities, murder, and rape of defenseless Urdu-speaking civilians. The news from Dinajpur and Thakurgaon was even grimmer. These towns were among the worst hit. Delay in the army reaching them meant the rebel EPR soldiers and the *sacha seboks* had all the time to carry out a complete annihilation of the defenceless Biharis. Even their women and children were not spared. Hashmat began to contact the army higher ups to see if he could travel with their convoys to Thakurgaon or to anywhere in the north.

Someone heard his desperate pleas, and toward the end of April, Hashmat was finally able to travel to Thakurgaon on an army helicopter. Talking to the survivors, he began to piece together what had happened in that town and how the events led to his family's final moments. In all that despair, he heard one piece of good news: one of his brothers, probably Shahid, had survived and crossed over to India. But no one could tell him where he was headed. He could be in one of the numerous camps that had sprung up across the border in India, perhaps planning to return to search for survivors. If it was Shahid, he could have even left for Darbhanga, because at sixteen, he was old enough to know that his grandmother lived in Kumhrauli somewhere in that district in Bihar. But if it was Zahid or Sajid, it was unlikely that either was capable of making it alone to that village. A week of searching yielded no clues, and Hashmat returned to Dhaka exhausted and heartbroken. But he hadn't given up hope. A week or so later, he took another helicopter ride with the army to the north.

The EPR camp in Thakurgaon had been retaken by the Pakistani army and served as its command centre in the north. Hashmat stayed at the camp, since it was not safe for him to go to our empty house. His host, the young, dashing Captain Cheema of the Pakistani army, had already earned the reputation of being a brave soldier. He had arrived in that town with only a handful of soldiers from Saidpur, clearing roadblocks and braving sniper fire. The young doctor's plight moved that brave soldier enough that he was prepared to go to any length to help him.

"Don't worry, doctor, we will find your brother and bring him here," he promised.

Hashmat was shown the living room next to the captain's office in the camp where he was going to stay as long as it took to find his brother. That night the two young men scurried through the maps of this unfamiliar territory, identifying the villages and the towns that Shahid may have travelled through. Hashmat knew so little about the countryside that he was of no help. As he lay on the sofa trying to sleep, something told him that God must have sent this man for him and that he could trust Capt. Cheema with his life.

By nightfall the Pakistani army was confined to their camps. So, they had no choice but to wait for daybreak. Even during the day, whenever they went out on patrol, they were likely to encounter sniper fire.

The next morning the captain announced at the breakfast table that he had found a local who would accompany them to search for Shahid. He had established his bearings about the adjoining areas, and they could leave by midday. The captain took a couple of soldiers and Hashmat and drove straight to the border village where Shahid had reportedly spent the night before he had crossed the border some four weeks earlier. It was almost foolish for Capt. Cheema to venture out in the remote countryside. "I could be fired for this," he said. Hashmat knew he was not joking.

By the time they located the village, it was well past 4:00 p.m., and they had just over two hours of daylight left to get back to the camp. After asking around in the village, they were taken to the house of a Hindu trader who was known to arrange border crossings. Luckily, the trader did not flee upon seeing the Pakistani soldiers. When shown his picture, first he denied, hesitated for a moment and then admitted helping Shahid cross the border. He had probably calculated in his mind the benefits of cooperating with Pakistani soldiers, as the tables had now turned.

Reaching under his desk, he took out a packet of money. "Here, you can have this back." He threw the packet at the captain's feet. It was the money that Lal Chacha had paid him to take Shahid across. "I only helped this boy out of pity for him. You can ask him how well I looked after him if you ever find him. And it is not my business to arrange border crossings." He wanted the captain to know that he was neither a smuggler nor a human trafficker.

At that point the captain did something so unorthodox which stunned even Hashmat, but he did nothing to protest. All he wanted was Shahid's recovery, and he did not care how that was achieved.

The captain asked his soldiers to take two of the trader's family members to his jeep. "They are going to stay with me in the camp until you bring Shahid back," the captain said. In other words, these people were being taken hostage. He also told the trader that he had five days to do this, after which he could not guarantee the safety of the trader's family. The captain asked Hashmat to write a note for Shahid asking him to return with the trader once he found him. Hashmat tore open the cigarette packet in his pocket and wrote quickly on the inside of the cover.

All this happened in a matter of minutes, leaving the trader with no time to recover from his shock. The two hostages in the back of the jeep began to wail and mutter their prayers simultaneously.

"Bring the boy, and take your family back. Remember, you have five days." With that the captain jumped back into the driver's seat and pressed the accelerator.

Dozens of villagers who had come out by then watched the spectacle in disbelief. This was a totally no-go area for the Pakistani army, not safe for them to stay much longer. Hashmat sat speechless as the jeep sped through the winding dirt tracks back on the main road toward Thakurgaon.

It's time for a miracle in my life too, Hashmat thought.

This was a cruel twist of fate for the unfortunate Hindu trader who had helped Shahid escape; hardly the payback he had expected. The clock was ticking for him. Left without a choice, the trader crossed the border that same night and reached the town that Shahid had arrived at in the jeep with the Bengalis from Thakurgaon. He headed straight for the refugee camps. One by one he walked through the camps, which were spread over many miles, stopping people and asking about Shahid, showing them his photograph, and describing the vintage jeep that carried his group. By the end of the third day, he was all but losing hope of finding Shahid. No one had seen the jeep, and no one recognized Shahid from the photo. Each hour that passed brought his own family, in the custody of that mad captain, closer to death. He kept cursing the day he met the young boy and everyone else in Lal Chacha's family. Dejected and tired, he arrived at the railway station and sat on the bench outside the tailor shop. He ordered tea from the chaiwalla next door and began narrating his plight to another customer to lighten his burden.

"Wait, wait a minute, what did you say the boy's name was?" the tailor asked, having overheard the conversation.

The trader swiftly took out the picture from his pocket. Within moments they had established that it was indeed the same boy. The tailor informed him how he had found Shahid by his shop next to the very bench on which the Hindu trader was sitting. He remembered the boy telling him that his grandma lived in the village called Kumhrauli in the district of Darbhanga. The tailor had helped him buy the ticket to the nearest station and had him board the train. Then he recalled the all-important information that Shahid's uncle was the *mukhia* in that village, even though he couldn't remember his name.

By the following afternoon, the trader had reached Kumhrauli. The shrewd trader had no difficulty in finding the house of Shahid's uncle. But when he arrived there, Uncle flatly denied any knowledge of the young boy coming from East Pakistan. He was afraid the man could be from the police or from the intelligence agencies. Who knew what trouble this man would cause if he was found to be harbouring a Pakistani boy.

Almost expecting the denial, the trader unfolded the carefully preserved cigarette packet on which was written Hashmat's note for Shahid, and Uncle began to relax. Forever afraid of the law, Uncle had hidden the sixteen-year-old in another house next to the primary school with some relatives a few miles away. By then Shahid had spent nearly five weeks incognito with the elderly couple who taught at that school. To pass time during the day, he was teaching the young children at the school.

The trader and Uncle reached the relatives' house the same night at around 2:00 a.m. Shahid was woken up and shown Hashmat's letter. He immediately began to get ready and left with the trader at daybreak, not giving himself any time to go to Kumhrauli to say goodbye to his grandma. The grandma passed away a few years later without ever seeing Shahid again.

The situation at the border had been changing fast. Arriving back by train at the border town, they learned the border crossing had become much riskier over the past few days, with intermittent firing from both sides. The

Pakistani army was firing from their positions to keep the infiltrators at bay while they themselves were coming under sniper fire from the Mukti Bahini. The trader informed Shahid of his decision to rest that afternoon, and his plans to cross the border on foot that night.

Fortunately, the rains hadn't arrived, so the rivers were still shallow, and the swamps and ditches had mostly dried out. All night they walked through the bushes, the knee-deep rivers, and the rice paddies. They were lucky it wasn't a full moon, so they could not be spotted easily by either side to take a potshot at them. Physically drained, Shahid felt little pain or emotion, and he was no longer afraid of being killed by the border guards or being hit by a sniper bullet. The Hindu trader kept calling on all his gods for safety, not forgetting to curse the captain every now and then for forcing him through all this. For once that night both the Hindu and the Muslim gods seemed in agreement to protect the two on the ground.

Shahid dragged his swollen feet, which had expanded within his shoes, making them numb. But he didn't complain, fearing it may cause his companion to slow down. So grateful to God that Hashmat was alive, he was determined to meet him before his luck changed again. He thought of me in Karachi, the city he had never seen, with a sense of relief that at least one brother was safely away from all this and wondered if I had any idea what had befallen the family. He kept praying that I didn't make the mistake of coming back to look for them. He wanted to live, if only to meet his brothers again.

By daybreak, the two arrived at the border village of Ruhia inside East Pakistan. From there they took a bus to Thakurgaon, arriving at the army camp just before noon. It was already the fifth day since the trader's family had been taken hostage. With every passing hour until they reached the camp, the trader's anxiety kept rising, along with his prayer chants. That afternoon at the camp, there were two emotional reunions, one for the trader and his family and the other for Shahid and his brother.

XXXXX

THE NEWS OF THE MASSACRE of Biharis in East Pakistan started to hit the papers in Karachi by early May. Despite the government's strict censorship, some papers decided to break their silence. Eyewitness accounts published in the *Guardian* and the *Times* by journalist Anthony Markeranhas were reprinted in the local press, stunning everyone in Pakistan. Sitting in Karachi, I had little choice but to read those dreadful accounts or listen to the Nine O Clock news on television. It wasn't until mid May that the true scale of the massacre began to unfold.

No matter how grim the news was, I still had not allowed myself to imagine the worst for my family, believing the small town they lived in was far away from politically charged Dhaka and Chittagong. Besides, unlike most other Biharis, our family was well assimilated in society. They had many Bengali friends who could shelter them and hide them if required. My imagination refused go beyond that. The only worst-case scenario I figured could be that our house had been looted, and the family had either moved to our land in Pran Nagar or taken refuge in a Bengali friend's house. My main concern until then was my father's health, knowing he suffered from high blood pressure.

For days I tried to book telephone calls to our home in Thakurgaon and sat by the phone. Each time after hours of waiting, the operator would inform me that the telephone lines to the northern part of East Pakistan were still out of order. After a while they stopped accepting the booking outright, saying no calls were possible.

A traveller from Dhaka brought a letter from Hashmat around the first week of May that mentioned the widespread massacre of Biharis in Dinajpur and Thakurgaon. He also wrote that he was trying to go to Thakurgaon as soon as the train service or the bus service resumed.

"Pray for everyone, and be brave," he wrote, preparing me for worse. I knew instinctively that he was not telling me everything he knew. But I could not contact him since he had stopped going to the hospital, and there was no telephone at his apartment.

One evening that same week, Ehsanul-Haq, from Thakurgaon, who was married to my cousin, Jhanna, came to meet me at Siddique Sahib's house. On a business trip to Karachi, he had gotten stranded when flights to Dhaka were cancelled. I had come to Siddique Sahib's house from my university hostel to try to make some phone calls to East Pakistan.

Taking one look at me, Ehsan realized I knew nothing about what had happened to my family. So, he took Siddique Sahib and Baji to the next room and shut the door. Minutes later I heard Baji sobbing and Siddique Sahib trying to comfort her. Utterly confused, I lowered the volume of the TV to listen in. Before I could join them in that room, the door opened again. Ehsan came out first. He switched the TV off and began to walk toward me. My heart sank.

"What happened? Tell me what happened," I pleaded as I stood up.

Ehsan reached out to embrace me and started to cry like a child. "We have lost everything; everything is lost." His sobbing continued, and he kept repeating the same words. I knew what he was about to tell me could only be the worst news I had ever heard.

"Please just tell me what happened, for God's sake!" I demanded, raising my voice as I struggled to free myself from his embrace.

Holding my hand, Ehsan sat down, almost pulling me down on the sofa with him. He opened his mouth halfway, as if searching for the right words, and then gave up.

"No one in the family is alive. The bastards didn't spare anyone. Not even my baby." He broke down.

I felt the world spinning around me as Ehsan's words echoed in my ears. Then the carefully disguised words from Hashmat's last letter flashed in my mind.

"Which family are you referring to?" I demanded to know.

"I mean everyone, my dear."

"What do you mean? "

Ehsan couldn't figure out what more to say and kept sobbing.

"But how do you know? You are not there." I told him about the letter I just received from Hashmat. He was going to Thakurgaon to find out. "No one knows anything. How can you be so sure? Please don't say such things!"

I was getting agitated at Ehsan Bhai, as we called him. By then I could hear Baji's sobbing from the next room, but I remained unmoved. Dumbfounded and scared to death, I was still unable to understand why she or Siddique Sahib had believed Ehsan Bhai so easily.

"This is true, my dear, at least a lot of it is true," Siddique Sahib said. Adding that Ehsan bhai had eyewitness accounts from survivors who had reached Dhaka, and now people arriving at Karachi from other parts of East Pakistan were also talking about it.

"We have to pray there are some survivors; let us not lose hope yet." Siddique Sahib sat down next to me and reached out to hold my hand lightly. "I was too young at the time of partition, but I have heard of God's miracles after the riots in Calcutta. People thought to be dead came back to their dear ones from nowhere," Siddique Sahib said calmly as he gathered his composure.

By then I could hear Baji reciting the Quran in the other room, soon Siddique Sahib left to make his *wadhu*, to prepare for prayers, leaving Ehsan Bhai with me.

Once he settled down, Ehsan Bhai took an envelope from his pocket and unfolded the letter inside with great care. It was addressed to me from Iqbal, dated March 22. The letter had been hand-carried by a family friend, Muhammad Bhai, who made it out of East Pakistan and had reached Karachi. He had already learned about what had happened in Thakurgaon before he left Dhaka, but he did not have the strength to face me and didn't want to be the bearer of this terrible news after he arrived in Karachi.

With the firsthand account from Iqbal that I was holding in my hand and listening to Ehsan Bhai speak of what happened subsequently, it was becoming painfully clear why there was very little possibility for my family to have escaped the massacre.

My God! No! How can this be possible? My mind raced aimlessly in an effort to piece together every bit of the news that had reached me by then. I tried to imagine the likelihood of an escape for my family. What about Hamid and Munni? They were small children; why would anyone harm them? I dreaded to think any further.

"Look at me, Azmat," Ehsan Bhai said ever so gently. "I have also lost everything, my wife and my baby—" He could not complete the sentence, pausing for a few seconds before he continued. "Do you know what those bastards did to her? Poor girl . . ." He broke down again.

Siddique Sahib brought a glass of water for him and tried a few words of consolation, but I could not find a single word to comfort him. He stopped talking and just sat on the sofa next to me. I do not remember how long he remained in the room with me that night or when he left.

The next morning I felt a deep remorse in my heart that I had not said anything to comfort him. After all, his wife was also my cousin and very dear to our family. His adorable two-year-old daughter was a darling to everyone in the family. Ehsan left for Dhaka as soon as flights resumed. After the war and the creation of Bangladesh, Ehsan returned to his native village in Bihar. He never recovered from that tragedy. Five years later, at age thirty-eight, he died of a mysterious illness. We received a couple of letters from him after he moved to India, but we never met again.

Another letter from Hashmat was hand carried to me in the second week of May. He wrote that the initial reports from the district were grim, and he was proceeding to Thakurgaon to search for any surviving family members. Stranded a thousand miles away in Karachi, all I could do was pray for a miracle, but by then I was prepared for anything. I had stopped going to the university and was now living at Siddique Sahib's house. More than me, the deeply religious Baji and Siddique Sahib continued to pray for a miracle five times a day.

When I failed to return to the hostel after the weekend, my friends at Karachi University came looking for me at Siddique Sahib's house. From them I learned that Yousuf, my roommate from the university hostel, had not heard anything from his family in East Pakistan in nearly two months. The two of us felt each other's pain better than anyone else.

As I waited for more bad news, my only prayer to God was to spare at least one of my younger brothers, if only to give me a reason to live. I thought of ending my life, but I could not summon the courage to jump into the large water tank in the hardboard factory. I would spend hours sitting by the tank under the neem tree, heartbroken, confused, and in excruciating pain.

Whenever I was able to sleep, I saw my family in my dreams, mostly Mother and Iqbal, who would talk to me. "It doesn't hurt anymore," they would tell me. I thought I saw where they were murdered, and I was restless to visit that place. But I never saw Hamid or Munni in my dreams, which I read as a sign that they were still alive. I imagined the shock of all that had happened to the others may have caused them to lose their mind, and they might be just wandering around in some camps across the border. Perhaps some kind-hearted family was sheltering them in a remote village. Unless I went there myself, we would not be able to find them.

Around the end of May I received news through some relatives in Dhaka that Shahid had been found alive, and my hopes shot up. There was no confirmation whether Shahid was injured or whether he had already reached Dhaka. In his letter before departing for Thakurgaon, Hashmat had forbidden me to go to East Pakistan, asking me to stay put in Karachi where he could contact me and get any survivors to join me. With the telephone services still disrupted, we could not talk. My painful wait in Karachi continued.

Finally, on May 30 a letter from Hashmat confirmed that Shahid was back in Dhaka, safe and unhurt. Along with this great joy, any hope of finding anybody else was put to rest. Hashmat wrote of eyewitness accounts confirming to him that no one else in our family had survived. He had visited all those places and talked to anyone and everyone who was around. In a strange way, there was a sense of relief knowing that nothing worse could happen now, and our ordeal would soon be over when the brothers were reunited.

My soul had been torn, and I longed for some inner peace to preserve what remained of my precarious sanity. Almost out of reflex I began seeking solace in religion, frequenting the nearby seminary Dar-ul Uloom. My deeply religious host, Siddique Sahib, began taking me there for prayers. Initially, it was two or three times a day, which gradually reduced to once each day for evening prayers. One of the moulvis that Siddique Sahib got me to meet extolled me to come there to pray every day.

"You will feel good here my son," he said gently. "*Woh hamse achi jagah hain.*" He assured me in Urdu that the dead were in a better place than us, the living. It pleased my host that I was praying, albeit irregularly. Slowly, my visits to the seminary began to wane, and I even avoided the attention of that moulvi. Part of me wanted to pray for the departed souls, but part of me could not connect with the myth or the rituals. Those visits failed to provide the solace I craved at the time, and my attendance began to fall.

Homecoming Like No Other

Home is where you once ran to the sea
Because the place you once belonged to.
Now no longer remembers your name
—Nikita Gill

Civilian flights to Dhaka resumed in late June 1971, nearly three months after the massacre of the Biharis and the subsequent takeover of the province by the Pakistani army. I was getting restless to meet the two known survivors in my family, Shahid and Hashmat. Siddique Sahib, my gracious host in Karachi, tried to dissuade me and then yielded partly due to his wife's plea to let me go, which she thought was important for me to find closure. Around mid-July, Siddique Sahib came home with the ticket, and I boarded the plane the next morning to go to Dhaka without informing Hashmat or Shahid, who would have definitely tried to stop me.

India had banned Pakistani aircraft from flying over its territory. The plane had to go around the southern tip of India, the detour adding a good two hours to the standard two-and-half-hour flight. By then India was actively supporting the liberation movement in East Pakistan, surrounding the Pakistani army on all sides as the war for the liberation of Bangladesh loomed.

On a wet July afternoon, our lone passenger flight touched down on the tarmac. Looking out the window, I could see around half a dozen military planes and armed personnel carriers on the move. It looked like the Dhaka airport had been turned into an airbase. With no luggage to collect, I was out in minutes, only to find a deserted road right outside. The hustle and bustle of the rickshaw wallas and scooter taxis had been replaced by the occasional army truck moving toward the nearby military cantonment. Unconcerned by the light drizzle that nearly drenched me, I waited on the pavement for a rickshaw, competing with a handful of other passengers who I had not noticed until then.

The few rickshaws that I found refused to go to Mirpur, saying it was too far and that they would have to come back empty. The real reason was that the Bengali-speaking rickshaw drivers were afraid to venture into a predominantly Urdu-speaking locality after all that had happened lately. Eventually, one was induced when I offered extra *bhara* to take me to Mirpur, a place I had never visited before.

Since his miraculous recovery from across the border, Shahid had been staying with our cousin, Zafar, in Mirpur on the outskirts of Dhaka. The predominantly Bihari settlement had become exclusively so, inundated by fleeing relatives of residents like Shahid who had escaped death from other parts of the province.

Seeing me get off the rickshaw from the balcony, Shahid could not believe his eyes. He ran downstairs to hold me in his arms. Relief and happiness swept us over, and we stood there trying to make sense of the moment. It was great to find him in good health and well fed. I didn't want to start immediately, but finding him okay, we spent the next few hours talking about what had happened. I hadn't even said *salaam* to anyone in the house, but no one interrupted us while we talked on the balcony. It had begun to turn dark after sunset, which neither of us noticed. It was better that way as neither wanted our tears to betray us. Surprisingly, Shahid showed very little emotion describing his ordeal. Every now and then he paused to repeat one word "betrayal," a word that rang in my ears for many evenings after that.

When Hashmat arrived from work later that evening, from the balcony I only recognized him because of his motorbike. I had never known anyone to lose so much weight in so little time. The handsome young man had been reduced to skin and bone, almost beyond recognition. When he spread his arms to embrace me, tears that I had held back for the past few hours could no longer be contained. But Hashmat, like Shahid, showed little emotion. He would, if he could, cry in solitude, but his tears had dried out a few months earlier.

Over the next few days, I continued to beg Hashmat to let me go to Thakurgaon. The fact that neither he nor Shahid had seen the bodies of our loved ones made it hard to put our minds to rest once and for all. Lack of closure threatened to rob us of our peace of mind for as long as we lived. It was hard to say what I was looking for, maybe some remains that I could identify or perhaps one more miracle. Hashmat finally gave in, took leave from his hospital, and agreed to travel with me. Shahid was to stay back in Dhaka because we could not risk all three of us taking what was going to be a perilous journey through the countryside with reports of daily skirmishes between the army and the and rebel Bengali soldiers, now widely known as the Mukti Bahini.

Train service to Thakurgaon remained suspended since the railway tracks had been blown up in various places by the fleeing Awami Leaguers. Although the Pakistani army was back in command and had restored order in most cities, the countryside remained a no-go area where hit-and-run sniper firing was the order of the day. Each night the entire country was under curfew after 7:00 p.m. Being unfamiliar with the territory, the Pakistani army hired Bengali Razakaars (volunteers) belonging to Jamiat Islami and remnants of Bihari youth who had survived the massacre. Almost all the Bihari youth had lost their parents, their homes destroyed, and they had nowhere to go. Evidently, some were looking for revenge, but others were just happy to work for food and shelter, thankful to be alive.

For the first leg of the journey to Thakurgaon, we boarded a bus early in the morning for the Bahadurabad ferry terminal on the Brahmaputra River. The old Bedford engine roared as the bus struggled to pull out of the roadside mud, spraying black earth in the air. A nearby coconut vendor cried out in disgust, but no one was listening. With a gentle tap followed by two loud thumps of his palm on the side of the bus, the conductor signalled the driver to move on. Some passengers were still trying to settle down while the roadside vendors, who had not finished returning the change to the passengers through the windows on the bus, had to run a few steps alongside it.

Over the next few hours, the bus meandered through the countryside with a few small towns and villages in between. Most of them looked deserted, as if the entire population had been wiped out by an outbreak of plague or cholera. The exodus of the population was also marked by almost nonexistent traffic on the road, rows of closed shops, and even the absence of beggars in the various *haats* (bazaars) that we passed. Every time a vehicle crossed from the other direction, the drivers would stop to exchange information on the road ahead. Perhaps some of them were also passing on coded information to the Mukti Bahini still active in the countryside.

It took us around three hours to reach the banks of Brahmaputra River at the Bahadurabad Ghat ferry crossing. The passengers scrambled to board the ferry to cross the mighty Jamuna River. With the onset of monsoon season, the river had swelled and looked ready to flood its banks. The furious, swirling waters were noisy and ominous, ready to gobble up anyone who might fall off the slippery wooden walkway to the ferryboat. The river had become so wide by swallowing the adjoining plains that the other side was no longer visible. It took nearly two hours for the ferry to cross, the pilot struggling to keep the old British-era steamer on course as he battled the strong currents.

On both sides of the mammoth river, contingents of Pakistani army *jawaans* (soldiers) kept a watchful eye. The soldiers searched every passenger and their luggage as we disembarked the ferry and waited to board another bus on the western side of the river. At the outset the driver warned the passengers that if progress on the road was slow, they might have to spend the night somewhere on the way.

Like the last bus from Dhaka to Bahadurabad Ghat, this bus made frequent stops at every checkpoint or in the middle of the road for the driver to talk to vehicles passing from the other direction, evaluating the conditions each step of the way. Hardly anyone on the bus spoke, so it was hard to understand where they were headed. Everyone looked wary of others. Perhaps, like us, some of them were searching for their loved ones or quietly heading for the border to escape to the other side. It was hard not to doubt that some of them could even be from the Awami League or the Mukti Bahini who may have killed innocent Biharis in their respective neighbourhoods and were now running away. Occasionally, a passenger whispered something to another, but still no conversation was taking place. Every time the bus stopped at a checkpoint, fear and anxiety gripped everyone. In some places where the passengers were asked to get off for a body search, they would panic at every question the soldiers asked.

After an hour and a half on the road, we passed through the town of Bogra. I thought of the two smart-looking Bihari boys from a well-known business family who had been studying in our cadet college, a few years junior. I couldn't recollect their names but remembered that one of them had grey eyes just like my brother, Zahid. No one knew if they or any from their families had survived. Hashmat kept looking out the window as if expecting to see someone. I knew this was the town where his sweetheart, Dr. Nahar, lived. The lady Bengali doctor who graduated with Hashmat had been able to contact him to give the news that her family was okay. But she was ill, and her family was trying to move her to Dhaka for treatment. Like a child, Hashmat kept looking out as if he would catch a glimpse of someone he recognized, someone who may give him some news about his friend. I wondered what was going through his mind because he must have realized it would be impossible for a Bihari boy to marry a Bengali girl after all that had happened. It would be unthinkable; his own brothers would not accept such a proposition.

Like most passengers on the bus, Hashmat and I hadn't spoken for a long time.

"Are you hungry?" he asked when our eyes met.

"No." I shook my head.

"Catch some sleep if you want; just lean on my shoulder," Hashmat offered, realizing how uncomfortable the seats were.

While I was dozing off, the bus stopped, and Hashmat got off to buy some fruit. The fruit seller took ages to come up with the right change. By the time he got back, some passengers were angry at Hashmat for delaying the bus, which was ready to leave without him.

My eyelids were too tired to lift, and my head was spinning due to lack of sleep. A thousand voices screamed in my mind, singing, whispering, and taunting me. I tried to recognize them. I concentrated, I heard some music, and then they receded. I tried harder to listen.

Suddenly, the loud screech of brakes jolted me up, almost throwing me off my seat. It was followed by a heartrending cry of a dog hit by the bus. The conductor jumped out to check. "Shala kukur," he cursed the poor dog for sleeping on the empty road. I clutched Hashmat's hand in a reflex. "*Keya hua*?" I asked in Urdu.

Instantly, a few heads turned toward us; now they knew we spoke Urdu. That was a big mistake on my part, which I realized instantly just looking at Hashmat. But I was not afraid anymore, and neither was Hashmat. The

Bengali passengers on that bus could lynch us if they wanted. Or they could just stop the bus anywhere and throw us out on the road. There was no army to protect us in the deserted towns and villages we were passing through.

In a few seconds, the conductor got back on the bus and tapped the door twice, signalling the driver to carry on. "Shala kukur," he swore again. The almost human-like moaning of the wounded dog faded slowly as the bus moved forward. One passenger two or three seats behind us kept moaning too, holding his wrist in the air with his other hand. He appeared to have hurt himself when the driver applied the brakes, and he was thrown off his seat. It had begun to drizzle, and the cool air blowing through the window of the moving bus eventually helped to soothe his pain, and he settled down. Drops of rain were hitting my face and my hand on the half-closed window, which I paid no attention to until Hashmat reached across to close the plastic window pane before I got drenched.

By speaking in Urdu, I had managed to attract the interest of one fellow passenger, who kept staring intermittently at us, disgust on his face. I only became conscious of this as the daylight slowly receded in the distance. In that fading light, my eyes met his. He resembled one of the faces on the garland of human heads wore by the *Kali Maa* at the Kali temple near our house in Thakurgaon. I tried to avoid his gaze, yet every few minutes kept checking to see if he was still there. His gaze seemed transfixed on me, his unusually shiny eyes reflecting the dim lights on the bus's ceiling. With darkness descending outside, some passengers started to recite the *kalima* or whatever verses they knew. The prayer chants slowly engulfed everyone on the bus as they joined the slow chorus. We all seemed to be part of a funeral procession in which some of those taking part were soon going to join the ranks of the dead.

A few miles before Dinajpur, the driver stopped by a tea shop for a short break, announcing it would be the last stop before the final destination. Passengers got off for refreshments or to relieve themselves. The driver also disappeared behind the bushes. Glad to see the first sign of life after some hours, we got off and ordered tea and biscuits. The water in the large nearly burnt-out kettle on the wood fire had been boiled repeatedly, fresh tea leaves added every now and then. Despite all the sugar thrown in, the tea still tasted bitter, but the hot drink still soothed us before we got back on the bus.

"He is gone," I whispered to myself.

"Who?" asked Hashmat.

"Nothing." My voice was lost in the noise of the engine as the bus roared back to life and started moving again. We reached Dinajpur an hour after darkness, making the 200-mile journey from Dhaka in almost 10 hours.

Since the buses for Thakurgaon would now only leave in the morning, we had to find a place to sleep and move quickly because the curfew would become effective in less than half an hour. We found accommodation at a grocery shop owned by a Bihari near the railway station. The elderly owner, who we called Malik Dada, had known our father well. He instantly recognized us, hugged us, and kissed our foreheads. He knew well what had happened to our family and every now and then kept cursing the Awami League.

"They will all burn in hell. Mind you, Allah's wrath may not make any sound, but it always comes sooner or later," he kept repeating.

Arrangements were made for us to sleep with him inside that small shop, which was barely able to accommodate the sacks of rice, daal, and other provisions. The smell of chili powder and turmeric overpowered the odour of the bars of soap and hair oil on the shelves above them. Hashmat slept on the narrow *charpoy* and I on the *chatai* between the sacks of rice and flour. Malik warned us not to scream if we saw any rats at night.

Until late that night, the shopkeeper kept us awake with the details of the horror that had taken place in Dinajpur until I begged him to let Hashmat catch some sleep. Religious to the core, he found hints of messages from God in all that had happened in that town.

"This is nothing but a warning that the day of judgement is around the corner," he said calmly. "No one can deny it; the holy book has foretold this."

According to him, everyone we knew in Dinajpur was either dead or missing. He never showed the slightest emotion describing how it all happened, not even when he told us how two young boys, presumed dead, were pulled out from a pile of bodies near the bridge on Kanchan River. One of them was the son of our own *mouvli sahib*. Malik believed that returning from the dead was a miracle by God to remind us that He was still watching over us.

"He will carry Hadi Bhai's name in this world, just like you boys are left behind to carry the name of Ashraf Sahib."

I asked if the army was able to save any lives in that town. "They arrived after it was all over," he replied with a wry smile. "The Bengalis don't want Pakistan, and the Biharis are all dead. Don't know why they're here now. Who is the army fighting for?"

"They are fighting for the control of the cemetery called Pakistan," Hashmat, who had been quiet all this time, said, letting out a sigh.

In all that gloom, the shopkeeper was able to cheer us when he informed us that our *moulvi sahib* had survived. Two of his sons were killed, but two others survived. Our father's friend, Jaleel Sahib, and his wife and daughter were alive too. Jaleel Sahib lived in sector five of the satellite town built for Bihari refugees from India in the 1960s. Except for the periphery areas, the rest of the sector had remained largely unscathed due to the bravery of a few Bihari youth who kept vigil with only a few guns each night.

For the rest of the Biharis in other parts of Dinajpur, the carnage was extensive. In the localities of Paharpur, Neemtalla, Malda Patti, and Balubari the Biharis were obliterated. Their houses were empty, and entire neighbourhoods looked like ghost towns, as if no one had ever lived there. When the Pakistani army arrived, they found heaps of bodies of women and children rotting in the compound of Hashmat's old school less than a kilometer from the grocery shop where we slept. It was only the start of the monsoon season, yet in that strange, lifeless town everything appeared damp and rotting like the rat-infested shop in which we were sleeping. The humid air was laden with a strange smell similar to that of the *shamshan ghat* by the Tangon River, where the Hindus cremated their dead, the one we used to cross going to the lichi orchard.

When I got up in the morning, I found myself on the charpai, and Hashmat was not there. Before I could scream, I saw him returning with a packet of food. He had gone to fetch breakfast from Saleem's restaurant next door. The restaurant was no longer bustling with the early morning rush of the *nihari and paya* lovers that it had attracted in the past.

At around 9:00 a.m. we took a rickshaw to the bus stop south of town, from where we were travel to Thakurgaon. The bus stop had fewer busses and fewer people than before, but something else had changed too. Many of the buses here used to belong to Urdu-speaking transporters, who had dominated the business only a few months earlier. The vernacular of the bus drivers and the conductors was now exclusively Bengali, all replaced, along with the owners, in one go.

I had made that journey with my father and brothers so many times that every mile was familiar. The winding single-track road passed through swathes of agricultural land, two small rivers, three or four rain-fed ditches and a few small villages. The river near Birganj, halfway to Thakurgaon, had a modern bridge built in the recent past on that thirty-six mile stretch that, luckily, had not been blown up. Two of the villages on the way had been like second home to our family. First, the village of Pran Nagar, ten miles before Thakurgaon, where we had our farmland and where our Aunt Husna lived. Second, the village of Khalkhalli, some six miles from Dinajpur, where one of our family friends, Zillu Chacha, lived with his beautiful wife in his farmhouse.

Six miles from Dinajpur, we were passing the village of Khalkhalli, the farmhouse belonging to Zillu Chacha visible in the distance. Hashmat informed me that he had met Zillu Chacha's sole surviving brother in Dinajpur in May. The entire clan of around twenty were massacred at the farmhouse, which from a distance bore no sign of the tragedy and looked just as tranquil as before. I recalled spending a couple of days with our parents on that farm a few years earlier, around the time Zillu Chacha got married. As part of the *barat* (wedding party), we had travelled from there by bullock carts, then by train, and again by bullock cart to another village near Birol, where the bride's family lived. Like Zillu Chacha, his wife's family were also well-to-do landowners just by the border on the Indian side. Why they didn't escape by crossing over to India, we will never know.

Every time the bus stopped at a checkpoint or anywhere to pick up or drop off passengers, we would eagerly look out as if a familiar face would appear from somewhere. After nearly an hour on the road, the bus passed through the village of Pran Nagar. The empty houses of Aunt Husna and our father's uncle on the opposite side of the road appeared before our eyes. The houses were still intact, but not a soul was in sight, as if a plague had wiped out the little settlement.

"Do you want to get off for Fateha here? I can ask the driver to stop if you want," Hashmat said, the first time he had spoken in a long while.

The bus went past the houses before I could reply and passed the small orchard next to our aunt's home, one that my father had so lovingly planted over several years. Each one of our brothers and sisters had planted saplings there. Selected species of mango, sharifa, and kagzi lemon were placed neatly in different rows. They had grown much bigger than I remembered from our family visit less than a year earlier.

"I will build my retirement home here next to my sister's," Father used to say. "It will be so enchanting when the trees are fully grown that my sons will be attracted to visit us regularly no matter where they all live. Maybe I won't be there, but make sure you come to visit your mother," he would add after a pause. Mother would get angry each time she heard that; she never liked such talk.

The last two miles of the journey seemed to never end, and my heart began to sink as we got closer to Thakurgaon. The bus stopped by the small bridge near the EPR camp, which had become the HQ of the local army command. Hashmat took my hand as we got off. Without a word spoken, we walked into the camp and headed toward the officers' quarters. At the gate the guard recognized Hashmat and let us pass.

Less than one year earlier, I had been there on Independence Day, August 14, with my elder brother, Iqbal, who won the rifle shooting competition in the junior category. Nothing looked different today except that everything had changed for ever.

We walked into the main office of the camp commander and asked to see Captain Cheema. To our great disappointment, we learned he had been transferred to another location. Hashmat nevertheless was relieved to hear that at least the captain was alive and well. I had to wait another twenty-five years to meet the man whose extraordinary act of courage led to the recovery of Shahid from across the border, the man who had given me a reason to live and to whom Hashmat and I owed so much. Six months later when we learned of the defeat and surrender of the Pakistani army, we had presumed him dead, thinking a person like him would refuse orders for surrender and prefer to die.

The new camp commander took us to his quarters next to his office. The inner walls of the living room were full of bullet holes. As we looked down, we noticed that the bloodstained sofa had not been properly washed, just a white sheet placed over it. The captain said the Bengali soldiers who rebelled in the camp killed his predecessor and his young wife in that very room.

Their two little daughters, four or five years old, were killed a day or two later. The faces of the camp commander and his two lovely daughters whom we met the previous August at the Independence Day celebrations in that very camp were still fresh in my memory.

The new camp commander preferred to sleep in that room. He said it helped him maintain his resolve to fight for the integrity of Pakistan. For the time being, the enemy was invisible, had melted away, or had crossed over to India. They were reportedly regrouping and receiving training and equipment across the border in the Indian camps. An uneasy calm had descended over the town, and the camp was once again in the control of the Pakistani army.

By then I was getting restless to visit our house, which was only a mile away. The commander arranged for us to be dropped off in one of the jeeps, and we got off at the main square some one hundred meters from our house to talk to a shopkeeper named Zaheer, who we heard was alive. But the shop was closed, so we started walking toward our house, soon to be stopped by the SDO (sub-divisional officer), who was passing by in his car. The SDO, Mr. Masood, knew us well; he was the father of my classmate, Akhtar Masood. He hugged me and held me in his arm for a few seconds, which seemed like a long time as I struggled to free myself from his awkward embrace. Since he was my friend's father, I could not be disrespectful to him. Mr. Masood proceeded to explain how he tried in vain to bring order to that unfortunate town and how he had tried to protect my father's life until his luck ran out, and everything went out of his control.

"They [the Awami Leaguers] had taken over everything. There was nothing I could do," he said, still holding my hand, which I was trying to pull away.

Hardly interested in his sympathies, neither Hashmat nor I paid much attention to his excuses. When we mentioned where we were headed, he insisted on driving us to the place where my father, along with other prominent Biharis, was shot on the banks of the Tangon River. That spot was close to the jail where they were held in captivity and not too far from the SDO's residence.

From where we stood, it was difficult for us not to assume that, hiding behind that boundary wall, Mr. Masood could have easily witnessed what happened that morning of April 12. The weak, spineless administrator had allowed his authority to dwindle away bit by bit, unable to stand up to his responsibilities. More than anyone else, it was he who bore the responsibility for my father's death, since my father was in the custody of his administration. If my father had any doubts that the smooth-talking SDO and the father of his son's friend would do nothing to protect those in his administration's custody, he may have taken other measures to protect himself. Father had told Iqbal that he and other Bihari family heads had no option but to trust the SDO and the newly elected MPA of the Awami League, Mr. Fazlul Karim. In their joint custody, they would have drawn comfort from their personal relations with those gentlemen, who had vowed to protect them if they cooperated with them by opting to come under their "safe custody." Together, these two people had the option to free their captives or at least tip them off after the EPR rebellion when things began to slip out of their hands.

Hashmat and I prayed at the spot where a large mound of sand stood by the river. We said goodbye to the SDO and walked back to the town centre.

While Hashmat was talking to someone he recognized, I kept walking toward our home, already visible from there. If Hashmat noticed, he did not stop me. Most of the small shops on the way were closed, even in the middle of the day. One or two that were open displayed empty shelves and had no customers. Some of the closed shops belonged to Urdu-speaking Biharis, like Quddus, the grocer; Yasin, the cloth merchant; Zaheer, the paan walla; and the two restaurants of Ghosyar Khan and brothers Rabbani and Jilani facing each other by the main square we called the *chowrasta*. Most of those shopkeepers had perished along with their families, except for Rabbani's partner, Jilani, and one of Ghosyar Khan's sons, Barakalaah. Just a few Bengali faces appeared to look familiar, I felt some were looking at me, but I kept walking.

The waiter at Peltoo's restaurant waved at me and called out to his co-worker. The two kept looking at me without any exchange. After so much bloodletting, everyone seemed afraid to talk to a Bihari, driven partly by guilt and partly by fear of being branded as a Pakistani collaborator should things change again.

The last shop in the row was the stationery shop that I had visited regularly for years to buy pencils, newspapers, magazines, and so on. From there I could walk to our house with my eyes closed. The first stop was Uncle Niamat's house, then Beju's workshop, then Keramot Mukhtar's house, with its beautiful garden, and finally our own house just before the large fields of the old British clubhouse. The other beautiful garden opposite our house belonged to Uncle Moharrir. It lay in waste, overgrown bushes having replaced the colourful seasonal flowers. Like most of our neighbours, the Moharrir family had fled to India. Had the prominent Bengalis of our town not been such cowards and protected their Bihari neighbours with whom they had no quarrel, there would have been little reason for them to flee after the arrival of the Pakistani army.

Except for the odd rickshaw looking for passengers, the street was largely deserted. As I got closer, I noticed our house appeared to be intact, as if nothing had happened there. A small pool of rainwater had gathered on the front lawn where we used to play badminton. Since the front door was locked, I walked around the side of the house through the mango and jackfruit trees. Some wild grass had grown by the tube well, almost hiding the passage that led to the side door, where a padlock hung from the outside. There was no sign of the house being ransacked, although I had been told that nothing was left inside. Even the picture frames on the wall had been taken away.

Held together by a loose chain and a rusty padlock, the side door had a sufficient gap through which the courtyard inside was clearly visible. As I sat down on the steps, I thought I heard some giggles, children playing in the courtyard. I called out each name one by one: Hamid, Munni, Zahid, Sajid, Iqbal Bhai and Ammi. Voices were still whispering, calling and beckoning behind that door. There was still no one I could see through that opening.

Fallen leaves had formed a carpet around the back of the house, which had not been swept for months. When they rustled in the wind, it felt someone was approaching me. Instinctively, I turned around to look, but no one was there. I don't know how long I sat there before I got up and walked back toward the front, where Hashmat was waiting patiently for me.

"Do you want to go to Dr. Yusuf's?" he asked.

"Hmm", I nodded.

Without saying anything, we had already begun to walk in that direction, two blocks north, to the house where our mother and siblings had spent their final days.

On the street outside the house, we bumped into someone who seemed to have been waiting there to meet us. We were not certain how he knew, but it seemed he had expected us to visit Dr. Yusuf's house one day. The *maulana sahib* who taught Islamiat at the school grabbed us and started hugging and kissing as he sobbed inconsolably. He needed to tell us something in order to take a huge weight off his chest.

"My children, my children, God is my witness that I tried, but I couldn't save them. You will see, those *zaalims* will soon meet their fate." He was trying to comfort us and himself at the same time. He gave us an eyewitness account of their last few minutes while he kept cursing the perpetrators as *kafirs*, *jaanwars* etc. "I fell on my knees and begged them to spare at least one child, little Hamid or Munni." He fell on the feet of one of the EPR soldiers who was waving his gun at the family, ordering them to board the van. "These *mauras* are our enemies!" the soldier shouted in anger. "They must not be allowed to live!" One of the soldiers pushed him so hard that the maulana sahib fell on the ground. Then he threatened to shoot him if he tried to stop him again.

We didn't want him to go on. To accept any explanation or sympathy from one who failed to act when it mattered most seemed pointless. Who knows? Had he stood his ground or been really brave that day, he might have saved at least one life. Or the old man might have chosen to give his own life for the sake of his students. Who else was in a better position to do that than him? We hugged the weeping man one last time but could not bring ourselves to thank him for at least trying. Leaving him standing there, we entered the gate of Dr. Yusuf's house.

The doctor's family had been our close friends for as long as we could remember. His daughters, Lipi and Lita, were close friends of Munni and went to the same school. The two little girls looked visibly traumatized by what had happened to their best friend's family and did not speak a word. Perhaps in their hearts they felt the guilt of their father's failure to protect them. Here was one family that genuinely tried to do something. But throughout the time we spent at Dr. Yusuf's house, one thought kept crossing my mind. Had this man been half as resolute as Lal Chacha, my mother and the two youngest could have stayed back with them in their village and survived. The doctor struggled for words, and his wife kept sobbing and repeating that they did everything possible. They said they were helpless before God's will. We could not say anything for fear of adding to the grief of their lovely daughters, who looked to be suffering this tragedy equally with us.

"It was that shameless rascal Khokon. Had it not been for him, they would still be here today." Dr. Yusuf's wife disclosed that their neighbour Moharrir's son, Khokon, had come to know from the cook that our family was hiding in their house. She had no doubt that it was Khokon who informed the EPR soldiers of our family's whereabouts.

I remembered playing with Khokon as a child, visiting each other's house, and searching for eggs in the nests perched on the trees in their big beautiful garden. For some reason he dropped out of our group and gave up his studies; no one knew why. I used to feel sorry for him until one day I recalled his mother came to our house, shouting abuses at her son. She was holding her wrist, which was wrapped in a wet white cloth. Khokon had hit her with something. Soon the neighbours came to know, and Khokon was ostracized by practically everyone. The children in the neighbourhood no longer played with him. Dr. Yusuf told us that after the army arrived in Thakurgaon, they had picked up Khokon, and he had not been seen since. I was sorry to hear that, if only because it robbed me of my one chance for revenge on someone who could be identified as a culprit.

There was still one hour to sunset, but it was too late to catch a bus. Dr. Yusuf asked us to stay for the night. When we declined, he insisted we take his car with his driver.

When we got up to leave, Mrs. Yusuf handed me a small black purse that I instantly recognized as my mother's magic wallet, one that had never let us down in times of need. "We found this in the room where your mother was staying," she said. She also handed me my mother's ring along with a couple of earrings that were found on the dressing table, which I also recognized. "Please keep them safe, my son, these are your memories now . . ." She could not finish, just reached out to hug me, a drop of her tear fell on my arm.

It was going to get dark soon. Seeing that the Bengali driver looked nervous at the thought of driving through various checkpoints we would encounter on the way, Hashmat took the wheel. I sat next to him.

As we drove away, I took out the black purse from my pocket. Holding it in my hands brought back the memories of how that little wallet had saved the day for me and my brothers on so many ocassions. Whenever we needed money, and we made it out to be a matter of life and death, Mother always yielded. She would smile, hand us five or ten rupees, and then put her wallet carefully back in the steel *almirah*. That purse of magical powers was never empty.

Soon we passed the village of Pran Nagar. Almost instinctively Hashmat slowed down and stopped in front of my Aunt Husna's deserted farmhouse to look for any sign of life. The place looked like the set of a movie where the filming had ended and the cast had left for the day. Tomorrow the cast and the crew would return. The director would call "action," the people would start to move, and the camera would begin to roll again.

This village appeared so lifeless that except for the invisible birds chirping in the large trees above, we saw no animals, no chickens, and no movement.

"Stop, stop!" I shouted, when the car began to move again. Hashmat almost veered off the road as he slammed on the brakes.

"Did you see him? Did you see?" I shrieked.

"See who?" Hashmat's voice filled with anticipation.

Even before the car came to a complete halt, I jumped out and ran toward the trees. There he was, covered in dust, his torn shirt pocket dangling like a handkerchief. He was wearing a pair of shorts cut out from some oversize trousers, and his bare feet were covered in dust. His shiny black skin had turned dirty brown, and he looked a good ten years older than his age of sixteen or seventeen.

"Chotu, remember me?"

"Bhaia, this is Chotu," I called out, turning toward Hashmat, who had caught up with us by then. "Do you not remember him?"

Chotu looked so terrified. Suddenly, he turned and started running. We ran behind him.

"Stop, Chotu, stop! I swear we won't harm you. For God's sake, stop! You idiot!"

He kept running as we closed in again. Too weak to continue, he tripped, almost hurting himself .

"You stupid Chotu, what happened to you? It's me, Azmat" I yelled when I finally caught up with him. "Don't be afraid. Come on, and get up now." I extended my hand and pulled him up.

The physical contact served to revive him, assuring him that we meant no harm. Chotu was Aunt Husna's servant. He arrived at her house when he was only nine or ten and had lived with her family ever since.

"Tell us what happened here," I demanded to know. "Is anyone in the family alive?"

Chotu pointed his finger toward the river that ran parallel to my aunt's land behind her house. "They didn't spare anyone, no one survived." "There." He pointed toward the river and began walking toward it. We followed.

The *sautal* community that Chotu belonged to was from the almost extinct bush dwellers in that part of northern Bengal who, until the 1960s, were living like aborigines with their own distinct dialect and culture. In the desolate forests of northern Bengal, the sautals lived in perfect harmony with nature. Their men wore scant pieces of cloth around their waist. Their women carried their babies on their back tucked safely inside baby slings made out of the clothes they wore. Although some of them had begun practicing subsistence agriculture in remote areas or in the riverbeds, until the 1950s the sautals were known to hunt for wild boars with arrows and spears.

On our frequent visits to our aunt's farm, Chotu who inherited part of the skills would teach us how to use his bow and arrow. Despite several expeditions in the jungle with him, we could never master his weapons. He, nevertheless, was always able to trap the odd rabbit or catch some birds—*charuis, mainas,* and doves— with all kinds of contraptions. Aunt Husna would scold him everytime we returned from our expeditions, and he would swear that we hadn't gone across the river in the forest.

"Amma," as he called Aunt Husna, "is buried there." Chotu pointed to a spot on the banks of the small river where Aunt Husna was buried with the rest of her family. We counted four large and three small heaps in the sand.

Chotu sat down by those graves and narrated the events of the last few days in the lives of these people. On the fateful day, he had gone to the village market, the *haat,* with Jamal, aunt Husna's son. Some people got into an arguments with him, and started calling him "Maura Bihari." In no time a dozen or so people pounced on Jamal and began to beat him up. Bewildered, Chotu could not understand what Jamal had done or what those people had against him. He dragged Jamal back home, leaving his bike behind, as Jamal could no longer ride it.

As they neared home, they heard loud cries of the ladies in the house. People armed with sticks, spears, and *daos* had surrounded the house. Chotu had never seen the men before. "They were not from Pran Nagar," he swore.

Jamal asked Chotu to take him behind the bushes, where he could hide. The heartrending cries of the women inside the house grew louder and louder before they subsided. In a few minutes, they saw the men dragging the ladies and children toward the river. As luck had it, one of the attackers spotted Jamal, half-dead, hiding behind the bushes.

"He is hiding here!" the man shouted.

Their head count for the household was now complete. Within seconds four or five of them descended on Jamal. They stabbed him several times. His calls for mercy in Bengali subsided as he slumped on the ground.

"Shala Bihari, aita tomar desh nai!" ("This is not your land!") one of them scolded as they turned back to join the others, dragging the rest of the family toward the river. The men did not bother to ask Chotu who he was.

After they were gone, Chotu realized that somehow Jamal was still alive. He dragged him inside the courtyard. Jamal was still breathing, and his eyes, which were open, seemed to be asking where his mother and sister were.

No longer able to hold back his tears, Chotu fell silent for a while. When he resumed his story, he said he told Jamal that he would go looking for them when he got better. Until then he would stay with him. Chotu gave him some water, which he could not drink, so he just sat next to Jamal, staying with him long after he was gone.

The following morning, Chotu's father helped carry Jamal's body to the riverbank. It took Chotu and his folks all day to carry the mutilated bodies of the others to the riverbank. Being sautals, they did not know how to perform the Muslims' last rites. They dug a large trench on the riverbank and laid the bodies side by side.

"Where are your folks?" I asked. "Didn't they live next to the river?"

He nodded pointing across the river. "Do you want to go inside?" Chotu asked, pointing at aunt's house.

The doors had been tied loosely with a jute rope from outside, probably by Chotu, who was still the housekeeper there. He had been looking after the empty house, hoping for his masters' relatives to turn up looking for them one day. The bamboo fencing on the side leading to the courtyard had collapsed along with the side door that lay on the floor clinging to the fallen rain-soaked mud wall. We simply had no stomach to enter the empty house.

"Who buried your family in Thakurgaon?" Chotu asked calmly.

"What did you hear?" I asked, taken aback by his question.

He told us that he had been to visit our family home in Thakurgaon after he heard the news. A neighbour told him that no one had survived, but he knew nothing more. His joy at seeing the two of us alive was written all over his face.

We asked Chotu about the family of Aunt Husna's Uncle Munif (we called him "Dada"), who lived across the road from her farm along with his second wife and two daughters. He informed us that everyone except Munif Dada, who was too old to walk, had run away before the attackers arrived. Munif's son, Nasim, and his son-in-law were in the police, posted in Lalmunirhat. They were the first casualties in that family, killed by their Bengali compatriots in the rebellion around late March. The rest of the family never returned even after the army arrived and presumably had gone across the border. Munif Dada was killed where he sat on the veranda outside the house, next to his rope-making wheel. We spotted his stick still dangling on the veranda. Now we knew the fourth adult grave by the riverbank was that of Munif Dada and not of Zareena, as we had presumed. The first three adult graves were for Aunt Husna, her daughter, Chanda, and her son, Jamal. The three small graves were for Chanda's three younger children. Her beautiful grown-up daughter Zareena, nearly sixteen, was not killed. She was taken away by one of the men. Chotu believed she may have been taken across the border or killed somewhere else. This was the second young Bihari girl that we heard was abducted or saved by the perpetrators. The first was Akhtar Sabib's daughter, Shaheen, in Thakurgaon who was saved by a Bengali neighbour who later married her and looked after her as his wife. Zareena probably was not that lucky, and years of searching after that yielded no information about her. Some years later, we heard about a third young girl saved by a Bengali family.

We walked through the bushes back to the riverbank one more time to pray at the place where my aunt's family was buried, then prepared to leave. Chotu started to weep as we reached the car.

"We have to get back to Dinajpur before it's dark, Chotu," "Take care; we'll be back," I said without any thought. Chotu's look told us that he knew it was a lie.

On the way back to Dinajpur, we crossed several checkpoints but only had to get out at one near the small town of Birganj for body search. A thirteen or fourteen-year-old kid with a rifle in his hand startled us as he approached us.

"Azmat bhai, salaam."

"Recognize me: I am Shabbir, Shobrati's younger brother."

"Yes, yes, I do now. What are you doing here?" I asked.

He smiled as his eyes lit up, showing off his rifle, which was almost as big as him, and his position of authority. With his long hair kept in place by his cap, he looked a child version of Che Guevara.

Shabbir informed us that Shobrati (who was half Bihari and half Bengali) was killed by EPR rebels, who took him to be Urdu-speaking. Like the unfortunate Shobrati, Bengalis from Murshidabad were largely bilingual, often married to Urdu-speaking people, and mingled well with the Biharis. Shabbir also informed us that a Hyder mechanic who had married a Bengali woman and used to live behind the club next to our house was killed along with his sons and brothers.

With nowhere to go, Shabbir had little choice but to join the paramilitary, known as Albadr, a force largely raised from the victims of the massacre of Urdu-speaking people and also from the Bengali Jamaat Islami workers who supported the federation to assist the Pakistani army. It is hard for those who have not suffered the kind of atrocities these young men did to understand why some of them were on a revenge spree and why they were working with the newly arrived Pakistani army, who also seemed to be avenging the loss of their fellow soldiers and their families killed in the uprising by the rebel Bengali soldiers.

Shabbir called out to another young friend, who looked no older than Shabbir himself.

"I know you; you are Uncle Ashraf's son." The young boy quickly held out his hand, excited to see us. He told us that he knew everyone in our family and knew what had happened to them. He belonged to the Muhajir Para in the southern part of Thakurgaon near the graveyard. Without a hint of emotion, he told us that he was the sole survivor in his family, just like Shabbir. I felt sorry that I couldn't recognize the shy, timid kid, who didn't even look fourteen. I wanted to ask him about his family, so I could place him better, but it would have served no purpose. Daylight was fading, and we had to get going.

"Who's that man tied up on the roadside?" I asked, pointing at a man on the grass who had been moaning in pain ever since we had stepped out of the car.

"Don't know. I think he's an informer, Mukhti Bahini maybe," the boy answered calmly.

In the fading light, it was still possible to see that the man's ankles were bruised, and he was bleeding from the cuts on his wrists caused by the jute ropes used to tie him up. His hands and legs were tied around a bamboo stick, which made it difficult for him to sit up. His captors had probably beaten him to extract information. Groaning in pain, he kept pleading, "I don't know anything. I don't know anyone here. Please let me go, for God's sake, let me . . ."

I have no idea what atrocities Shabbir or that nameless boy may have participated in. I never found out what happened to those unfortunate kids after the war. Having seen so much blood at such a young age, they had little regard for human life, burning in hate and unable to forgive.

At every checkpoint after that, I kept looking out for more Shabbirs, hoping by some miracle that I would find someone I recognized.

Back in Dinajpur we were told that some Bihari survivors from the adjoining villages had been brought to the Iqbal school camp. The shopkeeper with whom we spent the night on the way to Thakurgaon had told us there was little hope of finding anyone we knew, but we decided to look for anyone we could recognize.

"This is not a camp; this is a graveyard," the guard told us. When the army arrived, they had to remove at least 200 bodies from the school, almost all women and children. Those who were still there did not have any place to go. After we left Dinajpur, we learned from neighbours from Thakurgaon that Uncle Yasin's daughter, Ambia, only recently married, had survived, but her husband was missing. We also heard some years later that the wife of Uncle Mahmood, a friend of our father's, was also among the survivors. We looked around but found neither of them in that camp. Over the years after the genocide, I was able to meet several survivors from the district who owed their lives to one miracle or another. Their accounts helped me piece together what happened in that enchanting town.

Dinajpur had a large population of Urdu-speaking people, 15,000 to 20,000 by some estimates. Like Thakurgaon, the town, being farthest away from Dhaka, bore the brunt of the killings, where around 15,000 Biharis perished. No one knew the exact numbers, and no such statistics were ever compiled. Just like Thakurgaon, the formation of peace committees, followed by the disarming of the Biharis, had begun around mid-March, soon after the postponement of the assembly. The biggest operation against the Biharis coordinated secretly between the Awami League, the police, and the EPR command, code named operation "Baton Day" (or payback time, as the connotation went), was set for March 28 when the Pakistani soldiers and/or their Urdu-speaking colleagues were to be killed by the EPR soldiers. The rebellion at the Peelkhana camp was to be preceded by the rebellion of the local police. The police had already looted their own arms depot and killed their non-Bengali colleagues, like my father's second cousin, Naseem Akhtar, and Naseem's brother-in-law. Then the rebels had broken open the district jail in Balubari and distributed arms to the prisoners, who quickly went on a looting and killing spree in the Bihari neighbourhoods.

Large-scale killings started around March 29, when scores of Biharis, especially young men, were rounded up and trucked to the banks of the Kanchan River. They were ordered to line up and then shot under the railway bridge known as Kanchan Bridge. Bodies piled up as more and were brought there to be shot. One survivor I met a few years later was our moulvi sahib's son, Zubair, who was shot in the arm and in his back and left for dead. Miraculously, he was still breathing when the Pakistani army arrived a few days later and began burying the bodies. Another place in Dinajpur where the army had to bury hundreds of bodies was the site of a dry pond by Iqbal's school since the bodies were too decomposed to be removed. Bihari residents of localities like Malda Patti, Balu Bari, and Suihari, were largely wiped out.

Only a handful of survivors were able to hide or flee to the satellite town sector five, which was a Bihari majority area. That was the locality where the exceptional courage of a few young men led by an officer on leave from the Pakistan navy, Mahtab Ahmed Siddiqui, put up a resistance that saved nearly 3,000 residents. Their story of courage and human endurance would live with the survivors; to be told and retold to their children and grand children for years to come.

The predominantly Bhiari settlement, called the "satellite town," was surrounded by well-armed EPR soldiers and *sacha seboks*. They made several announcements on the megaphone asking people to surrender their weapons and promising they would not be harmed if they did so. But these residents knew what had happened elsewhere in Dinajpur. Those who chose to surrender their weapons around the periphery of that sector were murdered quickly. Surrounded by a far superior force, the rag-tag group had a few brave young men who refused to surrender. In nearly two and a half weeks of siege, these young men, armed with a few shotguns and rifles, were able to hold the attackers at bay. As luck had it, they received reinforcements of some weapons and ammunition from a Pakistani army officer who had survived the uprising and managed to flee from the nearby EPR camp. In the two-week standoff that followed, a few old and infirm died due to lack of food and drinking water, both of which were cut off by those who had laid the siege. Some felt compelled to take chances by trying to escape, but they were shot by snipers perched on the nearby water tank. Finally, on April 13 a contingent of Pakistani soldiers arrived from the Rangpur garrison, and the attackers vanished into thin air.

Leaving Dinajpur for the last time, the emotion that gripped me was different from the one I had experienced when I was leaving Thakurgaon and Pran Nagar. For once I was not only grieving for my own family but for all the family friends who had perished in that town which was our second home, where we used to spend many weekends mostly to watch newly released movies at the Bustan or Modern Cinema.

In all that pain, a few pieces of good news trickled through about those who had reportedly survived, although we could still not meet them because no one could tell us where they were. We knew we would probably never see those broken souls again. But their faces kept popping up in my mind: Uncle Jalil, Uncle Mahmood's wife, Ambia, our own moulvi sahib, Dr. Saba, and others. We could not risk staying there longer to keep looking for them. That failing has tormented me ever since, and my guilt of not staying back in Dinajpur and not making much effort to search for those survivors while we were there will stay with me for as long as I live. Many years later I learned that Mrs. Mahmood, a housewife from a well-to-do family and the lone survivor of that household, spent the rest of her life (nearly twelve years) working as a maid in a house close to her own, which was occupied by new owners that she had never met before.

Just like Thakurgaon, not a single Bihari family in Dinajpur had escaped the brutalities of the *sacha seboks*, the rebel EPR soldiers, and the rebel police. The handful of survivors I have met over the years who managed to make it to Karachi believed without a shred of doubt that one way or another, the entire Bengali population was complicit in a planned ethnic cleansing of the Bihari community. True, a small minority of kind-hearted Bengalis did not agree with what was happening. A few even managed to save some lives by hiding them, and undoubtedly some brave men like Lal Chacha risked their own lives to save a few Biharis. Barring the exceptions, in town after town, the pattern of events pointed to the Bengali community's miserable failure to save even their close friends. They had proven themselves to be what Uncle Ansari used to call them, *buzdil*, due to the historic absence of gallantry or valour in that land.

Returning to Dhaka, the only Bengali friend I met was Hamid, my classmate from cadet college. After the army action, his family had shifted from their Mohammadpur house, a predominantly Urdu-speaking locality, to old Dhaka for reasons of safety. Barely six months earlier, Hamid's house had been my second home in Dhaka, where I spent the bulk of my evenings. Hamid and I were freshmen at Dhaka University in the Economics Department. Almost every other evening, I would eat and sleep at his house until I left for Karachi in January 1971. At the time it felt like I was leaving two families behind in East Pakistan, my own in Thakurgaon and Hamid's in Dhaka.

Hamid's father was one of the senior-most Bengali engineers in Wapda, reputed for his integrity as well as his competence. Although his son had performed brilliantly in school, securing first position in the board in SSC and second in HSC, his father was least prepared to spoil his son. He had set extremely high standards himself, winning numerous scholarships and awards in his time. Hamid's mother, on the other hand, was just a simple devoted housewife. Like my own mother, she appeared oppressed and timid in front of her husband's towering personality. This probably drew me closer to her during my stay in Dhaka, when I was missing my own mother. Hamid's only sister, Labli, five or six years younger than us, possessed the most beautiful eyes I had ever seen. Almost as a reflex whenever I entered Hamid's house, I would search for those dark, sparkling black eyes. Everyone in Hamid's family seemed to be fond of me and made me feel at home. Labli happily teamed up with me when we played badminton in their little front yard and attended to small chores for Hamid and me.

In just a few months, the world had turned upside down for both our families, stunned by the atrocities committed by our two communities against each other. Like us, they were torn apart by the hatred between the Biharis and the Bengalis. Nothing would be the same again. Restricted indoors due to the curfew in the evenings and the lack of public transport on Dhaka's streets, during the two days that I spent at Hamid's house, we did not attempt to venture out. We spent most of our time sitting in the small living room where Hamid would continuously try to engage me in aimless conversation. Labli and her mother took their turn bringing food, tea, and so on. Except for "Salaam" and "How are you?" I do not remember talking to them during those two days. They looked extremely distressed for me, their pain was written on their faces. Once or twice I noticed Labli and her mother would sit nearby praying silently or listening to the one-way conversation of Hamid trying to keep me composed.

Forced to live away from their own home, the lives of everyone in Hamid's family had changed too. They did not know when or if they would return to their own home. Trapped in a time capsule, Hamid and I were no longer talking of the grand plans for our future, not even of any plans for the present. Neither of us wished to trivialize the recent tragedies by talking about the country's politics or our own safety. Everything seemed meaningless, and we all appeared to be locked in a world where our despair seemed like they would never end.

Events were clearly pointing toward an all-out war for the independence of Bangladesh. Dhaka was bound to see many months of terror and tragedy. While leaving Dhaka, this time for good, I could not help but worry about the safety of Hamid's family. It was difficult to predict whether everyone would survive the difficult times ahead and whether they would ever be able to return to their own home in Mohammadpur.

"Look after yourself." Hamid snatched the words out of my mouth, leaving nothing for me to say. With his mother and Labli watching silently, he stood still as I climbed into the waiting rickshaw, not knowing if we would ever meet again.

1971 – BENGALI REFUGEES HEAD TOWARD THE INDIAN BORDER.

1971- INDRA GANDHI (INDIAN PM) TALKING TO BENGALI REFUGEES IN INDIA

While the plight of the Bengalis was well publicized in the world press, the tragedy of the Biharis was missed by all, since the dead cannot speak.

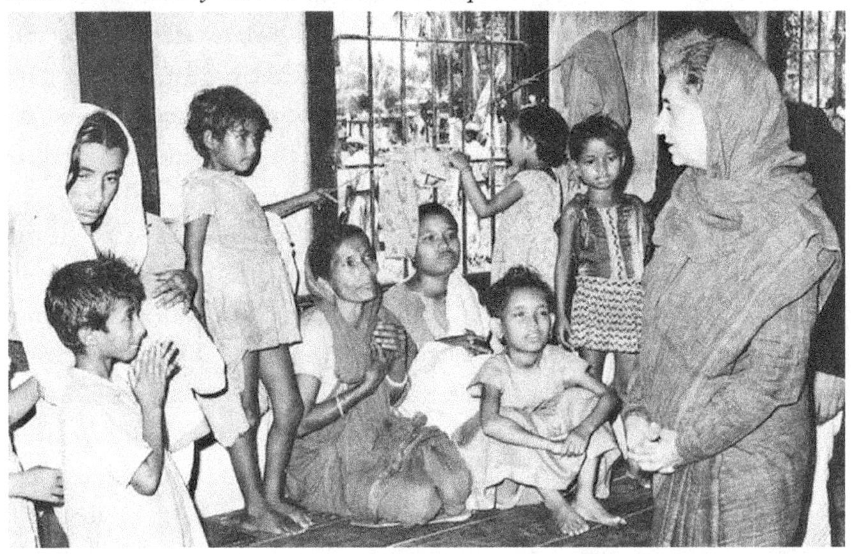

1971 – EAST PAKISTAN/BANGLADESH (MAJOR TOWNS AND MILITARY INSTALLATIONS)

Given the topography, which consists of a dense network of rivers, and with many bridges blown up by the rebellious Bengali soldiers, the movement of the Pakistani army was hindered, requiring several weeks to recapture the garrisons and restore order. This gave the rebels ample time to massacre the Urdu-speaking people (Biharis) at will.

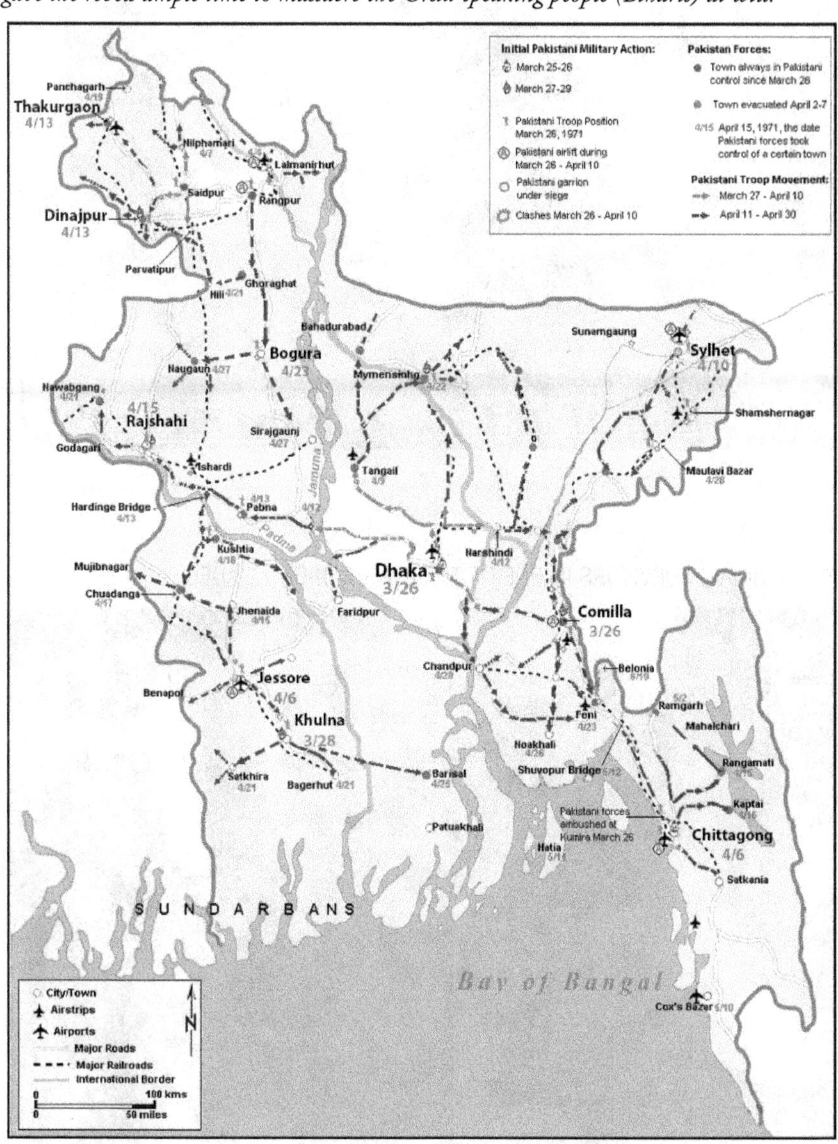

1971- AT THE END OF THE BANGLADESH WAR, BIHARIS FEAR FOR THEIR LIVES AS THEY ARE ROUNDED UP BY THE VICTORIOUS MUKTI BAHINI

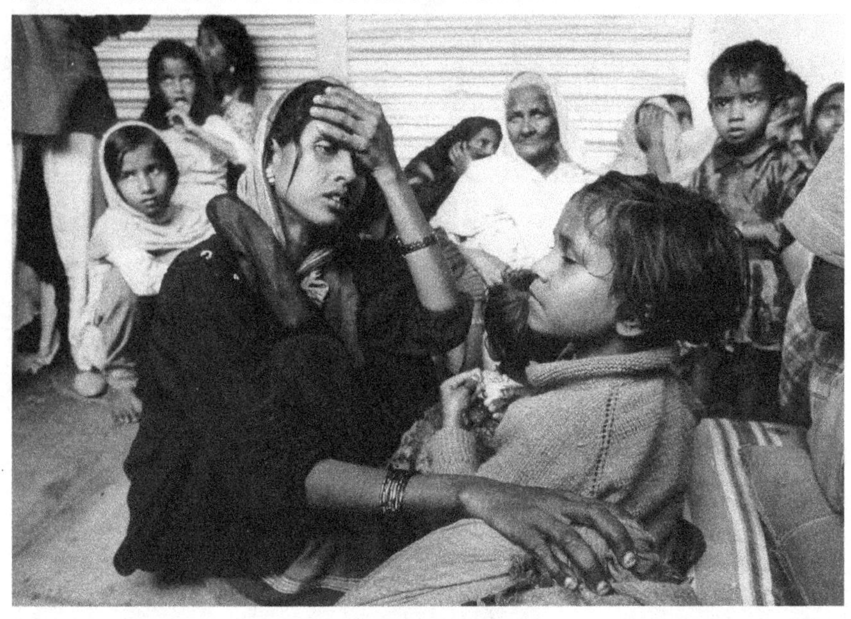

1972 – BIHARI SURVIVORS IN ONE OF THE CAMPS IN BANGLADESH

SECOND MIGRATION

So tell me, where should I go?
To the left, where there is nothing right?
To the right, where there is nothing left?
—ANONYMOUS

Barely a few months ago, I had arrived in Karachi as a student, intending to return home after my studies. But it had turned out to be a one-way ticket. Having lost my home in East Pakistan, I had no place to return to, and by default I had completed my second forced migration at the age of eighteen, my first had taken place in my mother's lap when I was a year old.

Returning from Dhaka to Karachi for the last time, I found that the Pakistani papers had finally begun to echo the gloom that I had left behind in East Pakistan. Along with that were reports of Indian troops massing on the country's border. Once again it was the villain India that was trying to break up Pakistan, which had done little wrong. Everyone there bemoaned the fanaticism of the Awami Leaguers and blamed Shaikh Mujib for playing into India's hands. "Crush India" car stickers were on display in abundance around Karachi. Pakistanis appeared to be bracing for a decisive war with India, a few still believing that Pakistan was going to thrash them.

Practically no one understood the follies of the Pakistani rulers or recognized the realities on the ground in the unfortunate eastern half of the country. All this while a full-scale war that Pakistan was doomed to lose appeared to be inching closer. For anyone doing a reality check, East Pakistan was destined to become Bangladesh.

Waiting for me in Karachi was a letter from the ex-principal of Ayub Cadet College asking me to meet him at the Mauripurpur airbase public school. When a short, frail man in white pajamas opened the door, I took him for the family cook until I heard his unmistakable voice.

"Kya haal hai mera beta?" ("How are you, my son?") He had been waiting for me at his door since the guardroom had called him to announce my arrival. "I am glad you look fine, my son," he added a few seconds later.

He certainly didn't look fine; weighed down by his own tragedies. He had grown a beard that had turned completely white, making him look like a thinner version of Santa Claus. I had been postponing calling on my ex-principal from cadet college, Wing Commander Syed, since my arrival in Karachi. Initially, it was due to laziness, but later the events in East Pakistan had completely grounded me. As soon as Mr. Syed heard about my tragedies, he phoned and asked me to visit him. When I failed to turn up, he wrote a letter. Mr. Syed was serving out his last years prior to his retirement as the principal of the air force school at the Mauripur air base on the outskirts of Karachi.

He embraced me, then took me by the arm and pulled me toward the sofa in the living room, sitting so close that I was almost in his lap. Then he called his entire family to meet his student. To my embarrassment, he introduced me as his "star student." Far from being a top student, all I had managed during his tenure as principal was to avoid being expelled. I neither deserved not received any praise from him when he was principal at the cadet college. Yet, it still felt great that he had been following the progress of his students.

"You're not saying that just because you feel sorry for me," I asked hesitatingly, realizing instantly that I had unnecessarily poured cold water onto his warmth.

"We are all in the same boat, my son. I feel sorry for myself too," his said, giving me a somber gaze.

In total command of his emotions, he informed me that his journalist brother, Rahman Syed, was also killed in East Pakistan. That instantly sent me back three years in time. I remembered the fine radio documentary that Mr. Rahman had made about our cadet college some years earlier in his baritone voice. His phrases like "the pompous Padma" and "the lush green velvet of Shardah" were used by many others after him to describe the great river that ran next to the college and the greenery that surrounded it. Journalist Rahman had been travelling back to Dhaka from an assignment in Chittagong when his train was attacked by the Mukti Bahini. The Urdu-speaking passengers were asked to get off and were butchered; no one survived. There are different accounts of them being held as prisoners first in a nearby village for a couple of days before they were killed.

Rahman's wife sat speechless in her white sari next to Mrs. Syed on the sofa opposite ours. Mrs. Syed, who we simply used to call "Madam," had also aged quickly. No colourful sari and no hint of the subtle makeup that used to be her hallmark back in Rajshahi. She was doubly touched by that tragedy, since Rahman's wife was her younger sister. Two brothers marrying two sisters was common in those days. Also in the room was the son of his youngest brother, Squadron Leader Syed, who had died of a heart attack at age of only forty-eight. Resembling the picture of his father in uniform on the side table, the son had grown up to be a fine young man and, keeping with the family tradition, was planning to join the air force.

It was painful to watch an entire family in mourning, particularly the family of the man we feared so much in school. In the twilight years of his life, with his dreams in shambles, faced with a failing health and the responsibility of looking after three families, the old lion was merely a shadow of his past self. For a moment I forgot my own problems, watching this wounded, aging man whose towering personality had intimidated me so much only three years earlier. On the flip side, it was gratifying to see how this devoted teacher had kept himself up to date with his former students' progress.

"Remember, I am your guardian here in Karachi," he reminded me when I was saying goodbye, insisting that I call him regularly and come to him for anything I needed.

Torn between two worlds, my Bengali friends from cadet college in East Pakistan—Saif, Taneem, Mustafiz, and Bazlur—were stuck at the military academy at Kakul in the northern part of West Pakistan. Physically, they were pursuing their course in the Pakistani army, but their hearts were in strife-torn East Pakistan. They no longer believed they had a future in Pakistan, and most of them were planning to run away. Some wrote to console me in their own way. Being Bengalis, they felt extreme guilt and remorse at what their fellow Bengalis had done, lost for words to express their feelings. The future of these fine young men, who had so much potential, hung precariously in the balance with the growing conflict in their minds viz a viz their duty as army cadets in Pakistan on one hand and their conscience on the other. With the news of the Pakistan army's excesses against their own people being splashed all over the world press, they were on edge.

Saif phoned from the military academy to say he was coming to see me in Karachi during the upcoming break. A week later he turned up at my door along with our mutual friend from cadet college, Bazlur Rashid. I knew it was not a simple visit from the moment I saw them. After dinner that evening, we went out for a walk without Bazlur, who was watching the evening news on TV.

"We are going to India." Saif broke the news as we sat by the water tank in the factory compound where I was staying with Siddique Sahib.

"You mean you're defecting?" I asked.

"So, this is where you come when you need solitude," he said, changing the subject. He was repeating what I had already told him before dinner.

In the evenings that was the darkest corner behind the main factory building, and it was peaceful since no one went that way at night. The burnt-out light bulb hanging from a small pole next to the pond had not been replaced, and the resulting darkness hid the heap of *raddi* (rejected cardboards) from the factory next to the tank, making the place look neater than it actually was. A large wooden scale stood next to the heap. Each Friday it was used to weigh the raddi, which was sold to the junk dealers. The faint moonlight guided us to the small bench at the edge of the tank. The moonlight falling on the water in the tank made it glow. The reflection of the neem tree in the water created a calm, serene atmosphere despite being only yards behind the noisy, dusty factory that never slept.

"Have you learned to swim yet?" Saif laughed as he recollected how I had almost drowned back at cadet college. He reminded me how our college mate, nicknamed "Goda" (neither of us could recall his real name), was teaching me to swim.

"Very good, you got it." Goda was coaxing me to move toward the deep while supporting me lightly by the waist. Seeing how far I had gone, I lost confidence and panicked. I clutched his arm, almost pulling him down with me. The newly dug pond was quickly declared out of bounds for those who could not swim.

"How will you cross the border?" I asked.

"Not sure. There is someone in Karachi who arranges the border crossing through the Thar Desert." Saif had never met the agent but had spoken to him on the phone.

There were two routes, one via Kabul, which was much safer those days with a porous border and known smugglers' trails. Upon reaching Kabul, he could take a plane to Delhi. The other route was the direct crossing into India through the Thar Desert in lower Sindh. Although the latter was riskier, it was the fastest and cheapest route. He had heard that Bengali soldiers defecting to India were being welcomed across the border by the Indian army. They were being fed and trained for the war of liberation in several camps that had sprung up near the other border with East Pakistan, a thousand miles away.

"I don't want to miss out on this once-in-a-lifetime opportunity," Saif said, looking at me as if for approval. When I didn't respond, he continued. "I would never forgive myself if I missed out on it; my life would not be worth living." He had never sounded that serious before.

"Why did you come to me? I could have you arrested. Don't forget I'm Pakistani."

"Actually, that's what some of my Bengali colleagues at the academy also told me," he hesitated to admit. But he did not want to go without seeing me, so he decided to take the risk.

"Just remember, Azmat, things change. Bad times don't stay forever. Whatever you do, never give up. You have *Chotay*," as he affectionately used to call Shahid. "Consider yourself lucky that you have a brother like Hashmat who can take care of your needs." Saif kept talking while I listened.

"If you make it to Thakurgaon, will you look around for any survivors in my family?" I interrupted.

Shahid's recovery had rekindled my hope for another miracle which is what I thought about all the time. I asked Saif to also look for people from our district in the camps bordering India. Then I shared with him the dreams I had been having, in which my mother was trying to say something. I wanted him to visit those places I had being seeing in my dreams. We went on until the early hours of the morning. By the time we got back to the room, Bazlur was fast asleep.

Although by then I was practically living at Siddique Sahib's house, I had not surrendered my room at the university hostel. Saif asked me the next day to move him to my room at the hostel while Bazlur stayed at Siddique Sahib's house with me. He needed to contact certain agent who was going to take them across the border. It was not safe for him and Bazlur to move around together. With their army haircuts and pidgin Urdu, they would attract unwarranted attention.

Two days later, Saif phoned and asked me to meet him at the Village restaurant, where he had arranged to meet the agent. It was the same place where American journalist Daniel Pearl had been lured to meet a clandestine terrorist group. From there he was abducted and brutally murdered many years later, in 2002.

Saif called again asking me to meet him in the lobby of the Metropole Hotel next door from where we were to walk to the Village restaurant at 8:30 p.m. Bazlur and I arrived at the appointed time and found Saif waiting for us in the lobby, hiding his face behind a newspaper as he pretended to read it. Together at the restaurant, we ordered our food and waited in one of the dimly lit bamboo cabins where the noise of the live band was more tolerable. Mixing western music with 1960s hits, the band was playing our favourite songs, "*Akeley na jaana*" and "*Kahaan ho tum ko*." The contact failed to turn up. After waiting for over two hours, we gave up and left.

The next day Saif phoned again asking Bazlur and me to meet him at the same place along with Bazlur's handbag, the only luggage the two had. We were a few minutes late, which was making Saif restless. He had called the house to check exactly when we had left. We were shocked to see that Saif had a bandage on his head. Before we could ask him, he began to explain.

"Your hostel friends are up to no good. First they discussed politics with me, knowing I'm Bengali. Then they started hurling abuses. But when I abused them back, they attacked me. Tell me, what was I supposed to do?" he pleaded, looking sheepishly at us.

We examined the slight bruise under the bandage on his head.

"You need a bandage on your brain," Bazlur said.

I had missed telling Saif the frame of mind my roommate, Yusuf was, in those days and why he could have been so easily agitated. We found ourselves a booth in the farthest corner and ordered our meal.

"We're leaving tonight," Saif said, lowering his voice. The mood suddenly turned somber. The music in the background grew louder as we quietly finished our dinner without further conversation.

"You don't have a watch; you'll need this." I took off my watch and handed it to Saif. "Sell it if you need money."

We hugged each other, bid goodbye inside the cabin and then left separately.

Saif and Bazlur rode away in a waiting rickshaw. Left standing on the pavement I just wondered if we would ever meet again. They would probably be shot crossing the heavily guarded border with the two armies standing eyeball to eyeball. If they didn't, they still had a war to fight after that. Long after they disappeared into the traffic, I stood motionless, thinking of all that I wanted to tell them which had remained unsaid and may remain so forever.

Shahid arrived in Karachi from Dhaka in September to join me as soon as he finished the especially arranged board exams at the cadet college, which had been postponed twice and eventually held under the army's protection. Relieved he was safely out of East Pakistan, we both began to live in Siddique Sahib's newly constructed house in the northern part of Karachi. My stipend of 150 rupees per month from the university was a bonus because I was enjoying free boarding and lodging. Although Shahid had a school-leaving certificate, he was still waiting for a transcript of his matriculation results from cadet college, which never came. In those extraordinary times, his school-leaving certificate sufficed, and he was granted admission in HSC at the national college. The college authorities showed a lot of flexibility in Shahid's admission and in allowing him to start in the middle of the term.

In the city, where everyone spoke Urdu, Shahid and I very soon began to feel at home. We wondered why our parents had not chosen to migrate to this part of Pakistan twenty years earlier instead of East Pakistan. Within months we had developed a sense of belonging in Karachi that East Pakistan had not provided us despite our years of residence there.

Hashmat had waited back in Dhaka for his employment papers from the UK to arrive and left for the UK as soon as they came. To see us in Karachi, he stopped over for a couple of days.

"You are now your own guardians," he said while leaving. "I will try to take you to the UK somehow," he promised. "Just make sure you don't let your grades slip, not at any cost."

Hashmat was proud of his brothers' academic achievement, which was also his only hope for taking us out of Pakistan. If we didn't get any scholarships, he would not be able to support the two of us in the UK with the meager salary he had been promised as a junior doctor.

A semblance of normalcy returned to our lives as we got down to our studies once again. Despite the pressure to obtain good grades, it was hard to forget everything so quickly. A sense of fatalism kept creeping up from time to time, making it difficult for us to take much interest in studies. At the university I was naturally drawn to the students who had come from East Pakistan who would be easily recognizable given their distinct Urdu accent. Some made fun of their accent and others sympathized, knowing the upheavals these young boys and girls were going through in their lives. Most offered helping hands whenever the opportunity arose. The university waived our tuition fees for the year. Unlike their counterparts in Dhaka, the students in Karachi appeared far less politicized, were more outgoing and fun loving. The girls were fair, tall, and stylishly dressed, and most of the boys were bigger and broader and much better in sports compared to their brothers from East Pakistan. But when it came to studies, their smaller brothers from Dhaka enjoyed an edge. Those from East Pakistan banded together and spent the free periods in the arts lobby discussing the latest news and never stopped worrying about the relatives still left behind. Aftab, Aqueel, Wazeer, Anis, and my roommate, Yusuf, were all in the same boat and the same state of mind.

Sometimes humour provided relief, and sometimes a story of someone's lucky escape or unexpected reappearance after he was presumed dead provided joy. We also heard jokes about the hapless Pakistan army *jawaans* bogged down in the unfamiliar territory of East Pakistan. Like the one about the Pathan soldier asking for the "denty card," to check the identity of a journalist invited to the governor's house for a press briefing.

"Saary bondhu, can't let you in."

"Aarder nahin hai," he declared when the journalist failed to produce his identity card. Brandishing a printed invitation card to show that he was indeed an invitee, "Look here, you can't stop me," the journalist handed him the invitation card. But the soldier still didn't budge. "Where is the law?" the journalist protested.

"Here is the laa." The soldier tore the card to pieces and handed it back to the journalist.

WE HEARD ANOTHER ONE ABOUT a Punjabi soldier guarding the telephone exchange on a dimly lit Dhaka street.

"Who goes there, friend or foe?" the soldier shouted at a civilian passerby.

"Sir, it's me. I am a *foor* Bengali," came back a voice from the dark.

The soldier shot the passerby, thinking he must be from the Mukti Bahini.

"Who goes there? Friend or foe?" he asked the next one.

"It's me, sir, I am a Bihari," the smart Bengali answered.

The soldier let him go.

"Who goes there?" He asked a third passerby.

"It's me, sir, I am a *fonzabi*."

The soldier took one hard look at him, then shot himself. "If he is a Punjabi, then who am I?"

The jokes reflected the hopeless mission the soldiers were assigned by their leadership, how a professional army had been reduced to a hated occupying force in an unfamiliar land and was now locked in a battle they were doomed to lose.

IT WOULD BE DIFFICULT FOR anyone who did not know Siddique Sahib and Baji to appreciate how well they looked after the two sons of their late friend, Hayat Ashraf. Before they had shifted to Karachi some years earlier, they were already our favourite relatives in East Pakistan. Mother was especially fond of Baji, who was our most effective weapon whenever we needed our father's consent for a picnic or to go to a movie. The way Baji and Siddique Sahib reminisced about our family was extremely gratifying for both of us. They would talk to us about the wonderful time they had with us in that country and always had good things to say about our parents. Five times a day, Siddique Sahib would remember our family in his prayers. Even though it was a temporary arrangement for us until our British visas arrived, we could not have wished for a better home in Karachi. We had found a perfect surrogate family.

Our hosts had three children: Nizam (8), Moin (6), and Roshan (12). Nizam and Moin quickly adopted us as their gurus and accepted our authority over their lives. Being a girl, Roshan remained shy and somewhat aloof. For nearly a year and a half, we ruled over the lives of our newfound disciples like Kung Fu masters, commanding more authority over them than their own parents. Baji was smart enough to know what was best for her children, having seen the benefits of strict discipline at our home back in Thakurgaon. Given Siddique Sahib's lax attitude towards discipline, she was happy to see the boys had some fear and respect for their elders and at the same time had someone to look up to. Our students soon learned to compete fiercely between themselves to defend their gurus' honour. Nizam was Shahid's protégé while I was Moin's lord and master. Their loyalty at the age of six and eight was unquestionable. In return they enjoyed frequent outings and permission to play cricket matches in the lanes where we lived or in the barren, dusty park nearby. Unfairly aided by two grown-ups, the young boys' team was soon doing well, and they grew in confidence. The boys finished their homework on time and their grades improved.

Outside our new home, the situation remained precarious as the country lurched toward an inevitable war. Within a few months of Shahid's arrival in Karachi, in December 1971 war broke out with India. Except for a few bombing raids at the port oil facility, our lives in Karachi were not directly affected, since the thrust of the war was a thousand miles away in the eastern theatre. There the Mukti Bahini, aided by the Indian army, was fighting for the liberation of Bangladesh.

The onset of full-scale war brought back the fears of a major catastrophe for the remaining Urdu-speaking community in East Pakistan. I thanked God that Shahid was now safe with me, but we all remained concerned about relatives still left behind.

Karachi received a few sorties of Indian air force bombings targeted at oil storage tanks by the port and at the airbase. A few misdirected bombs fell on residential and industrial areas without causing any extensive damage. We had to huddle under stairs on two or three occasions when we heard the air-raid sirens. To the surprise of many Pakistanis, the Indian jets were almost freely flying over Pakistani airspace, challenged only by the anti-aircraft guns below. The much talked about Pakistani air force remained pretty much grounded after the first few days of the war. The Indian surface-to-air missiles (SAMs) had practically decimated the firepower of the Pakistan jets. The F-104s, so successful in the 1965 war against India, and the new Mirages were no match for the Indian Mig-29s. A few days into the war, the inevitable happened.

"Have you heard the news?" Aftabuddin, my friend from university, asked on the phone early in the morning.

"What news?" I replied, sensing from his voice that it was not good.

"Bloody Niazi has surrendered." He was hardly able to contain his anger.

Only the previous week General Niazi (commander of the Pakistani forces in East Pakistan) was quoted in the press boasting that Dhaka would fall only over his dead body. Aftabuddin's brother-in-law, a senior civil servant, had recently been transferred to Dhaka. His wife and children in Karachi feared for his life.

Although the end of the war was predictable, the reaction of the Pakistanis' was not. The news of defeat in East Pakistan was greeted with shock and disbelief in Karachi. It only served to confirm how little the people in Pakistan understood what had been happening in East Pakistan. The heavily censored press had managed to keep the public in the dark. People were angry at the surrender and humiliation of 65,000 or so Pakistani troops who had been taken prisoner by India and at the politicians who had thrust an impossible war on them. The image of the Pakistani army, which had already been tarnished in the international press due to the large-scale atrocities they allegedly committed, fell to an all-time low within Pakistan. When they saw the picture of General Niazi signing the surrender document in front of the world press, the final insult had been delivered. The humiliated president, General Yahya, stepped down, ceding power to the runner-up in the 1970 elections, Z. A. Bhutto.

1971 – PAKISTANI FORCES IN EAST PAKISTAN SURRENDER TO THE LIBERATING INDIAN ARMY.

My first thought after hearing about the breakup of Pakistan was for the two child soldiers I had met in July on my way back from Dinajpur. It would be a miracle if they were still alive. If they were not killed in the war, they would surely have been lynched by the Mukti Bahini when their checkpoint was overrun. After seeing the pictures of the public execution of collaborators or *razakaars*, as they were called by the Mukti Bahini, appearing in papers around the world, I shuddered to think what might have happened. Their lives were of no value to anyone anymore.

For my Urdu speaking cadet college alumni now in Karachi and many others whose families had suffered atrocities in East Pakistan, it was painful to see that a large number of West Pakistanis, who had no family ties with the eastern province, appeared happy at what they considered to be a "good riddance" or the shedding of an economic burden on Pakistan. Many commentators and pundits on television talk shows accepted that what happened was inevitable. Those whose lives had been destroyed would never understand why, if it was inevitable, it had to be paid with their blood. They were deeply hurt by the absence of any remorse in Pakistan for the loss of hundreds of thousands of lives. It puzzled them to no end as to why the public at large did not demand a serious investigation after such a catastrophe.

One afternoon a couple of months after the war, I was waiting at the university bus stop to return home. Suddenly, I caught a glimpse of Qamar, my classmate from East Pakistan, in the window seat of a passing university "point bus." In an instant I found myself running behind the bus shouting, "Qamar, Qamar!" at the top of my voice. Just as I was about to give up, the bus slowed down, thanks to the traffic in front of it. My screams finally drew the attention of Qamar, who turned around and saw me running. He jostled his way out of the overloaded bus, nearly falling on the roadside as he jumped out.

"I've been looking for you all over ever since *we* arrived in Karachi!" Qamar's excitement could not be contained. He began to hug and kiss me, totally unconcerned about the onlookers. I had heard about the large-scale killings in Shantahar but could not miss hearing the word "we" from him.

"Who else in your family is here?" I inquired.

Qamar knew what I actually meant: "Who else in the family is *alive*?"

He took me straight to Nazimabad, where his family was staying in a small apartment. Neither of us could wait to hear each other's tale of survival and all that had happened to our respective families.

In East Pakistan, Qamar's family lived in Shantahar, where nearly 10,000 Urdu-speaking people worked and lived in a railway colony next to what was a major railway junction. Like Thakurgaon, Shantahar was among the worst hit. His family was amongst the lucky few, losing only two members. His elder brother was abducted while returning home from work; his body was never found. His father, a railway engineer, was stabbed to death in front of the entire family when he refused to be taken away. Qamar himself was miraculously saved by one of his teachers, who intervened when Qamar was being dragged away to be killed by the same people who had killed his father. Qamar's mother and sisters fell on top of him and begged the attackers to kill everyone rather than just take Qamar away. A local schoolteacher, who knew Qamar's family well, was a volunteer conducting the house-to-house search of the Biharis. He had a change of heart, somehow he managed to persuade the attackers to leave them alone at least for that day.

That night the teacher arranged for the family to flee the town and took them to his village near Noagaon close to the border. The same teacher helped them again when the army arrived, so they could make their way to Dhaka. A few weeks later the family was able to fly to Karachi.

The trauma of losing their father and eldest brother followed by nearly two months spent in hiding had deeply affected the family. Qamar's mother had lost her mental balance from which she never fully recovered. She used to wait all day on her prayer mat for her son to return from university. From the moment he returned home, her eyes would follow him everywhere until he went to bed. This pitiful creature was permanently perched on the prayer mat; her ordeal only ended with her death a few years later.

From Qamar we also learned that our other school friend from Shantahar, Arshad Jamal, and two of his siblings had survived the massacre, but he had lost his parents and his sister. We had no way of knowing if he was still alive after the war.

Gradually, Qamar and I found out from our contacts about some of our Bengali friends too. We learned some had been killed in the reprisals by the Urdu-speaking people or during the army action by the Pakistani soldiers.

Among them was Momin, one year our junior in cadet college, a sweet, good-looking boy who was full of life, a keen sportsman, and a valuable member of our house hockey team. Also killed was my roommate Munnaf, an unusually quiet and mild-mannered boy who wouldn't hurt a fly. At the height of the military action, the Pakistani army had arrested these young men, wrongly believing them to be members of the Mukti Bahini.

Such was the irony of the time that the killers went scot-free, and the blood of the innocents on both sides was spilled freely. The senseless killings of people like Momin and Munnaf shattered the moral high ground that some in the army (people like Capt. Cheema) wanted to take by punishing only those who had killed their Pakistani colleagues or committed atrocities against the Urdu-speaking civilians before their arrival. It was known to all residents belonging to every side in East Pakistan during the months leading up to the war that all those involved in the killing of innocent Biharis had fled when the army arrived in their towns. By then the murderers were operating either from the remote countryside or from across the border. Unfortunately, the target of the backlash were the innocent Bengalis who had not fled since they had done nothing wrong.

Yusuf, my ex-roommate from the university hostel, still had not heard anything from his folks in East Pakistan, which was gradually turning him into a nervous wreck. By joining a student movement that was demanding repatriation of stranded Biharis from Bangladesh, he found an escape and a purpose. The movement was gaining strength as Bhutto kept delaying a decision on the matter. First it was lack of finances, then opposition from nationalist groups in Sindh. The odds against repatriation increased with a newly enacted political move with regard to the imposition of the Sindhi language in the province. Language riots broke out in Sindh cities like Karachi and Hyderabad, providing the political excuse Bhutto was looking for. Eventually, Bhutto relented, and a few thousand Biharis were repatriated to Pakistan.

The Bihari repatriation movement started by the students continued to draw impetus from the thousands belonging to divided families and from those feeling the moral repugnance against abandoning the very people who gave their lives for Pakistan. Yusuf pulled me into the movement, making me participate in their processions and sit-ins. Then I missed one demonstration where things got a little rough. Yusuf escaped with some bruises, but the leader of the movement, Laeeq Azam, was arrested and beaten up by the police.

"Aray baap re! Sala Harami hit me." That's how Yusuf described how it happened, to the amusement of his friends. The stick-wielding police hit him on his back and then tried to grab him as he fled, tearing his sleeves off his shirt.

"Why do you want to be a politician?" we asked. But we all knew the state of his mind after months of no news from his family in East Pakistan. "The next time it could be worse," we warned.

The repatriation movement that Yusuf had become an integral part of continued to gain strength. A few months later, Yusuf was detained and beaten by the police. I only met him once more after that encounter. Yusuf left for Bangladesh to search for his family; no one ever heard from him again.

A few months after the Pakistani army's humiliating defeat in East Pakistan, President Bhutto signed a peace agreement with India that led to the repatriation of Pakistani POWs from Indian jails. It also opened the door for a limited repatriation of stranded Pakistani civilians from Bangladesh. Those who could prove their family links in Pakistan were permitted to return. Pakistan's interest in repatriation of the remaining Urdu-speaking people began to fizzle out by late 1972, ostensibly due to budget constraints and waning public interest. Out of a total of 250,000 or so who wanted to return to Pakistan, around 80,000 were reportedly repatriated. The numbers are quoted differently by different sources, demonstrating the lack of a serious effort to establish facts.

As soon as Hashmat settled down with his job in the UK, he began to approach various colleges for our admission. It wasn't until we applied for our passports that we realized how difficult that was going to be. Meeting the requirements without birth certificates and a schooling history in West Pakistan was nearly impossible.

My hopes rose when I heard one of my classmates from an influential family brag about someone from the passport office delivering his family passports to their residence after renewal. He was fully aware of the difficulties we were facing, but he never offered to help. This was an important lesson for Shahid and me, one that brought home a realization that seeking favours only made one weak and deterred him from fighting his own battles.

After months of running around, we finally came across a travel agent who agreed to help if we were prepared to spend some money. Shahid left for the UK in September 1972, but I had to wait until November because my admission papers arrived late.

I was trying to get some sleep because I had to get up early to go to the airport. In my dream I heard the voice of my Uncle Ahmed Karim from Dhaka. That was followed by the familiar voices of my cousins and my aunt. The voices got louder, jolting me awake as I struggled to open my eyes, somewhat confused that I was in Dhaka. The voices were still there, clearly audible, right outside my door. My watch said 3:00 a.m., and I was fully awake, sitting up in bed. By the time I realized it was not a dream, the doorbell rang. I knew the voices coming from outside the gate too well and rushed toward the door but turned back to knock at Siddique Saheb's door to inform him first.

Two taxi loads of guests that Siddique Sahib's family had not planned for: my uncle, aunt, their three sons, one daughter, and five grandchildren. We hadn't heard from them in ten months since the war ended. It was wonderful to see them alive, but they all looked like they had just been freed from a concentration camp: weak, pale and thin. Cousin Zia had to help his father climb the two steps to the living room. We hugged each other and made space for everyone to sit in the small living room.

It was not the time for them to start talking about their ordeal, but I had very little time. So, I tried to rush them, asking questions and interrupting their replies.

"Where is Shahid?" my aunt asked as soon as she noticed that he hadn't joined us.

I told her that Shahid had already left for the UK but how lucky I was to have met her that morning. A few hours later it would not have been possible because I too was leaving. She began to sob, then asked me to sit next to her once she composed herself. Her joy of meeting the *nishani* of her beloved brother must have lightened the burden of her long, arduous journey, even though it was so short lived.

While Baji prepared tea for everyone, cousins Zia and Zafar summarized the story of their survival and their incredible near misses after the fall of Dhaka. The Mukti Bahini raided their house repeatedly on one pretext or another. Terrified, they decided to sell their jewelry to buy their freedom. They crossed the border to India and headed for Nepal. The journey took over two weeks on foot, by train, and by bus. At the Pakistan embassy in Katmandu, Zia, who worked for a Pakistani bank, got assistance from his employer in proving their family's links with Pakistan. After weeks of painful waiting, down to their last penny, they were issued special permits and allowed to fly to Pakistan via Bangkok.

Uncle Ahmad Karim sat in the corner supported by his granddaughter. He looked particularly pale and exhausted by the long trip. He showed me a lump that had developed around his vocal cords, which had been bothering him lately. A chain smoker of the Bengali *bidi* for years, he was diagnosed with terminal cancer soon after I left for the UK. A great believer in God's infinite mercy, he passed away peacefully in his sleep after a relatively short illness, content that his family was safe in Pakistan, which was all he had asked God for.

Siddique Sahib, Baji, and the kids came to see me off at the airport. Saying goodbye to them, I suddenly remembered my mother, Hamid, and Munni, who had come to Dhaka with my father to say goodbye to me less than two years earlier. Mother's eyes were transfixed on me, treasuring every moment that we spent together, not knowing when she would see me again. Hamid and Munni, too young to realize we wouldn't be able to see each other for some time, were quietly playful but uneasy about saying goodbye. Then I remembered how Iqbal had hugged me while saying goodbye a week later at the Dhaka airport, almost embarrassing me in front of my friends.

Until a few hours earlier, I had forgotten all about the past in my excitement about going to London. But a strange empty feeling gripped me as I left Baji, Siddique Sahib, and the kids behind. They had become so used to us in such a short time that I felt it was unfair, especially for the boys at their tender age. I was somewhat worried about Baji coping with the three children, who had been stirred into a life of outdoor living by their two elder keepers in transit through their lives. Happy that I was going to join my brothers in London, Baji had no right to stop me, and she didn't want to. But for her children's sake, she must have wished that Shahid or I had stayed a little longer in Karachi.

"Allah kay havalay," ("In God's care") Siddique Sahib said, as always, but this time with a long sigh. Having taken care of his friend's sons at their greatest hour of need, he prayed for Allah to look after us in a faraway land.

"I will write to you and send you lots of photos," I promised the boys as we reached the departure gate. I knew I would never be able to repay the family for what they had done for Shahid and me.

THIRD MIGRATION

These Strangers, in a foreign world,
Protection asked of me—
Befriend them, lest Yourself in Heaven
Be found a Refugee—
—Emily Dickinson

November 1972. It felt like I had stepped into a giant freezer as a gust of cold air hit my face. Barely a few steps out of terminal three, I saw my breath blowing out in the cold air. The frigid November evening in London was my first taste of really cold weather. Despite being wrapped in heavy winter clothes, my legs shook inside my trousers, and I struggled to pull my suitcase with one hand, holding my handbag with the other.

Since Hashmat was working 200 miles away in Sunderland, he had asked his friend, Saeed, to receive me at the airport. The PIA flight from Karachi arrived almost six hours late, and Saeed had given up and left for home. I couldn't afford a hotel and didn't know anyone in London, so I waved for a cab to take me to Saeed's house. With only a few pounds in my pocket, I watched nervously as the meter turned at the speed of a cash till. My eyes remained glued on that meter until I arrived at #7 Woodside Close, Wembley. By then the total bill had exceeded the amount in my pocket. My gracious host came to the rescue by insisting on paying my taxi fare.

The next morning Saeed drove me to Kings Cross, where I boarded a train for Sunderland. Shahid and Hashmat received me at the station. It was a relief to see that the change of scenery had already had a positive effect on Shahid, who had started going to a local college and was even playing football in that football-crazy town. But Hashmat's sadness had not left him.

He had become a very private person, devoting most of his time after work to reading medical books and preparing for his FRCS exams. He had made no effort to make new friends. Whenever he found Shahid and I having a laugh about anything, he looked resentful. We wanted to forget the past, but he was not prepared to bury his grief yet.

The cold, windy town of Sunderland where Hashmat worked appeared as economically depressed as parts of Pakistan. Most of the houses in that region had no central heating. At 1 Hadley Road, where we lived, a coal heater adorned the living room downstairs. Twice a day we had to fetch coal from the backyard to feed the messy fireplace. Once inside the house, we would huddle by the fireplace, where we spent most of our waking hours. To supplement the heat generated by the coal fire, we would often bring the electric heater from the bedroom. At night we would carry it back upstairs. Poor insulation in those old houses meant the heat was lost as soon as the heater was switched off or the coal fire was put out, which forced me to wear thermal undergarments most of the time.

Each day on our way back from the college, we would stop at the hospital cafeteria for supper, mingle with the doctors and nurses, and read the papers. The menu varied little from one day to the next. Roast beef, pork chops, steak-and-kidney pie, shepherd's pie, and fish and chips. The bland English food was hard to swallow, and we had to find an alternative. That's when Shahid discovered a cheap Chinese takeaway not too far from the hospital.

"Whatever you sell us, it must be pork free," Shahid took pains to explain to the Chinese owner, who understood very little English. "No pork, please, understand?"

"Yah! No pok, Yah! Yah! Hokay," the owner acknowledged.

Satisfied that the man had understood his request, Shahid became a regular client. It didn't take us long to suspect that the Chinese man hadn't understood Shahid after all. We had been eating a lot of what we wanted to avoid, little red pieces of meat in the rice and the telltale smell of lard in everything fried. That forced us to start cooking for ourselves. Srimi, the wife of a Sri Lankan doctor friend, showed us an Indian grocery shop in the nearby town of Newcastle, and we were all set.

Shahid and I reached an agreement whereby he would cook, and I would wash the dishes. I was satisfied that I had the better deal because I wouldn't have any worries until I had eaten.

We were not the only ones who opted to cook to escape the bland English cuisine. At the royal infirmary where Hashmat worked, Dr. Biswas from Calcutta was being forced to cook his own meals too. The nurses used to make fun of the curry-smelling doctor claiming that anyone could tell he had passed through the corridor long after he was gone.

"I swear I don't enjoy cooking, but I no longer trust anyone here," the doctor confided once he had become friendly with us. The cafeteria attendants at the doctors' mess had made him eat pig for months without him knowing.

Once he had found out, for a long time after that the very sight of meat made him sick. "But what do they care? Beware of those fat old ladies at the hospital cafeteria."

Eventually, we learned those poor girls did actually take care not to serve pork to the good doctor. But bacon and eggs for breakfast was something else. They had no way of knowing that even those tasty things were forbidden in Dr. Biswas's religion.

As we settled down in our new house, our visits to the doctors' mess became less frequent even though our desolate neighbourhood looked totally cut off from the rest of town after sunset. The dimly lit cemetery with large trees behind our house and the empty streets combined to create a scene from a Dracula movie. The cold nights meant the already sparse population would stay indoors after sunset, and very little traffic was seen on the streets. The cemetery's perimeter was separated from our row of houses by a mesh fence that ran behind our backyards. Some of the tombstones were close enough for me to read the names and the year of death from my bedroom, making it difficult for me to sleep even after the curtains were drawn. It felt as if I was back in the early 1960s before the arrival of electricity in Thakurgaon. My nightmares of Kali maa with her garland of human heads around her neck and her long bloodstained tongue hanging from her grotesque face came back to haunt me.

Besides the food and the weather, we had one more difficulty: the local dialect. After spending years in English medium schools, the last thing we had expected to face in England was a language problem. But Sunderland was a new frontier. The local dialect, called "Joddy," apparently because that's how they pronounced the name "George," was anything but English. Joddy was not easily comprehended even by people from the south of England. But as soon as we made some headway on the language front, we were completely taken in by the simplicity and friendliness of the people of Sunderland.

A keen footballer himself, Shahid became an ardent supporter of the local football team, which was on a winning spree that season. Sunderland won the FA cup the year we arrived, beating the favourite, Arsenal. Watching the victory procession of our new heroes riding a double-decker bus curiously provided us a sense of belonging. The most unpredictable football team, Sunderland, in some ways resembled the mercurial Pakistani cricket team, which we also supported.

With a home team and the language barrier broken, the only challenge that remained was the weather. Rainy, windy, and bitterly cold, Sunderland hardly seemed like a place that I would ever get used to. My mother used to cover me from head to toe whenever the mercury dropped below 12 degrees Celsius. What would she have done to protect her weakest offspring in sub-zero temperatures?

A semblance of family life came in the way of our first local friends, Dr. David Graham and his lively and talkative American wife, Elaine. Their newborn baby, Amanda (who we called Mandy), became our immediate attraction. Aware of our recent tragedies, David and Elaine were extra friendly. David was preparing for his American board exam and Hashmat for his primary FRCS. Impressed with Hashmat's academic knowledge, David spent time revising various chapters with Hashmat, quizzing and testing each other's knowledge of the basics of physiology and medicine. Elaine and Shahid would help out by cooking for them. In the process, Elaine soon learned to cook Pakistani dishes like korma, tikka, and curry. It began to feel as if we had known the Grahams for years. Our ethnic differences aroused curiosity about each other's culture, religion, and most importantly, food. This was our first close contact with a white family, the first of many such bridges we would cross in our new home.

Our family continued growing in Sunderland. Dr. Enam, Hashmat's Bihari friend from Dhaka, arrived in March 1973 to work at the nearby Ryehope Hospital. It was great to have someone in Sunderland that we knew from before. Dr. Enam liked everything about Sunderland except the incomprehensible dialect. Few in the hospital understood him. Frustrated, he would swear in Urdu, to the embarrassment of his colleagues from the subcontinent.

"Hadley Road," he told the driver of the bus as he handed him the coins.

"You wha me laad?" the driver asked.

"Hadley Road," Enam repeated.

"Sorry laad, say that again."

"When will you motherfuckers learn to speak English?" Enam murmured in Urdu with a straight face. Passengers behind him waited, and I looked for a place to hide my face.

"Oh, you mean Haadli Road," the driver finally understood, saving us further embarrassment.

A month after Dr. Enam arrived, Hashmat informed us that his Bengali girlfriend from Dhaka was coming to Sunderland too. It came as a huge surprise that Hashmat had stayed in touch with Dr. Nahar and had pulled every string to find her a job at a nearby hospital. We had nothing against Dr. Nahar, but we were not so keen to see her come back into Hashmat's life.

As things turned out, within days of her arrival, Dr. Nahar endeared me and Shahid to her. She was careful not to speak Bengali and made every effort to speak Urdu, which quickly improved with practice. If we laughed at her broken Urdu, she wouldn't get upset. Our apprehensions were soon forgotten, and we began to look forward to her visits on the weekends. They became more and more frequent, and Dr. Nahar started to spend much more time at our house studying with Hashmat as she prepared for some diploma, giving her the perfect excuse. She only went to her apartment at the hospital to sleep at night. Like an elder sister, she would often cook for us and show concern for our education, making us all feel that she was an integral part of the family. Dr. Enam, who had also known Dr. Nahar from Dhaka, became a frequent visitor too. We enjoyed their company as normalcy descended upon our lives.

By April, winter had departed, and we were suddenly greeted with an onslaught of colour and beauty. A riot of wildflowers sprouted around us, covering the entire landscape like we had never imagined before. We would often go for long drives and picnics down south to the Yorkshire dales and west to the Lake District. During the drives Dr. Nahar would sing old sentimental

Hindi songs, which brought back memories of the movies we had seen and of our beautiful carefree lives only a few years earlier. Her repertoire of classical love songs and duets from the hit Indian movies of the 1960s included those sung by Lata, Rafi, Mukesh, and Hemant Kumar. She generously obliged our request to sing a particular song that we liked in her gifted voice. These wonderfully innocent and romantic songs were typically tragic or melodramatic, given the Indian obsession with fate and futility of existence.

She would sing "Do Hanson Ka Jora," "Yeh Raat, Yeh Chandni Phir Kahan," and " Mere Mehboob Tujhey Meri Mohabbat Ki Qasam." Often we would join in and hum along with her. Shahid sang his favourite, "Abhi Tum Ko Meri Zaroorat Nahi," or I would sing my own favourite, "Chandi Ki Diwaar Na Tooti Payar Bhara Dil Toot Gaya."

Of all the songs, one that Dr. Nahar sang particularly well was: "Lag Ja gale Ke Phir Yeh Haseen Raat Ho Na Ho, Shayed Phir Is Janam Mey Mulaqaat Ho Na Ho; Ham Ko Mili Hai Aaj Yeh Khushiyan Naseeb Say, Jee Bhar Ke Dekh Lain Hum Ko Qareeb Sey . . ." It meant something like "Embrace me now, this night may never come again, this happiness is but a stroke of luck, take a close look at me, do not squander away these moments, lest they never come again."

Close enough yet so far, neither Dr. Nahar nor Hashmat were under any illusion that they could undo history. They appeared to accept that destiny intended their love to remain unfulfilled. Shahid and I liked and respected Dr. Nahar and wished her well in life, but we could not imagine her as part of our family. Our wounds were too fresh to consider a Bengali sister-in-law or Bengali children in our home.

One evening we had gone with her to the movies in the nearby town of Newcastle and somehow got separated coming out of the theatre. Dr. Nahar remained visibly anxious until we met up again. Noticing her affection toward us, Dr. Enam made a direct suggestion.

"She would be a good bhabi (sister-in-law) for you two."

"But how can that happen?" I replied sharply without thinking.

"Shhhh . . ." Shahid gestured that she and Hashmat were only a few steps behind us.

When our eyes met, I knew instantly that they had overheard us; it was written all over their faces. Both appeared deeply hurt, perhaps even insulted by our indiscretion. No one spoke much on our drive back to Sunderland,

It's hard to describe the helpless love of these two young souls who had fallen victim to a cruel fate. Even before that evening, it was gradually becoming apparent to Shahid and I that both of them were reconciled to their fate. All they wanted was to help each other get through those difficult times and perhaps steal a few moments of happiness and joy for themselves in the process.

One evening when they were studying together by the fireplace, Hashmat appeared frustrated that Dr. Nahar had forgotten what she had covered with him the previous week. "Seriously, how can I help you if you take things so easy?" Hashmat fumed. "You will never pass if you don't concentrate. Now listen to me one more time." He proceeded to explain again. For a second he sounded just like my father, that unmistakable voice of authority. And like my mother, Dr. Nahar listened sheepishly.

For hours that night I lay in bed thinking that we were all doing a great injustice to Dr. Nahar. Perhaps we should leave her alone and let her go her own way while she was still young and eligible. With Hashmat, she would get nothing but a lifetime of waiting. That was cruelty and was unfair to them both. So, Shahid and I decided to talk to Dr. Enam the next day.

"Do we not have to stop her for her own good?" we asked.

"Never underestimate the determination of this little woman," Dr. Enam said. "You have no idea of the sacrifice she has already made for your brother. Do you know that she ran away from her home on her wedding night last year?" His revelation stunned us both.

After the massacre of Biharis in East Pakistan, Dr. Nahar's family naturally assumed there was no hope of her marrying Hashmat, especially after Hashmat had left Dhaka for good. So, her parents arranged for her to marry a Bengali doctor in their hometown of Bogra. On the night of the wedding, when she was dressed up as the bride, she decided to run away. With the country in the midst of a civil war, the young bride risked her life travelling to Dhaka on her own. How she managed to cross numerous military checkpoints and how she reached Dhaka on her own, we never knew. Once she arrived in Dhaka, she was able to track down Hashmat in the UK, and there she was a year later. Her family would never forgive her for the anguish she had caused them.

We were awestruck by the iron will of this petite five-feet-two-inch lady. Inside she must have known she may never get married to Hashmat. Yet she preferred to sacrifice her life for her first love, to live with her memories if that was all she was going to get in the bargain.

Thirteen years later when I visited her in UK in 1986, Hashmat's old photo still adorned her dressing table. Hashmat had finally been persuaded to get married in 1984. But Dr. Nahar's love was total, and her sacrifices honoured her love until the end.

My admission papers from University College London arrived in August 1973. Soon after that came the confirmation of Shahid's acceptance from the Bolton Institute of Technology near Manchester. I was going to study economics, and Shahid was to study civil engineering. Thinking about the three of us separating again made us sad, particularly for leaving behind Hashmat, who had just started to normalize having spent a year together. He had gradually regained much of the weight he had lost earlier and was beginning to look a bit like his former self, or like Omar Sharif, as his colleagues would have him believe. Thus we tried to make the best of our remaining weeks together. Dr. Enam, Hashmat, and Dr. Nahar took time off from their work, and we went on a tour of the Lake District, Blackpool, and Scotland. The departing summer that year was generously long and warm, giving us days of sunshine on both ends.

To compensate for my imminent loneliness in London, providence had made some arrangements. One afternoon we were waiting for Hashmat to come home early because we had planned to go out together. The doorbell rang, and it kept ringing impatiently. I knew it could not be Hashmat. When I opened the door, I could hardly believe my eyes. Saif was standing outside in a three-piece suit, looking totally unlike his former self.

"Shala Bihari." That's the way he greeted me whenever he was excited. I didn't have to pinch myself after that; it had to be him.

Still dumbfounded, I didn't know how to react, so I pulled him inside. "Look who's here!" I screamed as Shahid came running downstairs.

"How did you get here?" I asked. "Who gave you our address?"

"I knew you were here; that's how I came here, you idiot. I wrote you so many letters. Why didn't you respond?"

"Bullshit! What letters? I thought you were dead until Hamid informed me that you were in Dhaka, but even he had not met you."

In his letter Hamid had informed me that Saif was injured in the war and had been awarded some medals for valor by the Bangladeshi government. People like him were known as Mukti Jodha (freedom fighters) in Bangladesh.

I was impatient to know more, and we hadn't even asked him to sit down. "No, I never received your letters. Did you put stamps on them?" Having missed the opportunity for so long, I couldn't stop pulling his leg.

There was so much to catch up on, that we literally spent the next couple of days talking non-stop. We hardly went out. Which of our class fellows were alive after the war? What were they doing? When Shahid was not around, Saif quietly informed me that he had verified with the few Bihari survivors that were left in Thakurgaon that nobody else in my family was alive. He had one eyewitness account and had spoken to a few who knew our family. All of them confirmed that no one was seen or heard from after those fateful days.

During the war of liberation, Saif commanded a small group of freedom fighters that had crossed over from the Hili border to liberate the Dinajpur district. One of the men under his command was a former EPR soldier who had rebelled against the Pakistani army and fled across the border to join the war for liberation. He used to brag about killing many Bihari civilians in Thakurgaon, never showing the slightest remorse. Saif couldn't tell whether that man was responsible for killing any of my family members but had decided to "dispose of him" toward the end of the war when he was of no use to him. On the day of the final assault on the border town of Hili, Saif's troops came under heavy fire. Saif was hit by a bullet that went through his left arm, but that ex-EPR soldier was hit in the head. A single bullet pierced his helmet, crushed his skull, and killed him instantly. Bleeding heavily from his wound, Saif made it back to the camp and survived.

After Bangladesh won its independence, Saif, like many of his compatriots moved to Dhaka, only to find a setup he thought he had fought to replace in another garb. Soon he began to despair of the political jockeying and the intrigues in Dhaka. An idealist and a proud Bengali, he was disappointed at the way Bangladesh was being governed by the sons of Shaikh Mujib and the band of sycophants surrounding them. Bewildered by the corruption, nepotism, and favouritism in his new country, he had no wish to be associated with any of that. He could not understand the point of so much sacrifice if the poor Bengalis still couldn't have true freedom. The elitist culture of the Pakistan days had resurfaced with a vengeance in newborn Bangladesh. Only the faces at the top had changed. Socialist at heart, Saif's disappointment ran deep.

"I have had enough of the army. I want to go back to my studies now. Tell me how I can get into a university here."

The next morning Saif and I left for London. We went to several colleges and polytechnics, one after another, for two days. Everywhere the requirement was the same: they wanted to see his academic records.

"You see, our country has been nearly destroyed by war. My school records are good, but I can't produce them right now. They were lost during the war. So, I really need your help," he took care to add after creating some sympathy.

Finally, he got lucky at the City Polytechnic. He impressed a kind soul in the admissions office enough who was willing to give him a chance. The admissions officer offered to help if the education counselor at the Bangladesh embassy issued a certificate in lieu of Saif's education record. The polytechnic was willing to grant a provisional admission to the BSc program in economics, which would be confirmed after the admission fee was paid and Saif's school records were submitted before the start of the term. Saif pulled all the strings and got his consulate to cooperate, and within the week his admission was confirmed.

Having accomplished this seemingly impossible mission, we returned victorious to Sunderland. There remained just one small problem: the tuition fee of 250 pounds, a significant amount in those days. Saif had a total of fifty to sixty pounds on him. Back in Sunderland, we decided to approach Dr. Nahar and Dr. Enam. After some convincing, each lent him one hundred pounds. Saif got his visitor's visa converted into a student visa once the admission papers were issued.

We both arrived back in London to start our studies at our respective colleges that September, me at University College London and Saif at City Polytechnic. Our first few months in London was a time of discovery and great fun for us. Saif took a tiny room, sharing a basement apartment with a Scottish boy and his girlfriend in Brick Lane, probably the most depressed part of East London. To his delight, his roommates turned out to be committed socialists like him. His room in the basement, without central heating, was quite a contrast to mine on Tavistock Square in a proper student hostel.

Initially, Saif visited me regularly. Sometimes we studied together; other times we would just go out for long walks on Tottenham Court Road through Soho, Leicester Square, and Piccadilly Circus, then on to the south bank and trek back. Freed at last from all our recent troubles, we roamed London's streets, making our own discoveries in the city we grew so fond of so quickly. With no money to support him, Saif was forced to do odd jobs and would disappear for days, not even bothering to call.

The only Bengali student in my class at UCL was Nisar Ahmed from Dhaka. From the moment he set eyes on me, he suspected that I spoke Bengali. But after several attempts he gave up when I failed to reciprocate in Bengali. One day when Saif was visiting, he said something to me in Bengali, to which I responded, immediately catching Ahmed's attention. Thinking about it that evening in bed, I could not contain my amusement at the irony that less than three years earlier my family and I had tried hard to hide our Bihari identity just to survive. And here I was trying to hide even knowing the Bengali language, as if I had arrived in a parallel world.

After spending two years mostly away from each other, Shahid and I decided to spend the summer of 1975 with Hashmat, who by then had moved to a small town called Dewsbury, near Leeds, as a registrar in general surgery. Like most foreign-educated doctors, the tradeoff between promotion and location was simple. To work in surgery, Hashmat had moved to an economically depressed small town in Yorkshire. But his main reason for going there was the newly introduced overtime for doctors in the NHS, which was available at that hospital, and Hashmat needed the extra income to support his two brothers in university. For us that place had another special attraction. Unlike most other hospitals where Hashmat had worked before, it had a grand separate residence for the doctors, aptly called the "mansion." It was large six-bedroom house with a huge lawn at the back, and it was inhabited by only Hashmat and two other doctors, including Hashmat's new friend, Dr. Gazdar, a jovial person who loved to talk on any subject and a good companion for Hashmat, who by then had nearly regained much of his previous self. Shahid and I shared the spare bedroom; the large TV lounge on the ground floor was used mostly by the two of us. Each evening we would cook, chat, and watch TV with Dr. Gazdar and Hashmat.

Looking for a summer job in that little town was going to be a challenge, but luck was with us. One small factory making industrial weighing machines, a remnant of England's industrial past, was hiring. The factory was under threat from competition from less-expensive Eastern Europe. For survival they preferred part-timers whenever the order book allowed. Both Shahid and I were more than willing to provide the cheap labour. The working hours were 8:00 a.m. to 4:30 p.m. with a one-hour break for lunch and two fifteen-minute tea breaks, the first at 10:30 and the second at 3:00. We turned up for work five days a week to earn a well-deserved weekend.

With so many breaks and so much time to spend, we were able to make some friends among our co-workers in the factory. The crane operator, Bill, was especially friendly and kind to us and spent his breaks happily reminiscing about his glory years with the factory. Reemployed at a meagre salary after retirement, around age seventy, he still seemed to enjoy his work more than most.

"Why does 4:30 p.m. come so late here?" I asked him one day.

"Son, when you're my age, you'll know how fast the clock turns. Then you'll wish 4:30 didn't come so soon," he said in his typical endearing Yorkshire accent.

Each evening when we got home, four hours of sunlight still awaited us, giving us time for our own cricket match. We would empty the driveway, which served as the bowling pitch while the large lawn next to it was enough for placing up to four fielders. Dr. Gazdar, Hashmat, and other doctors would happily join us whenever they could.

That season coincided with the first ever cricket world cup, which was held in England. We watched many of the matches on television. The long hours of the English summer were well suited for the newly introduced sixty-over matches. The commentary of Richie Benaud and Freddy Truman compensated for the lack of today's technology for replays, speed radar, and animations. Each weekend either Dr. Nahar or Dr. Enam would visit us from Sunderland, and we would go out for a drive, shopping, or to movies.

I hadn't seen Saif since leaving London at the beginning of that summer. Just as I thought I was missing him and his numerous girlfriends, which he had been able to cultivate on a shoestring budget, one evening he phoned to say he was not well. Some stomach pain had kept him up the night before, and it wasn't getting any better.

"Have you taken any medicine?" I asked.

"Yes, something for upset stomach."

From the way he described the pain in his lower abdomen, even without any medical background, I knew it was no ordinary stomach ache. Except for the mental episode back in cadet college, to the best of my recollection Saif had never been sick. The only thing I could suggest was for him to take the overnight coach and come straight to Dewsbury. He called again the next morning from the bus stop, and Hashmat picked him up.

At the mansion, Hashmat examined him on the couch in the TV lounge and immediately phoned the hospital. Saif's appendix had swollen and could burst, spreading poison in his blood. He needed to be operated on immediately; any delay could put his life at risk. Within hours he was operated on by Hashmat, who was the general surgeon on duty.

Saif recovered quickly with the help of good nursing care and a lot of hospital food. Thanks to Hashmat, he received the sort of special treatment reserved for private patients, something most patients on NHS did not experience. Having not eaten well for months, the hospital food was haute cuisine for him. "Bhooka Bengali" ("Hungry Bengali") we teased. Saif's close call followed by a quick recovery was a positive winding up of a very happy summer.

Decades later I still reminisce about two summers of my life, 1970 in Thakurgaon and 1975 in Dewsbury. While 1970 was a year of celebration, marking the success and achievements of various members of the Ashraf family, 1975 was a new beginning. Things had begun to look up for the three surviving sons of Hayat Ashraf. They had resumed their education and careers, made new friends, and the past was receding behind them, allowing them to start afresh. They had knit together a new family from the remnants of the one that had been lost. Hope, the bulwark of a refugee, sprang eternal. The future, with its promise of a better life, beckoned once more. While all the other intervening summers have come and gone, 1975 in Dewsbury remains vivid and alive in my memory, just like 1970 in Thakurgaon. During that summer, for the first time it felt that despite all that we had endured, there was still a future for us.

The icing on the cake that summer was the good news from Bangladesh that our cousin Firoza was alive and well with the family of my younger brother's math tutor, Sadequl. Our Hindu neighbor who saved her had handed her over to them before crossing the border permanently for India. Sadequl's family had to go to great lengths to protect her, even faking her death by creating a mock grave and falsely claiming she was buried there to keep the killers who came looking for the little girl at bay. That little girl was now sixteen. Sadequl's family had grown fond of her and decided to wed her to their only son, Sadequl. The Bengali boy turned from her protector to her husband, and they have been happily married ever since.

One of my hostel mates at the commonwealth hall where I had moved in my final year at UCL was an amiable Bangladeshi student who often reminisced about his time in Pakistan as a child. In early 1976 he had two visitors from Dhaka. One of them introduced himself as Bazlul Huda, an ex-officer in the Bangladeshi army. I remember his name because it was similar to my old classmate from cadet college. While having dinner in the cafeteria, he turned to me and said, "If it is any consolation to you, I was among the soldiers who killed Shaikh Mujib."

Stunned by that revelation, I did not know how to react. I had heard about the assassination but no longer had any interest in Bangladesh's politics. Yet, coming face to face with someone who had indirectly avenged the blood of my own family was most disconcerting. I listened silently to his description of how it all happened that fateful morning of August 1975. Long after the soldier left that evening, my shock of coming face to face with someone who had administered "divine justice" to the man whose movement less than five years earlier had torn our lives apart lingered heavily on my mind. For months after my family's murder in 1971, I spent many a desparate hour contemplating revenge against faceless, nameless perpetrators if I ever came across one. That night I had understood that nothing would bring my family back, and nothing would make their loss easier for me. The pain would remain in my heart as long as I lived. Whether that officer was bragging or he was actually part of the group that killed Mujib mattered little to me. Nearly two decades later, I learnt that the young officer was not merely bragging that night. His name popped up in the news when he was tried and sentenced to death in Bangladesh for his role in Shaikh Mujib's assassination.

My final year at university, 1976, was serious business and required me to exercise some discipline. I saw Saif less and less and Hashmat probably only once in nearly six months when he visited London to appear for his final FRCS. The Royal College of Physicians was walking distance from Russell Square, where I lived. We met that afternoon. Hashmat was in a great mood, having become a fellow at the Royal College of Surgeons. We played squash at the commonwealth hall and went out for dinner at an Indian restaurant on Tottenham Court Road to celebrate. That afternoon while taking pictures of Hashmat at the Royal College, I thought of telling him how proud Father would have been today, but I held back, thinking he must also be feeling a void in some corner of his heart.

Hashmat was soon promoted to senior registrar that brought a pay raise along with a new job in thoracic surgery at Swansea. Having never visited Wales, Shahid and I were already looking forward to the next summer. I would be graduating in a few months, and Shahid would start his apprenticeship with a construction company in Scotland as part of his sandwich course in civil engineering.

At the top of my to do-list that summer was getting a driver's license, the key to freedom and happiness for which I had spent countless hours in Hashmat's car practicing on the roads of Swansea. Too eager to pass, in haste I forgot to take off the handbrake, quickly realized and corrected, but the big mistake had been made. No longer expecting to pass, I had ceased to be nervous, which doubtless saved further mistakes. At the end of the test, I parked the car and waited for the dreaded yellow paper. The instructor glanced down at the handbrake, which was now duly pulled back as required, smiled, and handed me a white sheet of paper instead.

"Congratulations, you passed. A bit of advice, son. Only a relaxed driver is a good driver, so always take your time." He had made my day.

I had no plans to go back to UCL or LSE for a master's in economics, which would open doors toward teaching or research, neither of which I would be good at. So, I decided to apply for the MBA programs at the London Business School, UMIST, and Bradford Business School, in that order, the last one merely as an insurance policy. The cost of the MBA programs was high, and I did not want to remain a burden on Hashmat, who had already done more than any brother could ever have. Himself, living on a shoestring budget, he rarely bought new clothes, preferring to wear what Shahid or I rejected. Even squash rackets or joggers were first used by Shahid or me before he got to use them.

By the time my BSc results arrived in July, it was clear that my grades were no longer good enough qualify for any scholarship. Rejections from UMIST and LBS came by early August, sending me into panic mode. Barely two weeks before the start of the session, I received my acceptance from Bradford University, my last remaining hope. With the final paycheck from my summer job came a hefty bonus of fifty pounds and a kind letter of reference. With money in my pocket and my plan back on track, I was all set for business school.

The oil boom had arrived in Saudi Arabia by the late 1970s when Shahid and I were finishing our education in England. In contrast, the economic slowdown in the UK meant that many young graduates, especially those from Asian countries, were looking toward the Middle East, where new doors were opening for employment. While waiting to start business school toward the end of that summer, we heard that Mr. Shamim was coming from Saudi Arabia to meet us in the UK. Back in the 1960s, we recalled Father talking about his exceptional nephew, Shamim, who lived briefly with him in Jamshedpur, India. Aunt Husna, Shamim's mother, used to tell us stories of how her defiant son had run away from home and how he had finally made it in Saudi Arabia. Their separate accounts of Shamim's childhood adventures had left us with a sense of great awe and admiration for him. Since the tragedy that struck our respective families in 1971, Shamim had kept in touch with us. On one of his business trips to London, he was going to take time out to meet the three surviving sons of his favourite uncle.

Mr. Shamim arrived from London by train. Stepping out of the first-class compartment, the diminutive five-feet-five-inch man clad in a designer suit looked like a mafia don. Our first impression of this unusual person would continue to be revised as we got to know him better. Within the two days that we spent together, we discovered he was a brilliant chess player, a successful manager, and an extremely generous person. A man of boundless energy, he possessed a level of self-confidence that was inversely proportional to his size.

He was managing a fair-sized shipping business spread over three continents. With a penchant for poetry and a ready stock of verses suitable for every occasion, he was, above all, great company.

Mr. Shamim offered to share the cost of my business school, which Hashmat politely declined. Since he hadn't brought any gifts, while leaving he gave 200 pounds each to Shahid and me, almost doubling our net worth in one go. Before leaving he also planted in our minds that the future belonged to the oil-rich Middle East; a tectonic shift was in the offing. His visit changed the course of my life. Soon Saudi Arabia became my next home. I had also met the man who would gradually take the place of my late father and become my mentor and a dear friend for the next twenty-five years. The exceptionally rewarding relationship endured until the final hour of Mr. Shamim's life on October 3, 2001.

Mr. Shamim suggested that we look beyond a temporary parking spot for ourselves and seriously consider Saudi Arabia as a future home. He believed the country was keen to provide citizenship to highly educated and technically qualified people, an assumption that later proved to be incorrect. Although many of his wife's relatives were Saudi nationals, Mr. Shamim's own application for citizenship had remained in limbo for years. Only after we arrived did it became apparent to us that the Saudi government did everything possible to discourage foreigners from trying to settle there. In rare cases where citizenship was granted, it had to carry the direct recommendation of the royal court and be approved by none other than the office of the king.

By the time Shahid and I were leaving the UK, Hashmat had already obtained a British passport after his expired Pakistani passport was not renewed by the Pakistan embassy on the grounds that it was issued in East Pakistan. He had nothing to prove his ties to what remained of Pakistan. A full-fledged heart surgeon by then, Hashmat was beaten by the bureaucratic process of his own country but accepted by another with open arms.

Along with Hashmat, we had also become eligible to apply for a British passport, having spent five years there. But neither of us were comfortable with the subtle touch of racism in British society, though it was nothing that we could not tolerate, having faced far worse in life. Perhaps it was our vanity or misplaced self-confidence, ironically provided by the British education system itself that we didn't wish to join the ranks of the "wogs," a phrase commonly used to describe the brown-skinned British in those days. The British sense of superiority over their former colonial servants was understandable. Conversely for us, after living in the UK it was difficult to reconcile the image of the fictional *gora sahib* with the exemplary work ethic and punctuality that our earlier generation had us believe. British industry suffered terminally from poor work culture, and the Brits appeared just as prone to racism as the rest of the world. In the end the petrodollar won. Shahid and I decided to seek our future in the oil-rich kingdom of Saudi Arabia.

FOURTH MIGRATION

Rafiq in Saudi Arabia

We journey toward a home not of our flesh.
Its chestnut trees are not our bones.
Its rocks are not like goats in the mountain hymn.
The pebbles are not like lilies.
We journey toward a home that does not halo
Our heads with a special sun.
—Mahmood Darwaish

October 1977: It seemed like we had landed on the moon. The city of Jeddah was dug up everywhere with large gaping holes where multi-storey buildings were going up. Every direction we looked, there were trenches for the sewerage, electricity, and telephone lines. US, German, French, and Korean contractors had taken over the city. It was hard to find a single kilometre of road without a detour leading to the back alleys of old Jeddah. Once in those treacherous narrow lanes, there was no option but to follow the other cars until one came out anywhere except the place one wanted to reach. Almost every car, new or old, had scratches and dents primarily caused by impatient young drivers negotiating their way out of one traffic jam into another. The sight of badly bruised brand-new Japanese and American cars reflected the attitude of the Saudis in looking after their vehicles, which were readily disposable in that gold rush country.

Even without the detours, the traffic would have been chaotic with the way the Saudis had taken to the roads. A law unto themselves, the young men with big American cars and scant regard for safety or courtesy to other drivers made it difficult for anyone to drive. The young men wore flowing white robes and a red-and-white checkered dish dash on their heads. It was held in place by a round black rope that looked like a halo. But these were no saints; they ruled the rough streets of Jeddah as if they owned them. Insurance coverage, generally discouraged in Islam, was very uncommon in Saudi Arabia in those days. That made it more likely that each accident would lead to verbal abuse and the occasional scuffle. But the damage to the cars was inconsequential compared to the high number of human casualties, especially on the highways to Makkah and Medina.

Petrified foreigners, especially those who could not speak Arabic, stood no chance with the traffic police if the other party in an accident was Saudi. None of the police officers, called the *maroor,* spoke any language other than Arabic.

Every driver lived under the threat of blood money hanging over their heads. If the accident caused a death, the driver was sent to jail, to be released only after paying the blood money. Dozens of prisoners who could not pay the blood money would eventually be released a year or so later by royal pardon. The office of the benevolent king or other compassionate rich Saudis from time to time paid out the blood money, releasing the driver from prison. That act of compassion was sure to please their God.

The first duty of a Muslim when he arrives in Saudi Arabia is to head for the holy city of Makkah for *Umrah,* the minor pilgrimage. So, the night we arrived, donning white robes called *ahram*, Shahid and I proceeded to the holy city in Mr Shamim's car.

A few kilometres before Makkah, the police at a checkpoint were scrutinizing IDs to ensure that only Muslims entered the city. Non-Muslims are forbidden to enter Makkah, and the punishment for trespassing is death. No one knew if that punishment had been awarded to anyone in recent times, probably because no one had dared take that chance since T. E. Lawrence back in the 1920s. But I heard about one lucky person who did that recently and got away. A British engineer working in the adjacent city of Taif had landed in Makkah by mistake one night. Probably under the influence of alcohol, he missed some turns and also an inconspicuous checkpoint at one of the city's smaller entrances. As soon as he saw the large floodlights next to the great mosque Haram, he realized he had landed in the Forbidden City. Too afraid to ask anyone, he kept driving until he spotted road signs to Jeddah that led him out of the city, and he lived to tell the tale.

It was difficult not to be struck by the majesty of the Haram as we entered the holy city. The tall marble towers dazzled in the floodlights as a strange, powerful feeling overwhelmed me, something I would never forget. Once inside, circling around the black square of the *Kaaba*, my entire life began to flash by in my mind. I stopped to touch the heavy black *Kiswah* that draped the Kaaba and closed my eyes. The images of my late parents and my siblings floated before my eyes clear, more vivid than ever before. I prayed to God to grant them a place in heaven, to forgive their sins and to have mercy on them. They had suffered enough in their lives. I cried unashamedly. Then, almost as a revelation, I felt an inner peace, as if something was telling me that my prayers had been granted. No voice from anywhere, just a strange feeling of reassurance that they were safe in heaven, free from all earthly sufferings. It was the middle of Ramadan, and the Haram was packed with hundreds of thousands of worshippers, yet I was standing right next to the Kaaba comfortably holding its cover in my hands and not being swept away by the human tide. In the midst of a sea of humanity, I had the exclusive attention of my Creator, and He was listening. After that night, I visited the Haram on many occasions, both for Hajj and for Umrah. But that experience of solace and peace of mind was never repeated.

As soon as the Eid holidays were over, the serious business of looking for jobs in Jeddah began. With construction activity all around, Shahid, being a civil engineer, had no problem landing a job within the same week with an American construction company. In contrast, my MBA degree was little understood by the local companies. Some foreign companies and banks that did understand my education had no ready stock of work visas. Before long I began to feel somewhat deflated.

Mr. Shamim took time out from his extremely busy schedule and introduced me to his contacts. Into the fourth week of our search, one of his friends, Mr. Mohammed Ali, obliged by placing me in the advertising department of the *Arab News,* an English newspaper. My starting salary was lower than Shahid's, which hurt my pride and kept the pressure on me to keep looking for a better job. After a few months, I finally got lucky. A newly incorporated investment company was looking for an MBA from a western university. It was a joint venture between the First National Bank of Chicago and a well-known local group, Abdul Latif Jameel and Co. The job seemed truly cut out for me, even though it was a start-up company.

There was just one small problem: I had been living illegally in the country since my Umrah visa expired a few months earlier. Converting my Umrah visa without leaving the country was a risk I was advised not to take. Had it not been for our brave host I would have given up on the notorious lack of flexibility in Saudi Arabia's immigration system.

So, I continued my illegal stay hoping that Mr. Shamim had enough friends who could get me out of jail if I was picked up at any of the frequent street checks for residence permits, called *iqama* by the local police, known as the *shurta*.

Going to jail in Saudi Arabia was no big deal. People who had committed traffic violations, possessed expired documents, or simply not carrying their papers on their person would go to the detention centres every day. Many would come out the next day or, if they were unlucky enough to be picked up on Thursday, would be freed after the Saudi weekend on Saturday. Thousands of third-world citizens were landing every day in Jeddah on Umrah visas intending to look for jobs. Many would find work and live without work permits for as long as they didn't get caught. It was, therefore, only a matter of luck as to how much time one had before their investment in the air tickets paid off. For the construction companies requiring menial labour, these workers were cheap, disposable, and easily replaced by the fresh arrival of more illegal workers.

The unprecedented construction boom in Saudi Arabia could not have been achieved without the hundreds of thousands of illegal workers from India, Pakistan, Egypt, Sudan, Bangladesh, Ethiopia, and Somalia. The Saudi bureaucracy was aware of this, but they were simply overwhelmed by the request for work permits. The exclusive use of Arabic meant that every document had to be translated into Arabic and certified. The volume of work was such that even the US or the British government would have found it hard to cope. Yet the Saudis were not prepared to relax their laws for their own good.

The avalanche of foreigners had turned a traditional and hospitable people into the most xenophobic society that one could find on earth, one that awarded a derogatory title to every foreigner. Pakistanis were called *Rafiqs*, Philipinos *Sidiks*, Egyptians *Ali Awads*, Africans *Taqroonis*, and whites were generically called *Khwajas*.

Until our residence papers were regularized, Shahid and I remained petrified to venture out on our own in public after work. Seeing our fear, Mr. Shamim would laugh. "One must learn to take risks in life," he would say. Not having complete work papers was illegal but not criminal, the logic being that we were neither harming anyone nor had a bad intent. Knowing we had no local driving licence, he would lend us his car and encourage us to drive to get used to the city.

My good luck with the *shurta* continued until one afternoon when I was driving Mr. Shamim's oversize American car and was stopped by the police for a routine check. With no residence permit and no local driving licence, I knew I was in big trouble. The combined punishment on the three counts could be immediate detention followed by deportation.

"Hath rukhsa," the *shurta* commanded, asking me to produce a licence.

I began to explain in broken Arabic. "Wallahi, shoof, kaan naem ana," something to the effect that I woke up and forgot my wallet.

"Fain rukhsa, au fain iqama." The officer asked for my papers, clearly getting angry due to the long queue building up behind me.

I was calling for God's intervention fast but tried my best to lie in broken Arabic. The cop could see my hands shaking when I finally managed to produce the photocopies of the car's registration papers, pretending I hadn't understood what else he wanted. The man chose to believe that I had forgotten my wallet at home or something similar.

"Imshi, yalla roh." He waved at me in disdain to move out, throwing the papers back in the car. Then, quite unexpectedly, the policeman asked me in broken English to turn around and head home immediately, warning me that there were more police spot-checks farther down the road.

Another brush with the law came a couple of years later after my residence papers finally got regularized, and I was able to obtain a driver's licence. I had mistakenly entered a recently converted one-way street in the Souk Sharqia area from a side road where no "one way" sign was posted. No sooner had I entered from the wrong side than I was stopped by a cop as if it was a trap laid for unwary foreigners. He promptly confiscated my driver's licence and ordered me to report to the traffic police office in the north of the city the next morning. Before giving me any time to react, he drove away on his big bike.

Afraid I would be locked up, I asked one of my Saudi colleagues to accompany me. It took us a while to find the new traffic office, which, like every government department in those days, kept shifting to new premises to cope with the rapid expansions. After some inquiries back and forth between several windows, we were finally told to meet the senior officer in charge, the one with the two stripes, on the first floor. Arriving in his office, we found the officer surrounded by half a dozen Saudis holding one paper or another in their hands. A number of half empty glass teacups lay scattered amidst the piles of papers that overflowed the officer's unusually large desk. Next to the desk between the sofa and the officer, more files were piled on the floor in no particular order.

After greetings and kisses, my Saudi colleague patiently explained in Arabic the purpose of our visit. Halfway through his explanation, the officer opened his drawer and took out a bundle of recently confiscated licences. When he found what he was looking for, he gave me a long gaze, looked up and then down at the licence to match the photo with me. "This is a serious violation. He has to be . . . " he paused to think of a suitable punishment while I waited nervously.

Fearing the conversation could be going in the wrong direction, I promptly asked my Saudi companion to explain that the one-way street had only recently been so designated. No signs were posted where I had entered. As such my mistake could have been made by anyone. I volunteered to take the officer to the scene to prove my point. Disregarding my explanation, my friend signalled me to shut up. He proceeded politely to ask the officer for compassion and consideration, making me feel like a total idiot. But his approach worked, and he succeeded in getting my licence back. On the way back, Muhammad gave me a useful tip. "Never argue with the *shurta,* especially in front of others." That was tantamount to challenging his authority, something that never went well with the Arab psyche.

Thanks to Mr. Shamim's many years in the kingdom and his large circle of family and friends, I was gradually provided with some sense of belonging in a place that, for many foreigners, must have seemed downright hostile. Many of his relatives in my age group were either Saudi nationals or Saudi born and spoke Arabic. That helped me build a rudimentary vocabulary of my own to deal with taxi drivers and shopkeepers. Before long I began to feel at home in Jeddah.

Saudi Arabia was not a country for anyone, let alone a foreigner, to attract female companions who were hidden behind their veils. The limited number of social occasions that I attended practiced total segregation even within family circles. From behind their *abayas* or from inside their quarters, the girls could see the boys, but the young men were not allowed to peek in. Occasionally, when one did catch a glimpse of a young girl, it would only be by design, meaning when they allowed it. There is a saying in Urdu "Chirag taley andhera," which means "Shadow underneath the lamp." Somehow I had missed the special care that I had been receiving since my arrival from Mr Shamim's eldest daughter, Fatma. It was not the maid but Fatma who was ironing my clothes and tidying up my room when I was at work. At times she would arrive at my door asking me for some errands that I could tell were not urgent. But making advances to a girl nearly ten years junior would not only look stupid but could backfire.

Fortunately, the Arab girls—Fatma, for all practical purposes, was Arab—grew up fast behind their veils. I could not fail to notice her self-confidence and her straightforward manner. She would never say anything just to please anyone, something one normally doesn't see in the girls from the subcontinent. I thought of the romantic games my Bengali friends played back in East Pakistan even in their teens. How effortlessly they found poetic dialogues to write to their cousins and neighbours and then bragged about any reciprocity from them. Unlike my school friends, I was never good in literature and could recollect nothing to say or write to impress a young girl. I thought of Saif back in London, who never had a problem finding a girlfriend wherever he went. For me in Jeddah, the best I could do was go shopping with Fatma, chaperoned by her sisters, or fetch the odd Indian movie from the numerous movie shops in the Bani Malik area.

The guest room where I was residing was considered outdoors for the girls. As soon as the family sensed the chemistry building between the two of us, Fatma was asked to observe *purdah*, as per Arabic tradition. She was not to come in front of me without her *abaya* and never to meet me alone. At the age of seventeen, she was finally declared a grown-up girl. Oddly, it was her disappearance that made me want to see her more than before. So, I began calling her from work for no particular reason, asking if she wanted me to bring anything home.

One evening on the way back after dropping her mom at the weekly movie night at the Indian consulate, I suggested we go to the seaside. She had already begun to find excuses for not joining her mom for the movies, preferring to return with me after dropping her mother. As an insurance policy, she would have her youngest sister accompany her.

"Will it take long?" she asked, concerned about the traffic on the corniche road. "Maybe next week when Abbu is travelling." Her willingness was tempered with her instinct for self-preservation.

When Hashmat came to visit us in Jeddah in April 1979, he soon became aware of our growing affection for each other. So, he asked me directly if I liked her enough to get married. His manner of asking also told me that he was not sure if that was the best choice for me, given the big age difference. He feared I have been driven by loneliness in Jeddah to make a hasty decision. Years after the wedding, once he had gotten to know and like Fatma, he admitted his doubts. But my determined "yes" had left him with only the task of fixing a date for the wedding, which was set for November 7, 1979.

In the strict Muslim tradition, Fatma was taken out of circulation as far as I was concerned until the day of the wedding. I rented an apartment and began to ponder the responsibility of having a family. Fatma made me commit that I would let her finish university, which she was to start after the wedding.

I continued to spend a lot of evenings with my would-be father-in-law who, until recently, had been only a second cousin. But my immediate hesitation was short lived, thanks to Mr. Shamim's affection toward me. While I began to come to terms with the protocol of our new relationship, nothing had changed for him. On the weekends we played bridge. On other days we would talk about history, religion, sports, and so on but never politics, which he considered a waste of time.

"You must get a return even out of your pastime," he used to say. "Either you learn something or you earn something. Discussing politics, you achieve neither."

On the day of the wedding, my trustworthy assistant (Fatma's brother, Tariq) who loved to fiddle with my car spent the entire afternoon decorating it. The so-called *baraat* or wedding party, which consisted of the groom and his two brothers, was to travel in that car on the wedding night. It may have been the smallest wedding party on record that arrived at the bride's house at 8:00 p.m. on the dot, just as it was written in the invitation card. In the culture of the Indian subcontinent, the baraat arriving on time was unusual if not rare. Most of the guests had not arrived. Even Fatma's father was still in the shower.

There was a bit of a debate about what the groom was going to wear that evening. The bride's family, as per tradition, had the wedding suit made for me. But a sentimental cousin of ours insisted that I must wear the suit he had brought for me. At age thirty-eight, Kamal was the oldest person representing the groom's side. The brown daywear suit was not the most suitable for the occasion, but we three brothers jointly decided to respect Kamal's wishes.

When the baraat was hastily received and everyone was seated, I could see the girls looking at us from the balcony. Unknown to me a small commotion was in the offing there. One of Fatma's friends ran up to her saying how lucky she was; the groom was so handsome and looked so happy in that black suit. A little later another friend of hers did the same, adding that he was tall and broad. By then Fatma's suspicion was growing. She asked her friend to take her to the window, so she could see for herself.

"You idiot! That's not my husband; that's his brother, Shahid."

Scanning the small crowd, she searched for her groom among the guests. "There he is, in that brown suit." She couldn't believe what I was wearing as she uttered those words.

Time passed quickly for the Ashrafs, and soon it was Shahid's turn to get married. Fatma and I had started looking for suitable girls in Jeddah, but Shahid's mind was somewhere else. So, we coordinated our vacations to be in Karachi at the same time. Siddique Sahib had added a floor to his house where, a decade earlier, Shahid and I had spent over a year following the 1971 tragedy. The extra rooms meant there was lots of room for Fatma, me, and Shahid to visit at the same time. Toward the end of our short visit, we heard what we had wanted to from the time we arrived.

"Excuse me for saying so," Siddique Sahib started at the dinner table. "We know our daughter is not the greatest match for Shahid who is a foreign-educated engineer." He hesitated and then continued. "We just thought we owed it to the two of you to ask at least once before we consider any other proposal for our girl."

Baji was getting embarrassed at her husband's beating about the bush. To guard against that she had asked her brother, Dr. Akhtar, to be present, preferring him to speak instead.

"Why don't we leave it to the two of them?" I suggested shedding all formalities."let's just ask them."

Shahid had already confided to me the inclination he had for Roshan once he had the opportunity to see her again after almost nine years. She had grown up to be a shy, quiet person, unlike her mother, rather thin with sharp features and bright eyes.

"We like Shahid very much, and we will respect his wishes. We just want you to know how happy we all will be if the relationship between our two families grows from here." "Your parents were so fond of Roshan and we believe they would have been very happy with this *rishta* too, we assume". Once again Siddique Sahib was struggling to conclude and he looked at Baji for help.

"Kah diya naa, Azmat nay," Baji interjected. She was always conscious that we must not be made to think that we owed them anything for all they had done for us in the past. Without a hint in public, Roshan and Shahid had been writing to each other for a long time, knowing well that both the families would only be too pleased with this *rishta*. Over the next twenty-four hours, we spoke to Hashmat in London and fixed a date for the wedding later that year.

Visit to My Birthplace and Catching Up with the Little Big Man

Most exiles do not take enough with them
Some obtain new lands, new identities
Others return to the empty corridors of their sleep
In a place they are always certain to call home.
—Nathalie Handal from *Exiled Sentence*

Poor relations between India and Pakistan had prevented me from visiting my birthplace for over two decades. A rare opportunity came in the summer of 1982 when the relationship between the two neighbours had thawed somewhat with General Zia's cricket diplomacy. Fatma and I visited India along with Fatma's entire family to attend the wedding of her only *mamu* (maternal uncle) in Patna. With a few days in hand while the wedding preparations were going on in Patna, we took time to visit my uncle and aunt in Kumhrauli, where I was born.

In the middle of the monsoon season, the small roads through that part of Bihar become a nightmare to drive because of the countless potholes hidden beneath the puddles. Every time there was any traffic from the other side, our van had to slow down, and one of the vehicles had to leave the narrow road to make room for the other to pass. As a result the 150-km journey took over four hours. By the time we reached Kumhrauli, my uncle was waiting patiently by the roadside with two rickshaws to welcome us. The two-kilometre rickshaw ride to the village took another thirty minutes. Before I could congratulate myself for remembering the smallest of details in that village, I realized that time had stood still there. The houses of our relatives, the numerous fish ponds dotting the village, the school, and the mango orchard on one side of the village, everything had been preserved in its original shape.

We were surrounded from the moment we arrived until we left by Mamus' numerous children and his wife. Dozens of relatives kept pouring in all afternoon and evening as we sat on the veranda answering the same questions again and again. Most of the relatives had come to see the Saudi *bahu,* Fatma. Their affection for us was pure. Still, so much pampering and attention was not easy to take after a tiring journey. Fortunately, nature intervened. It started to rain, providing us with a respite and an excuse to retire early. The thunderstorm we had left behind in Patna was mild compared to what we experienced that night. Not used to seeing much rain in Saudi Arabia, let alone an intense thunderstorm, Fatma struggled to sleep. But I could not stay awake. Sound of water pouring on the tin roof, the most exhilarating music from my past hypnotised me back to sleep.

The next morning we were told that we had slept in the same room that belonged to my mother. After her wedding she and Father always stayed in that room whenever they visited there, and I was also born in that room. I looked around for anything that might remind me of my childhood: the old bed, the broken chair in the corner, or the chest of drawers, but they told me that my grandma had everything redone after 1971. There were no pictures anywhere of mother or her wedding. I don't know what I expected to see there, but it felt like there was an effort to remove my parents' memory, so others could move on. My parents and I were only a part of their yesterday. I wanted to go away and never return to that village.

Returning to Patna, the sound of the torrential rains kept stirring the memories of my childhood. The endearing Bihari/Bhojpuri Urdu of everyone around that I had not heard in ages kept me amused to no end. Together it meant there was no hardship in being housebound, and I relished those lazy days. Mr. Shamim took up the Rubik's cube without once referring to the guide. It took him nearly two weeks to master the cube, coming up with his own formula, which was different from the one in the instruction manual. For us it was one more example of his philosophy in life, of never accepting that he couldn't do something another man could.

The rain didn't stop the shopping trips of Fatma and her mother. It seemed all the shopping for the wedding was left to these two ladies, and they did not take their job lightly.

My own idle time was filled with chess lessons from Mr. Shamim, who let me win every tenth or twelfth game to ensure I did not get disheartened or give up, or playing cards with the groom's relatives. Like me, Mr. Shamim was also visiting his country of birth after decades, a place where he had spent the first eighteen years of his life. The free time allowed for some reminiscing on his part and an opportunity for a project I had in mind. That was to learn more about Mr. Shamim's eventful life, something my parents used to talk about with so much admiration. I wanted to know about the time he had spent with my parents in Jamshedpur thirty or so years earlier and the circumstances that made him run away from home. Bit by bit I began to piece together the story of this incredible self-made man.

His year of "rebirth," as he called it, was 1952 when, at age eighteen, "Samee Akhtar," as he was known then, boarded a train to Bombay, a city where all Indians travelled in search of their dream. Samee travelled without a ticket, had no money in his pocket, and no idea what he would do in Bombay. There he stumbled onto a *muallim* who used to transport Muslim pilgrims by ship to the holy city of Makkah. The muallim agreed to try him out as a runner since Samee had asked for no salary, just food and accommodation. Samee turned out to be a hardworking and likeable boy, and in no time the muallim grew fond of him.

Samee had only one wish: to be on that ship one day. Without a passport or money to buy a ticket, it would not be easy. His opportunity came unexpectedly one night when the muallim sent for Samee, asking him to meet him urgently. Samee thought somebody in the family must have found out where he was and started mentally preparing to run again.

"You must come with me now," the messenger insisted.

"You must be kidding! It's ten o'clock at night. Just tell me who died." He was reluctant to go.

"I don't know," the man insisted, "but the boss wants to see you now."

For Samee, the muallim was no boss, just a kind-hearted man who had taken a liking to the hardworking young man. When Samee arrived, the muallim took Samee to one side and informed him that he had a passport for him. Someone of his age was not going.

"We will have to work on the photo. The name is Muhammad Shamim. So, there is room to write your family name since the Saudis require a third name for the Hajj visa and also for the vaccination certificate."

"Ashraf," Samee said without hesitation. He couldn't believe his ears that he may finally be on that ship, and he got to choose his name. There was no better way for him to honour his favourite uncle, Hayat Ashraf, than by adopting his surname. The change of name would also free him from the past, giving him a new identity.

"When do I travel?" Samee asked, controlling his excitement.

"The ship leaves tomorrow afternoon at 4:30 p.m. You have to be on board three hours before, so go and pack your bags." That part was easy since he didn't have much to pack, and he was least interested in further details.

Samee, now Shamim, was prepared for a rough time in the height of summer when he arrived at the port city of Jeddah two weeks later. He had endured the sultry weather in the shanties of Bombay without much difficulty, but the dry heat of Makkah and the sizzling daytime temperatures of forty-five to forty-eights degrees Celsius in Jeddah was not something he had experienced before. There was no running water in the muallim's quarters where he slept at night with the other workers. For the first few months, he bathed and washed his clothes in the sea. Freshwater was so scarce that it was only available for drinking.

Mr. Shamim had burned his boat, and there was no going back. He wasted little time in making local Arab friends. With their help, he taught himself Arabic, and within months he could speak, read, and write Arabic fluently. Having read the Quran in childhood, he was familiar with the Arabic script even though he didn't know the meaning of the words when he arrived. At work his responsibilities grew as he was given more and more to do by the muallim. He kept proving his worth and memorized all the suras and prayers to become a full-time guide. He would escort the pilgrims through the holy places, reciting the verses loudly for the pilgrims to repeat and helping them diligently complete the various tenets of the Umrah or the Hajj.

Learning fast did not mean his heart was in that job. The muallims in Jeddah and Makkah those days were merciless exploiters who made money by fleecing hapless pilgrims at every opportunity. Shamim needed to get away from that world.

The economy of Jeddah and Makkah in the 1950s depended almost entirely on the hundreds of thousands of pilgrims who, after performing their pilgrimage, would roam the well-stocked *souks* to shop for duty-free electronic goods, gold, clothing, shoes, perfumes, and exotic spices imported from around the globe.

There lay the opportunity for Mr. Shamim, who concluded that one thing all the traders needed was to correspond with the outside world in English. So, he bought some books to improve his English, learned some basic accounting, and also learned to type. Within three years of arriving in Saudi Arabia, Mr. Shamim left the muallim and started working with two different traders of Indian origin.

As soon he had some money in his pocket, Mr. Shamim decided to marry a Yemeni woman. "It was a mistake," he admitted. The marriage only lasted a year and a half. Mr. Shamim started looking to move out of Makkah to the port city of Jeddah both to forget his unhappy marriage and to seek better opportunities. After six years of being on the move, he found a regular full-time job with the central bank. Finally, he began to save to invite his mother from India for pilgrimage, the first responsibility of an able Muslim son. As things turned out, his mother decided to stay with him after her pilgrimage for a while to fulfil her own duty—to find a bride for her son to settle him down in life

A talkative lady with a penchant for befriending anyone, she endeared herself to an Urdu-speaking Indian family living in Makkah. Through that opening, before long she was able to find a bride for her son.

"I had only seen a photograph of her, but I always believed in taking chances," Mr. Shamim would say jokingly, letting his wife overhear.

Their first daughter, Fatma, was born in February 1963, the same year Shamim was promoted as the personal assistant to the governor of Saudi Arabia's central bank (SAMA). To make extra money, he kept working part time at another place, which meant he arrived home late each night. Practically each alternate year after 1963 one more son or daughter was added to the family until the tally reached nine by the mid-1970s. With each addition to the family, his prosperity increased, which reinforced his belief that every individual is born with his own *rizq* or ration from Allah.

The additional ration came at a cost. The punishingly long hours had begun to take their toll, and Mr. Shamim had angina in 1971 at the young age of thirty-eight. The same year he had to bear the terrible news of the massacre of the Biharis in East Pakistan. That included his mother, brother, two sisters, and the family of his beloved uncle and my father, Hayat Ashraf.

The angina did not deter Mr. Shamim for long, and he continued looking for a more challenging job, which he found in 1973 with a newly established shipping company. The 'round-the-clock job was ideal for a workaholic like him who by 1974 had taken over as general manager. Then came the unprecedented boom in the shipping industry that followed the oil boom in Saudi Arabia with the tripling of oil prices after the Arab-Israeli war of Oct. 1973. The business grew at a breakneck pace, and the owners kept increasing Mr. Shamim's remuneration just to retain him in the company, even surrendering to his demand for a profit-sharing arrangement. Shamim had finally begun to reap the benefits of his single-minded devotion to work.

Staying in the fast lane and not prepared to accept a less active life, he decided to go ahead with bypass surgery in the UK.

"I would have gone through the surgery even if the surgeon had given me a fifty-percent chance to live," he said.

His thirteen to fourteen hours a day resumed, and he was firing on all cylinders again, behaving as if he had never been ill. "No one should listen to everything the doctor says," he used to tell his coworkers.

He loved the total involvement and excitement of the shipping industry. The everyday crises that it brought tested his tenacity and negotiation skills with the locals as well as with the international businesses.

"You people are lucky. You're getting off to a good start in life, thanks to your formal education," he used to say. "At least you won't burn out like me so early in life, and you won't need bypass surgery at the age of forty-three."

Despite his personal struggles, Mr. Shamim lived a life of purpose and fulfilment. Over the years he was responsible for opening doors for many young men from Bihar and from Pakistan by giving them jobs or referring them unashamedly to his numerous personal contacts in Jeddah. His faith and his determination to succeed continued to inspire many who came into contact with him.

FOR SHAHID AND ME, WITH our tax-free income and comparatively easy work hours, life was a complete contrast from the Saudi Arabia of the 1950s, 1960s, and early 1970s that Mr. Shamim had to endure. Happily married, we continued living in Saudi Arabia while Hashmat's career was advancing well in London. By the early 1980s, Hashmat had joined the team of heart surgeons led by the famous Majdi Yaqoob to perform the first heart transplant in the UK. Featuring prominently in a seven-part BBC-TV documentary, the young Omar Sharif lookalike became a bit of a celebrity. We received calls from our friends in London and even from one in Singapore who recognized Hashmat on TV. The president of Pakistan invited him to start cardiac surgery in Islamabad, but Hashmat wanted to learn more and make money too. He chose to leave for the US where, according to him, much more was happening in his field.

Each time we travelled to Pakistan, we would look for a bride for Hashmat, who was now living all alone in the US while both his brothers were happily married. At his prime, he didn't marry because he had to pay for his brothers' education. That reason was no longer valid, but at thirty-eight he was past his prime by Pakistani standards.

He was reluctant to start a new relationship in life even though he was no longer in contact with Dr. Nahar. However, Shahid and I felt it was our duty to get him settled and continued our pursuit by showing him pictures of girls we had seen in Karachi or Jeddah. Our search ended when, through a mutual friend, we were finally introduced to Asma Farid and her well-educated family. The tall, slim Asma and her great personality caught everyone's attention. Her mother had singlehandedly brought up three amazing daughters and two sons after the untimely death of her husband and given them the best education and upbringing possible.

"We would be proud to call her bhabi," Fatma and I pleaded with Hashmat.

Tired of living alone, Hashmat was finally persuaded, and we began our preparations for the wedding in earnest.

For someone who did not know our family, it would be hard to imagine that a cardiac surgeon living in the US would wed a girl he had never seen. And he would do so only on the recommendation of his younger brother and his even younger sister-in-law. Elated and relieved, we cut short our vacation in the US and returned to Jeddah to start preparing for the wedding, which was fixed for January 4, 1984.

Things had gone a bit too smoothly thus far, and Hashmat had behaved rather well until he began to have the "pre-marriage frights." When he learned that Shahid had never met the would-be bride, he wanted him to see and approve too. But it was a bit late in the day, the invitation cards had been distributed, and the bride was now in *Mayon* which meant no male from outside the family could see her until the wedding night, when the groom would be the first to see her face. The bride's family declined this strange request, but Hashmat was adamant, throwing everyone off guard.

While the stand-off between the two families continued, the husband of Asma's elder sister, Colonel Pervez Musharraf, arrived from his posting in the north. It was a coincidence that Hashmat was also known by the nickname Musharraf in the family. The two Musharrafs hit it off rather well. On the way back from their squash game, Parvez pulled off a détente that all had hoped for. The next day Shahid and his wife were invited to visit the bride, and the tension subsided.

The third and the last wedding of the Ashraf brothers maintained the tradition of the simplest of ceremonies. Dr. and Mrs. Gazdar came from the US, Cardiologist Shakeel Qureshi from London, and Mr Shamim's clan from Saudi Arabia. There were only a handful of relatives from Karachi itself, since we did not have many. Hashmat's wedding brought immediate good luck to the family. The day before the wedding, Fatma went to pick up the result of her pregnancy test from the Sindh Lab in Karachi. She had tested positive. We were elated that our *bhabi* had brought us good luck. Our lovely daughter, Sarah, arrived later that year after a five-year wait since our wedding.

XXXXX

"DO YOU RECOGNIZE ME?" I asked

"Give me a hint." Arshad looked puzzled.

We had come to know of Arshad's arrival in Saudi Arabia when I was visiting Shahid in Jubail. That same afternoon we drove to Alkhobar some fifty miles away to meet him. He looked the same. Pimple-infested with dark weather-beaten cheeks, his distinctive hairstyle, and a generous smile, Arshad hadn't changed a bit. Granted, both Shahid and I had grown a mustache, but Arshad's inability to recognize us made us wonder how much we had changed.

"Ayub Cadet College," we hinted, which didn't work.

"OK, which one of us is Azmat and which one Shahid?" We granted him another hint rather than give up.

"Fourteen years is a long time Azmat bhai." Arshad opened his arms to embrace me. Tears of joy rolled down his cheeks as he reached out for Shahid after that.

Until the early hours that morning we kept talking, laughing, and sometimes turning somber trying to catch up with the last fourteen years. Arshad had gone through rough times following the killing of his family members in Shantahar. He had spent two years as a POW in India. After reaching Pakistan he and his younger brother faced poverty and degradation. Yet somehow they fought through all that to finish their education. Arshad had done his MBA, and his brother, Kaokab, was a civil engineer working in Pakistan. If there was an example to marvel at the strength that God provides in times of extreme adversity, this was it. Living proof that those who don't give up can rise from the ruins.

Despite being pregnant, Arshad's beautiful wife insisted on cooking dinner for us. From a Bihari family, she was young when her parents fled the troubles in East Pakistan but not too young to forget all that she had seen and heard. Her happiness in meeting her husband's childhood friends was infectious, making us feel all the more welcome. When her daughter was born a few months later, they decided to name her after our own daughter, Sarah, a tribute to start a beautiful friendship between the two families.

A Saudi citizen by virtue of nearly fifty years of residence in Mecca, Fatma's maternal grandfather (her mother's uncle), Abdullah Abbas Al Nadawi, was a source a great pride and a pillar of support to the Indian community in Saudi Arabia. A professor at King Abdul Aziz University in Makkah, Mr. Nadawi was a noted scholar and writer. Every other weekend his large house in Makkah played host to Fatma's numerous relatives. The atmosphere was a mixture of Saudi culture when it came to segregation and prayer timings and Indian, with the traditional Indian food mellowed down to the taste of the younger Saudi generation. The numerous empty rooms on the first floor provided adequate space for us to play carrom or table tennis. Five times a day at every prayer time, the Azaan would pierce our ears from the loudspeaker of the small mosque only feet from the window. Everything would come to a halt for the men, who were expected to be seen across the street at the Saadi Mosque built by a rich Saudi philanthropist of Indian descent. Knowing I had no option but to follow them, Fatma would joke that except Eid, there was no way to send her husband to the mosque except to bring him to her nana's house.

In October 1984 Maulana Abul Hassan Ali Nadawi of Nadwatul Uloom in India, one of the greatest Muslim scholars at that time, was visiting Makkah. We were invited to dinner at Fatma's nana's house, where the great maulana was staying. At the dinner was one of the imams of Kaaba; the president of the World Islamic League, Shaikh Ali Al Harakan; the deputy minister of Auqaf, Amin Al Attas; the secretary general of the World Islamic league, Mr. Abdullah Nassief; and half a dozen scholars from several countries. I had never attended such a congregation before, nor have I since.

On the way to Makkah to meet the great man, we heard on the radio that Indira Gandhi had been assassinated by her Sikh bodyguards that morning. Not surprisingly, instead of larger issues troubling the Muslim world, the topic of discussion at the dinner was soon deflected to the news of Indira Gandhi's murder. Someone commented on how "divine justice" catches up with everyone, something I heard many times in the future before fully realizing the significance of the coincidence. Indira Gandhi was believed to be the last of the three principal architects of the violent break-up of East Pakistan, which cost so many innocent lives, the other two being Bhutto and Mujib. All three had met a violent death, and all three eventually lost their male heirs to violence too. Those who had paid the price for Bangladesh's independence with their own blood fully understood what divine justice meant to them.

Life in Jeddah remained predictable, peaceful, and enjoyable with regular squash games, bridge every weekend, and occasional fishing trips on Mr. Shamim's boat. With so many friends and relatives, Jeddah was very much home, despite so many annoying peculiarities in that country. It was a society so full of contradictions, yet it offered us all the comforts of modern living. The arrogance of the Saudi *thobe* was balanced by the friendliness and generosity of the ordinary Saudis once we got to know them personally. The inhospitable summer was soothed by the mild winter and the open spaces all around Jeddah. The religious zeal of the *mutawa* was countered by the simplicity of *Wahhabism*. Unlike India and Pakistan where the very practice of religion was a source of deep division between the numerous sects and sub sects, Saudi Arabia forbade all sectarian tendencies. Most of the Muslims from the subcontinent living there seemed prepared to trade the obvious infringement of their civil liberties for the safety and security of life and property in that country.

The Forgotten Folks in Bangladesh

Say this city has ten million souls,
Some are living in the mansions,
some are living in the holes;
Yet there is no place for us, my dear,
there is no place for us
—W. H. Auden, from Refugee Blues

"You have to come; he is our last hope," Dr. Jawed Anwar insisted on the phone.

Unable to bury their past, some Bihari professionals like Dr. Jawed, whose clinic did good business in Makkah; his journalist friend, Mustansar; and a few bankers and accountants often got together to discuss the repatriation of the Biharis still stranded in Bangladesh for so many years since 1971. This small group of expatriates living in Saudi Arabia had not given up hope after all these years of procrastination by successive Pakistani governments to bring their folks to Pakistan. Branded as the "stranded Pakistanis in Bangladesh," around 200,000 people were still languishing in nearly 116 camps around Bangladesh in sub-human conditions. They were either orphans of the war or those who could not prove family ties to Pakistan. Those folks had only one dream, to go to Pakistan, for which so much of their blood had been shed.

That evening we met Lord David Ennals at the Al-Attas Hotel to discuss his upcoming trip to Dhaka and Islamabad. The tall, thin, frail figure barely walked even with the help of a stick. He was a retired deputy minister from the British Labour party and the lone crusader in the Western world for the repatriation of the Biharis for nearly sixteen years. He had spent a part of his personal fortune shuttling between Dhaka and Islamabad on behalf of these destitute people. In the final years of his life, despite his failing health he was prepared to make one more attempt.

The world had long forgotten the survivors of the genocide who, after Bangladesh declared independence, had opted for Pakistan. After several initial gestures, Pakistan had done everything to disown them. The Bangladeshi government did not want them either. The Red Cross, which had run the refugee camps since these people were made homeless in 1971, had declared it was going to close the camps because it was running out of funds. For a year after that evening, we met, talked, and some amongst us travelled to Pakistan and Bangladesh. Contacts were also made with the World Islamic League in Makkah and some philanthropic organizations in the UAE and Kuwait.

On one of his trips to Dhaka, General Zia was reportedly taken to the camps to see the plight of this unfortunate community, but he remained unmoved. He stated that his government would consider accepting these Biharis only if the cost of transporting them and the cost of their resettlement in Pakistan was arranged by foreign donors. The irony of his position was that under the same president, Pakistan had been drawn into a war next door and was now hosting nearly three million Afghan refugees. Yet Zia remained indifferent to the plight of 200,000 of his own citizens who had paid the price of being Pakistanis with their blood. Sympathizers of the cause in Pakistan gave Lord Annan's visit sufficient press coverage and published articles in various Pakistani papers in order to mould public opinion. Unfortunately, Lord Ennals's visit added to his own deep disappointment at what he perceived to be a lack of sincerity on the part of Pakistan in coming to terms with history. While the Pakistani authorities' delay tactics continued, international oil prices fell in the mid-1980s, and the promise of funds from various oil-rich Middle Eastern donors began to wane. Lord Ennals passed away a few years later, his dream unfulfilled. We lost the only friend with an international stature who was willing to fight for the cause of the Biharis left behind in Bangladesh.

In an odd way, David Ennals reminded me of the infectious enthusiasm of my friend Yousuf at Karachi University back in 1971, who I never met again after he left for East Pakistan to look for his folks. Then a handful of students like him were able to achieve some results by staging demonstrations and risking police excesses, forcing the government into bringing a few thousand

Biharis in certain categories of eligibility. But now, after coming tantalizingly close to much more resources, the cause was failing.

Nearly a year after Lord Ennals's death, another friend was found, one that we had long been praying for, the World Islamic League in Makkah. Around that time Dr. Jawed and his contacts had arranged a level of protocol that was normally accorded to heads of state for the young chief minister of Pakistan's largest province, Punjab, Nawaz Sharif, during a trip to Makkah. Sharif had been won over as a friend of the Bihari cause. In the past the main opposition to repatriation was from Sindh, a province that was already feeling outnumbered by non-Sindhis. Sharif's interest from the province of Punjab revived the hopes once again. A repatriation committee was formed under the auspices of the World Islamic League with its Secretary General, Abdullah Omar Al Nassief, as its chairman. Other members included Amin Al-Attas, deputy minister of Hajj and Auqaf, Saudi Arabia, a gentleman from Kuwait, and one from the UAE. In Nawaz Sharif's cabinet, one supporter of the cause of the Stranded Pakistanis was Ghulam Hyder Wyne, who later became the chief minister of Punjab when Nawaz Sharif became the PM. Nawaz, being a businessman, was clear from the outset. He sympathized with the cause, but somebody had to fund the repatriation cost including the travel expenses and cost of construction of housing.

The Rabta, therefore, started where Lord Ennals had left but with much bigger resources at their disposal and the ability to mobilize more. We were all elated after the first visit of the Rabta, only to meet stiff resistance thereafter all the way. On one of the committee's visits to meet the government officials, before the meeting started the secretary of the establishment division declared that the quorum was not complete.

"Quorum pura nahi hai," he said in Urdu. He was simply looking to kill the meeting for which donors have flown in from Saudi Arabia.

"Quorum pura hai bhai," Amin Attas, who understood the language a bit, replied, to the hosts' embarrassment.

By then politics in Pakistan had taken another turn, and Benazir Bhutto had become the PM for the second time. Her home minister, Nasirullah Babar, asked the visitors why Saudi Arabia didn't offer to settle the Biharis in that country. Qaim Ali Shah, the Sindh chief minister, kept saying the province of Sindh couldn't accommodate more Biharis, and there had to be some guarantee that these people did not leave Punjab and end up in Sindh.

"We are here to help you solve your problem by arranging the funds you had asked for," Amim Attas said. "Your internal issues are not for us to tackle." Disgusted, he got up to leave the room. Iqbal Hyder, the minister for law, intervened, and the meeting continued. But the damage had been done. After several subsequent visits, the committee grew tired of dealing with so many people with such diverse and conflicting interests. A purely humanitarian issue had been politicized, and a price was being extracted from those who had offered to help. Eventually, two flights carrying around 500 Biharis landed in Punjab and were settled in a few houses that were reportedly built for them from the initial funds collected by that committee. Years passed, the league came and went, as did the governments, and the poor Biharis were forgotten again. It is believed that some of the funds initially paid remain frozen in a bank account in Pakistan with no committee to move them.

RECENT PICTURES FROM TWO OF AROUND 116 BIHARI CAMPS IN DHAKA, BANGLADESH, WHERE NEARLY 200,000 PEOPLE STILL LIVE IN ABJECT POVERTY AND SOCIAL REJECTION.

Women filling their pitchers at the only water point for over 10,000 residents of the Town Hall camp in Dhaka.

Children playing in the narrow lane of the Geneva camp in Dhaka.

Decades of marginalization has condemned a once prosperous community to extreme poverty and degradation.

By the end of the 1980s, my daughters were growing up fast. Two of them were already going to kindergarten which brought home the realization that our days in Saudi Arabia were numbered. The country offered few options in the way of schooling for foreigners. Many of our friends with teenage children had started to send their families abroad, and we began thinking of leaving too. I was reminded of what my principal at the cadet college, Mr. Kayani, wrote in my autograph book, all those years ago, "All good things come to an end."

With restrictions on driving and on generally on free movement, mothers in my wife's circle of friends were finding it hard to attend to their children's growing needs. Our Saudi way of life now required change for the sake of our children. Even if I could afford a driver, finding a work visa was difficult. For domestic help we kept alternating between one illegal maid and another, always fearful that we may have to face the law one day. The citizenship application for the family of my in-laws, Mr. Shamim and his children, had moved to the final stages after years of follow-up. Except for Fatma, the others were expecting final approval from the royal court, putting an official stamp on their Saudi way of life. But the path forward for my wife and children was different.

It was around that time that Mr. Shamim had to go to jail for a crime to which he was not even remotely connected. One of the containers meant to carry tea from Sri Lanka on one of the ships that his company handled as agents arrived at the port loaded with hashish (cannabis). The owner of the shipment never turned up to claim it, and the authorities suspected that someone in the company was involved. The bizarre local practice demanded the owner or the GM be detained behind bars until the investigations were complete. The Saudi owner was away on a business trip, so Mr. Shamim was put behind bars. The onus of proving innocence was left to the accused, who was presumed guilty unless proven otherwise.

He was not allowed to meet anyone. However, the prison authorities, under a doctor's advice, made one concession, to allow food to be sent from home. Fresh clothes were also allowed in exchange for his laundry. The only time the family was allowed a visit, they were horrified to see him handcuffed. Even for a man of exceptional courage, Mr. Shamim was badly shaken by all this.

In two weeks or so, the owner returned and the case was resolved. But by the time the ordeal was over, Mr. Shamim's Saudi dream had been shattered. A country where he had toiled and succeeded for nearly four decades had shown him his worth. He decided to call it a day and take premature retirement and was planning to move to Pakistan, where he had never lived. Mr. Shamim's ordeal served as a wakeup call to others like me invested less heavily in Saudi Arabia. Suddenly, it seemed that we didn't belong there at all and that we had been walking on soft sand.

Second generation by birth, my daughters stood no chance of becoming Saudi nationals since their Saudi-born mother had married a foreigner before she could obtain her own citizenship. Neither Fatma nor I entertained any illusions or imagined a future for our daughters there. This was a society where a woman was worth half a man's share in inheritance, in blood money, and in the weight of her testimony in court. Even a happy housewife in Saudi Arabia knew her husband could, if he chose, deny her the right to travel, work, or study. Men could take another wife or divorce their wife with a verbal utterance, while women had to plead before an all-male sharia court to rid themselves of their husbands, if they wanted to exercise their own right. This was hardly the place where parents with any choice would let their daughters spend their lives. Shahid had already returned to Pakistan to start his own business, and it was only a matter of time before we left too.

FIFTH MIGRATION

Back in Pakistan

Dreamed I saw a building with thousand floors
A thousand windows and a thousand doors:
Not one of them was ours, my dear, not one of them was ours
—W. H. Auden

"You will not last more than six months there," my colleague in Jeddah predicted in earnest. "I bet you will soon be looking for a job back in the Middle East when your savings run out." He was disappointed in me for leaving a good-paying job in Saudi Arabia and dismayed at my intention to start a business in Pakistan, a sure recipe for losing my hard-earned savings. Senior in age, Shariq had lived and worked in Pakistan for nearly a decade before coming to Saudi Arabia, and he knew how difficult the business environment in Pakistan was. He swore there was no room for a professional to run a business in a land of limited opportunity where money was made through nepotism, corruption, tax evasion, and flouting the law.

Undeterred by my friend's prognosis, Shahid and I decided to prove him wrong. Joining us in that mission was our friend from cadet college, Arshad Jamal, and our newfound friend in Jeddah, Aftab Alamgir. The four of us with our hard currency savings from Saudi Arabia and part of our youth still intact were determined to take the plunge.

Soon after landing in Pakistan, Arshad set up a distribution business supplying pharmaceutical products from multinational companies to shops around Karachi. He acquired smart premises and leased brand-new vans and a computer to account for the inventory and growing sales. Arshad wanted his gains up front, dealt in cash not credit, and it seemed not much could go wrong. Shahid, Aftab, and I became his partners.

Shahid also started building houses for his contacts from the Middle East. In addition, in partnership with Mr. Shamim, Aftab, and me, he bought a furniture factory that was making kitchen cabinets and doors, providing a synergy to his construction business. Located in the north of the city, the factory was a good distance from his construction projects in the south, which required him to spend a lot of time on the road. This seemed like a small inconvenience at the time but in later years turned out to be a huge handicap when parts of Karachi were shut down for days on end due to troubles on the streets.

The good start Arshad and Shahid seemed to enjoy propelled me to plan even bigger things with Aqueel, one of the first friends I had made in Karachi back in 1971. Aqueel belonged to a prominent business family who, like us, was forced out of East Pakistan but was lucky to avoid any loss of life. Since arriving in Karachi, his family had done well to make it back in business but still were a shadow of their former selves. A graduate from Cambridge, Aqueel had the ambitions to match the larger resources of his family at his disposal.

My return to Pakistan could not have been better planned. My house was built by Shahid in time for my return. The most difficult task of all, admission to a good school for my daughters, was arranged without having to pull any strings. Since Aqueel, as the major shareholder in the textile mill, was going to manage the business, I decided to continue my banking career by joining an American bank.

Arriving back in Karachi in 1990, the first thing that struck me was how much the city had changed from the 1970s. Overcrowded bazaars and maddening traffic had choked out the beautiful shopping areas in Sadar and Tariq Road. The bustling nightlife of the 1970s, the nightclubs, and the cabarets had all disappeared during General Zia's eleven-year purification drive. The crime rate had risen, and it was no longer safe to venture out in the "city of lights," as it was known in the 1970s, after sunset. The sole entertainment left for the middle class was eating out till the early hours of the morning. Weddings had taken centre stage as the big social events: five to seven days of reveling and feasts starting from the night of *mehndi* and ending with *valima*, giving an opportunity for the rich to show off their wealth and young boys and girls to have some innocent fun. While the young ones were busy singing and dancing, matchmaking took place behind the scenes with the help of aunts and grandmas. Marriage halls had sprung up everywhere and were doing roaring business. Also multiplying in number were the mosques in each locality, most of which belonged to one sect or another and competed fiercely for funds and attendees. Each prayer time a multitude of loudspeakers would call for prayers from every corner simultaneously, competing to attract the faithful their way.

Not all had gone wrong for Karachi though. There was an apparent affluence on its streets, with luxury cars and big bungalows in that gold rush city, where money was being made by the lucky few using whatever means possible. Bankrolled for the Afghan war by the Americans, the economy in Pakistan had performed well during the 1980s. However, with the end of the war, the country was now left to cope with the enormous after-effects, including millions of refugees, a proliferation of illegal arms, and a thriving black market infested with drug money and illegal wealth. Hand in glove with the army, numerous linguistic and religious groups had prospered throughout the 1980s. They along with defectors from the mainstream political parties had joined the fray with General Zia in his eleven-year rule, which ended with his death in a plane crash in 1988. With Zia's departure, the pendulum had swung in the other direction, but his legacy looked set to haunt the nation for years to come.

For a brief period immediately after Zia, an air of change soothed the country, bringing a respite from the puritanical drive of Zia's regime. The darling of the west, the young and dashing "Daughter of the East," Benazir Bhutto, had swept the elections, riding a popular wave in December 1988. The optimists among us, being in the same age group as Ms. Bhutto, began to entertain the thought that a social revolution was in the offing. We thought it was destined to moderate a society that, for over a decade, had been held hostage by the extremist groups propped up by Zia's regime.

Alas, our optimism was short lived as the popular euphoria began to subside by the time we arrived in early 1990. Ms. Bhutto's inexperience and the sycophants surrounding her seemed to have gotten the better of her. The feudals had taken over the country like never before. It seemed no matter which party was in power in different provinces, a handful of families from their respective fiefdoms dominated the ruling class. The two major parties competing for power had brothers, cousins, and relatives with the same surnames in opposing camps.

In total contradiction to their socialist slogans, Bhutto's party had too many landlords, *waderas, jagirdars, chowdhries,* and *sardars.* Since these feudals came from their rural strongholds, an urban-rural divide especially in Sindh was pitting the Urdu-speaking *muhajirs* against the Sindhi-speaking largely rural residents. Within a few months of my arrival in 1990, law and order in Karachi had all but broken down as the two political forces in the province of Sindh fought their battles in the streets. At loggerheads with each other, the MQM represented the Urdu-speaking immigrants from India, constituting a majority of the urban population, while the power base of the PPP lay in rural Sindh with the Sindhi-speaking population.

Ominously, the linguistic divide in Sindh represented the dilemma we had witnessed in East Pakistan, where the Urdu-speaking immigrants dominated the economic life while the native Bengalis felt acutely alienated. The word "muhajir," a derogatory term only until the recent past, was being touted as a mark of political defiance and as ammunition in the hands of the MQM protesting the overall Punjabi domination in the country. By sidelining the mainstream political parties for years, General Zia's policies appeared to have divided the country dangerously on linguistic and ethnic grounds. Karachi's economic life was paralyzed. Scared investors were fleeing to other parts of Pakistan or simply leaving the country.

With the economy in a tailspin, Shahid's business was hurting. His factory was closed for days on end, and it was not safe for him to go there. Some of the most notoriously volatile spots in Karachi, such as Golimar or Leyari, lay en route to his factory. There were pockets of no-go areas designated by one group or another on those routes. Arshad's distribution business, which was doing well until then, was hit even worse as his vans could no longer reach the hundreds of shops they had to cover daily. Luckily for me I was still earning a salary to cover my living expenses.

There was little respite from the lawlessness. One afternoon while returning home from work, our friend Aftab's car was snatched at gunpoint. Before he could react, two men jumped out of the car in front, which had blocked his way in the narrow lane. One had a pistol in his hand.

"Get out of the car now. Don't try to be smart! Hurry up, behenchod," he swore when Aftab took a few seconds to open the door. "Hurry up, you behenchod, or I'll blow a hole in your brain." Clearly agitated by the delay, the man pointing the gun at him swore again.

Pushing Aftab out of the way, the two jumped into the car and drove away with at least half a dozen people watching from the corner shop less than fifty metres away. Aftab thus became our first friend in Karachi to fall victim to the rising crime in Karachi twice. Only a few weeks earlier his travel agency was robbed of cash.

The young robbers' audacity and their lack of fear of being apprehended gave credence to the theory that the political forces had let loose their young volunteers to collect *bhatta* from the masses to finance their own movements. The notoriously corrupt police had abdicated in favour of such criminals. Some reportedly even shared their booty with the police. The poor masses had no respite, and their confidence in the state's ability to provide safety and security of life and property was all but gone.

By that time the only business flourishing in Karachi seemed to be the private security companies that provided armed guards to protect those who could afford them. The other business doing well were the smugglers or *khepias* selling a range of electronics and consumer goods by undercutting those operating legally and paying their taxes or import duty.

After less than two years in government, Bhutto was removed by the president using his controversial powers to sack the parliament. Elections were held, and a new government was sworn in at the end of 1990. The new prime minister, Nawaz Sharif, belonged to a business family. His arrival had a positive effect on the business community, which had never run the country in the past. Aware of the negative effects of red tape, Nawaz Sharif quickly moved to deregulate the economy and free it from the stranglehold of bureaucracy. From famine to feast, suddenly things had never looked better for business in Pakistan. An upsurge of investments that followed the first-ever privatization drives woke up the sleepy Karachi stock market with a jolt. Within a year of the new government, Shahid and Arshad's businesses were limping back into profit, and their mood became upbeat and optimistic. The stock market boom that followed the first round of privatization gave us the opportunity to make some easy money for a change. Even the relationship with our big neighbour, India, seemed on the mend, and for once everyone seemed bullish about the future.

Calls from the Past

(1)

In 1993, nearly twenty years after deserting the Pakistani army, on an official visit to Islamabad, Saif took time off to be with us in Karachi. Dr. Saifullah Syed PhD, a distinguished economist working for the FAO (Food and Agriculture Organization), was travelling on a UN passport. In the small reunion at our house, he met seven of his Urdu-speaking Bihari friends from cadet college who had survived the massacre in 1971 and risen from the ruins to rebuild their lives in Pakistan. They included Qamar, Arshad, Tariq, Malik, Rizvi, Shahid and me. He was meeting the first five for the first time since 1971. All seven of them had lost their near and dear ones at the hands of Bengalis in those dark days and carried the scars of 1971 deep in their souls. The siblings or relatives that some still lived with in Karachi were the living dead in their families who had never recovered from their trauma and constantly reminded them of their past.

Not that they always banded together or even met regularly, but the strong bond among these young men provided the emotional shelter for these *blood brothers* of sort who shared a common purpose. That was to survive and prosper in what was a new country for all of them.

The way they received their Bengali friend Saif with open arms was not something anyone could have predicted. And Saif's joy and amazement at how his old school mates had rebuilt their lives after losing their parents, their homes, and their country while still in their teens was equally boundless.

Without anyone realizing, Saif's visit opened up other such calls from the past, a process that led to many visits from other old mates to and from Bangladesh in the coming months and years. Several Bengali friends arrived in Karachi to visit us, among them my dear friends Taneem and Hamid, Shahid's friend Shubro, and Arshad's friends Rumi and Manish Dewan. After so many years, it was amazing to discover that nothing had broken the bonds of friendship created in our youth, and the greatest of tragedies, no matter how difficult to overcome, could indeed be healed with time.

(2)

"ARE YOU CAPTAIN SARWAR CHEEMA?"

"Yes," the man replied.

"Do you recognize me?" Shahid asked again.

After taking an early retirement from the army, Colonel Cheema was working for a clearing and forwarding agent in Karachi, spending most of his time after work playing bridge at the Defense Club. He had lost much of his hair and his youthful looks but not his unmistakable mannerism. Over the past week or so, Shahid had meant to ask the man his name but had to wait until today when they faced each other across the bridge table.

"Were you in East Pakistan?"

"During 1971? Yes, why do you ask?" Cheema's anticipation was rising.

"Remember the young doctor whose brother you helped to recover?"

"How could I forget? Don't tell me you are Doctor Ashraf."

"No, I am the boy you recovered."

"Small world," they both mumbled as they jumped out of their seats and opened their arms for each other. Everyone around the bridge table watched in amazement.

The following weekend we played bridge at Shahid's house, interrupting every hand to talk about East Pakistan. Thanks to that chance meeting with Col. Cheema, I finally got my wish to express my gratitude personally to the man to whom we owed so much. Col. Cheema was one of the few outsiders invited to join our weekly bridge circle, and we spent many happy evenings together after that. A soldier at heart and soul, he did not enjoy his life outside the army. At times it was evident that he had been drinking or appeared to carry the previous day's hangover. After the war when the

Pakistani army surrendered in Bangladesh, Cheema became a prisoner of war. He spent nearly two years in an Indian jail before being repatriated to Pakistan. An otherwise brilliant career had come to a premature end. His new job did not befit his previous position, and he was struggling to make ends meet. He had not returned to his hometown Sargodha for months, and he never spoke about his family. That is how cruel life can be even for the finest among of us.

XXXXXX

BARELY TWO AND A HALF years after it had taken the local business community by storm and put the economy on a fast trajectory, Prime Minister Nawaz Sharif was also removed by the president using the same controversial constitutional amendment as had been used against Bhutto. In the musical chairs of Pakistani politics in the 1990s, Bhutto was back in power.

Her return brought back the confrontation with her arch political rivals, MQM, in urban Sindh. Within months of her arrival, Karachi's streets were in flames with a vengeance. At the height of that confrontation, scores of people were dying each week on the streets of Karachi and Hyderabad, paralyzing the lives of their residents.

Shahid's factory remained closed for months, and he was unable to meet the orders in hand. To add to his difficulties, the environment of pervasive corruption meant that even the payments for work completed were not forthcoming without greasing some palms. Contracts that were supposed to have earned a good profit saw the margins eaten up by the system. With his business going nowhere, Shahid was succumbing to inertia and irresolution. Arshad had already thrown in the towel, no longer able to carry on with his distribution business. Within two three months, his distribution vans were robbed of cash twice. Soon after those incidents, the car he was driving was snatched at gunpoint. In 1996 Arshad folded up and left for Canada after selling his business at a throwaway price.

But those were small setbacks compared to the family's largest investment, the textile mill, which was losing money faster than the partners could replenish the working capital. The margins collapsed in the wake of the increasing price of electricity, raw materials, and rising interest rates, pushing up the cost of servicing existing debts. The banks declined to provide further working capital or to fund the expansion of the number of looms that was necessary to bring the mill to its right economic size. Traditionally, the startups in the industry aimed to first establish their products and market. Thereafter they would gradually add more looms from the cash flow generated. Higher costs and lower volumes combined to push the mill to default on its payments to banks, forcing the partners to restructure the payments and pump in their last reserve of cash to keep the company alive.

The odds against survival in business were always high in Pakistan, but we were only wiser with hindsight as to how one thing or another in the system was always sure to beat us. Back in 1990, the government had advertised special incentives such as interest rate subsidies and cheap electricity for setting up manufacturing facilities in the less developed north. Our textile mill was located in that area and was critically dependent on those concessions to cover the additional costs of transportation and operation. But by the time the mill came into production, those incentives were unilaterally withdrawn, making the industrial units in the area instantly unviable. Hattar Industrial Estate, where the mill was located, turned into an industrial graveyard. Never mind the subsidized electricity, just to be connected to the electricity grid required huge amounts doled out as bribes.

Since coming to Pakistan, I had not given much thought to my former colleague Shariq's prognosis. Ill equipped as most in my group were for business in that country, we finally managed to blow our years of savings from Saudi Arabia. But that was only after we had outlasted my friend's prediction of six months by a good margin. Dejected, I decided to write to Sheikh Abdullah Abu Samh, a director at Bank Al Fransi, my former employer in Jeddah. Reminding him of his offer at my farewell dinner, I asked him to take me back. Within two weeks I got a call to visit Jeddah and returned from there with an offer of employment at slightly better terms than I had enjoyed in the past. But I was undone by the opposition to my returning to Jeddah, which came from the most unexpected quarter. Used to the freedom of driving around and the privileges of the house servants, Fatma was unwilling to return to Jeddah.

"We don't need more money," she said. "We already own our house, and your salary at the bank is enough for us to live comfortably here."

Most importantly, our daughters were happy and settled in good schools in Karachi. If we returned to Jeddah, we could forget about putting them back in those schools if we came back to Karachi. In any case, in a couple of years there would be no option for the older two beyond O-levels in Jeddah, and we would have to move. There was no way we would consider splitting the family and sending the girls to a boarding school. In other words we concluded that our lives had to move forward, not backwards.

Bhutto was fired for the second time for corruption and incompetence under a controvertial constitutional article 58, this time by the president of her own choosing, one from her own party. Once again elections offered limited choices to voters, the same old faces and the same two political leaders who stood apart by their dislike for each other and not by anything meaningful in their declared manifesto. "Do unto them what you do not wish done to yourself" seemed to be the motto of Nawaz and Bhutto, who continued to dominate the intermittent bouts of democracy in Pakistan.

As expected, the elections brought back Nawaz Sharif for the second time with a two-thirds majority, enough for him to change the constitution and secure his power for a long time. But the country had a new challenge to face. The outside world had taken note of Pakistan's inability to contain its religious extremist elements. Zia's legacy had spread like cancer in that failing democracy, where many still sympathized with the extremist groups that threatened to wipe those they disagreed with off the map.

Just as the pressure grew on Pakistan, the country decided to test the nuclear bomb in 1998, following in the footsteps of archrival India. Business confidence took a nosedive, and Pakistan was on the verge of being declared a "rogue state." Fearing reprisals from the West, business investments ground to a halt. Things had not looked so gloomy in years. The new scapegoat for the economic failure was the business community, dubbed as the villain who had looted the country.

Despite all that, thanks to my job as the country manager for a foreign bank with a chauffeur-driven Mercedes, my career had remained on course. I continued to enjoy a busy social life with my family, going to parties and attending endless dinner table deliberations, the favourite pastime of the Pakistani elite. Except for the missing peace of mind, things for us were not all that bad. Had it not been for the city's nagging law-and-order problems, there was a lot of fun too. We spent our evenings at the Creek Club where our girls went swimming and the men played squash or badminton. Our bridge sessions on the weekends also continued uninterrupted. We were once again living in a bubble, a bit like the year before the breakup of East Pakistan.

The crime rate in Karachi had shot up to a level not known before. Often we would wake up in the middle of the night to the sound of gunfire, after which it would be difficult to go back to sleep. Two of our immediate neighbours suffered armed robberies. Thanks to our stars, our daily precautions, and our trusted German Shepherd, "Rambo," we remained unscathed. But it was getting closer and closer. In a botched robbery, a friend's teenage daughter was severely beaten. The poor girl needed psychiatric treatment for months to overcome the trauma. The rising incidents of kidnapping for ransom forced my employer, like many others, to propose an insurance policy to cover kidnapping for ransom for a "potential target" like me. I dreaded the idea of being on any list alongside the rich and famous. That I believed could only be counter productive, by making an unknown person like me a potential target, so I refused. Nevertheless, my employer paid to have my driver trained in how to avert close calls by being vigilant about his surroundings when he drove me around. The daily precautions included taking different routes to and from work and not always at predictable times. As if all that were not unsettling enough, one of our defaulter clients against whom the bank had started legal proceedings had obtained our home phone number and hired someone to harass and threaten my family. Suddenly, it seemed like too many things were going wrong around us. There were so many signs telling us to escape, to run away. A country, which in my childhood was an example of socio economic progress in the developing world, had steadily slipped in the international league table to new lows over the past three decades.

In the midst of all that, in Oct 1999, Saif arrived in Karachi again to attend an FAO-sponsored seminar to be held in Islamabad. I flew with him from Karachi the next morning, using the opportunity to call on my clients and hoping to meet up with Saif again in the evening before he flew off from there. Seated two rows in front of us on the plane was Asif Zardari, husband of ex-Prime Minister Bhutto. He was handcuffed and escorted by armed police taking him to Islamabad for a court hearing on one of the numerous cases filed against him. He had remained in police custody ever since his wife's ouster nearly three years earlier. It gave Saif an instant flavour of Pakistani politics, and more was to follow that same evening in Islamabad.

"Have you heard the news?" Saif was calling my cellphone from the nearby UN office. His voice betrayed his anxiousness.

"What news?" I asked

"A coup seems to be in process. Troops are moving toward the TV station and other sensitive locations."

"This is not a banana republic," I said, rejecting his suggestion.

A few minutes later while still at that meeting, my host informed me that the PM had fired Army Chief Musharraf. Unaware of my relationship with Musharraf, my host, an ardent supporter of Nawaz Sharif, did not hide his pleasure at the news. According to him, that move by Nawaz would finally break the impasse between the two centres of power, the army and the PM. The news of Musharraf's dismissal was startling enough, and I presumed that's what Saif must have heard along with some added drama from the messenger.

"You don't know what's happening in your country?" Saif called a second time a few minutes later. This time his voice was clearly anxious. He informed me that the troops loyal to Musharraf were on the move, apparently seizing power. "Go straight to the hotel, and don't venture out. I'll meet you there as soon as I can." He implored me to move right away before it got dark.

I called my wife in Karachi, but she didn't answer the phone. So, I called my sister-in-law next door and asked her to switch on the TV. In minutes while we were still talking, Pakistani Television (PTV) went off the air. In the next hour or so, I managed to reach my hotel, but by then my cellphone had gone offline too. The sun had set, and the well-lit roads of Islamabad showed none of the unusual activity to which Saif had referred.

On my way back to the hotel, which was only a few blocks away but not too far from the TV station where the troops had reportedly moved in, I asked the taxi to make a detour, so we could pass by the TV station. But we were stopped by men in uniform and ordered to head back the way we came. That confirmed that something was going on.

By the time I arrived at the Marriott, Saif hadn't reached the hotel, and with the cellphones offline, I couldn't call to find out where he was. Before I could begin to worry, he called my room from a landline asking me to meet him at the house of his colleague from the FAO in sector F-8. Didier and his wife, Joel, had only recently moved to Islamabad from France and needed company at that uncertain time. We had dinner at their house and spent several nervous hours with them in front of their satellite TV watching CNN and BBC. Their home telephone kept ringing as worried relatives and friends called from outside the country. Then the embassy, the UN, and the FAO administration called one after another to check if everything was fine and whether they needed any assistance. Saif's wife, Francoise, called from Rome too.

The streets of Islamabad had normally been the safest in Pakistan. But this was a special night, so we made several calls to the hotel to ascertain if it was okay for us to drive before we decided to go back, arriving there in the early hours of the morning. By then the fourth coup d'état in Pakistan's brief history was complete.

With our business in ruins and a grim political future looming over the country, we began to seriously think of an exit plan. It mattered little to us that Musharraf was known to the family since we were neither willing nor able to play the "contact game" that happens in the third world. The only positive expectation some had from this government was that it may be able to reign in the mullahs and stop the current drift toward fundamentalism. But that could last only until the next coup, in case Musharraf moved too fast to deradicalize. Fifteen years ago Musharraf's persuasive skills had saved us an embarrassing stand-off at Hashmat's wedding. He will need much more than that to make any headway with the religious fanaticism especially with the reported infestation of the fundamentalist elements even in the army itself. A longtime friend who worked at the ISI told us that Musharraf had an almost impossible job at hand.

The "lost decade" of the 1990s, as it came to be known in Pakistan, coincided with the unsuccessful endeavors in that country attempted by our friends, my brother and me. We did not know whether to blame our luck or to just agree with the prognosis of my former colleague, Shariq, from Saudi Arabia, that our decision to move was a poor one. The only two countries where I had spent a considerable period of time since my uprooting from Bangladesh were Saudi Arabia and Pakistan. While Saudi Arabia could not offer any long-term choice for my daughters, it provided a sense of security I had never enjoyed before. Pakistan, on the other hand, offered everything except a sense of security of life and property.

There was no way to turn the clock back; just one more decision needed to be made. I had to find a place where our daughters could live and prosper without fear of persecution and where they could enjoy a stable and safe existence, not much more than what my father was looking for all those years earlier. I could not imagine a future for my daughters in a Taliban-like society, toward which the country seemed to be drifting. It was no longer possible for me to let them stay in a place beset by gloom and uncertainty.

Life had turned full circle on me since I first became a refugee half a century earlier, at the age of one. I was now looking for a place where I could live out my final years and be safely buried, a concession my father was denied. I wanted a marked grave that my children and grandchildren could visit, something my parents were unable to leave for me. My final resting place from where I could no longer be dislodged may provide the mooring in a land that my children would call their own. In the emerging new global village, it might not matter where their earlier generations came from.

When the blood in your veins returns to the sea,
And the earth in your bones returns to the ground,
Perhaps then you would remember that this land does not belong to you,
It is you who belong to this land. . .
—Anonymous Native American

1970 – LAST FAMILY PICTURE IN THAKURGAON, EAST PAKISTAN:
1 – Father, 2 – Mother, 3 – Iqbal, 4 – Uncle Ansari, 5 – Hashmat, 6 – Azmat, 7 – Zahid, 8 – Shahid, 9 – Sajid, 10 – Munni, 11 – cousin Firoza, 12 – Hamid.
Eight out of the twelve in the picture were killed in 1971

They shall grow not old, as we that are left grow old:
Age shall not wear them, nor the years condemn.
At the going down of the sun and in the morning
We will remember them.
—LAURENCE BINYON

2007 – THE SURVIVORS (L TO R): HASHMAT, SHAHID, AND THE AUTHOR IN CANADA

AUTHOR'S TEMPORARY HOMES AND MIGRATION ROUTES THROUGH THE YEARS

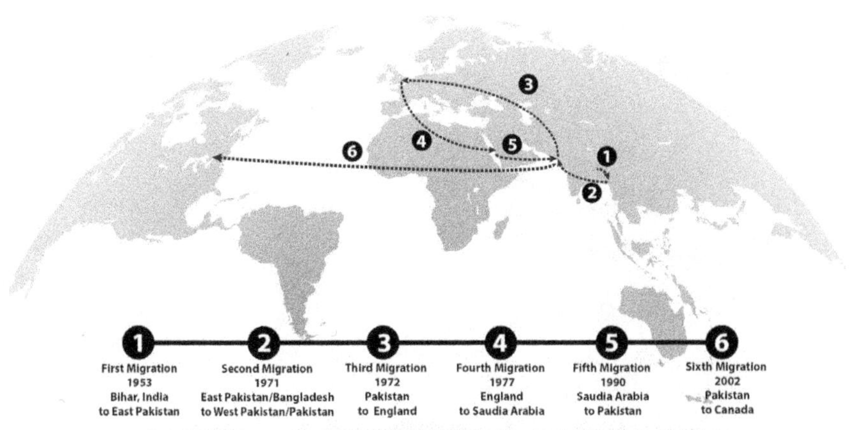

Acknowledgement

It is a small wonder that this book is seeing the light of the day after being in the making for so many years. I must begin by thanking my wife Fatma and my daughter Samia, who encouraged me to take on this project and collated my initial thoughts into a single document.

I would also like to offer my sincere thanks to dear friends Nizamuddin Siddiqui, Saifullah and his wife Francoise Syed, Kamran and his wife Zubaida Faridi who read the initial draft and offered their honest critique. Their comments and suggestions gave me the confidence to complete this project.

A special thanks to my brothers Hashmat and Shahid who read the manuscript for accuracy of dates and events. It must have been difficult for them to relive the past. Sincere thanks to my editor Kevin Miller and the staff at FriesenPress. Their expertise helped guide me through a difficult and at times exasperating process.

This book is a debt I owed to my parents, my siblings and countless others who fell victim to bigotry and violence that marred an otherwise legitimate movement for independence of Bangladesh in 1971. They remain nameless and faceless and largely forgotten by all except the survivors they left behind.

CPSIA information can be obtained
at www.ICGtesting.com
Printed in the USA
BVHW060657250321
603339BV00003B/198